The Story of
St. Agatha Home for Children

HOME KIDS

Nancy Canfield

Rita — this book
I hope you only
brings you only
fond memories
Love, Nancy

Silver Threads
San Diego, California

Home Kids: The Story of St. Agatha Home for Children

For information:

Silver Threads
3930 Valley Centre Drive, PMB 102
San Diego, CA 92130
858-794-1597 0149
www.silver-threads.org

Silver Threads is an imprint of Silvercat

Publishers Cataloging-in-Publication Data

Canfield, Nancy

Home Kids : the story of St. Agatha Home for Children / Nancy Canfield – 1st ed. – San Diego, Calif. : Silver Threads, 2006

p. : cm.

ISBN-13: 978-1-893067-06-6
ISBN-10: 1-893067-06-8
Includes bibliographic references

1. St. Agatha Home for Children (Nanuet, N.Y.). 2. Canfield, Nancy–Childhood and youth. 3. Orphanages–New York (State)–Nanuet. 4. Children–Institutional care–New York (State)–Nanuet. 5. Orphans–(New York (State)–Biography. I. Title

HV995.N162 S283 2006
362.73/2/09747/28–dc22   0510

printed in the United States of America

Contents

Dedication

To all the Home Kids and their families, all the Sisters and employees of St. Agatha Home, the New York Foundling Hospital, and the Sisters of Charity who helped us. Special thanks to Sister Rita King, archivist for the Sisters of Charity.

A special dedication to my recently departed friend, Craig Warren Andersen, who helped me transition from St. Agatha Home back to the outside world. (November 6, 1948 to December 5, 2004)

Many thanks to the Rancho Bernardo Writer's Group, Robert Goodman of Silvercat, and Peggy Lang, Editor, who dragged me through the morass of a manuscript.

Introduction

Saint Agatha Home for Children opened in Nanuet, NY in 1884, and has been continuously caring for children ever since. This is the story—a memoir, really—of how I came to live there and what it was like. To that, I've added the personal stories of others who lived at St. Agatha in every decade and have told me their memories. I share them here with you. We explore what we think happened to our families and why they couldn't care for us. We did not always know or understand why we were sent to St. Agatha. Some did not know what became of their parents, why no one else in the family could take them in, or even where they came from.

To the personal stories, I've added a collection of letters, reports, newspaper accounts, deeds, and photographs of the people and events as they unfolded. As St. Agatha grew, so did America. By the 1800's, unprecedented and unbridled immigration—along with prejudice, health epidemics, and public apathy—produced one hundred fifty foundling babies per month in New York City: babies left on doorsteps and in alleys. Many became "street Arabs," who were shipped out west on orphan trains as an alternative to living on the streets.

In the 1700's, children who needed a home because their parents died or went to debtor's prison were simply taken in by neighbors. When there were too many, such as during the great waves of immigration to the

U.S., huge orphan asylums patterned themselves after the successful penitentiaries built to house more than a thousand children at a time. Children came out of these institutions unfit to live in an unregimented environment and often ended up back in institutions: prisons.

Destitute children flooded the streets, were exploited, and became criminals to survive, as in Dickens' *Oliver Twist*. The need for smaller homes to care for and teach them trades, and not merely warehouse them, grew continuously. Public sympathy for these children and disgust at their living conditions, combined with indignation at the increasing nuisance the children presented, prompted attempts to remedy the problem.

The Sisters of Charity, like other orders, developed Homes to take these feral children off the streets. Their objective was to develop homes where all aspects of the children's lives were considered for their success: childcare, education, religious training, recreation, health care, and social development. To this end, the Sisters held fundraising events and planned construction, growth paths, and development programs while providing basic care to the youngsters, in hopes that their families would reclaim them.

As adults, former "Home Kids" sometimes reflect on their childhoods as fortunate because they were taken care of. Others viewed themselves as prisoners—treated without warmth and forced to do chores or attend to excessive religious duties. The one thing they all had in common was a longing to go home, often to a home and family that no longer existed. C.S. Lewis could have been speaking of their longing when he said, "We live in the Shadowlands. The sun is always shining somewhere else, 'round a bend in the road, over the brow of the hill."

I cannot say whose perspective is right in the care of the thousands of children who came to St. Agatha's doors. I can only try to retell what happened. Some opinions have changed with the passage of time and vantage points. As the "Kids" became adults, they had families of their own, watched society change, and made their own mistakes. Many have applied maturity, wisdom, and experience to their memories. They have a new understanding of the difficulties in rearing children by the hundreds. Others are too bitter, confused, or wounded to sort it out.

Grown men developed lumps in their throats or chuckled at the absurdities in the telling, but we got through their stories together. Here, middle-aged "Kids" and senior citizens who lived at St. Agatha in every decade relive some of their experiences, tragedies, and growth to share with you.

Part 1

Our Family

Home Kids is actually two stories in one, like one of those topsy-turvy dolls that you flip upside down. The black and white seersucker dress of the mama doll flops over her head, to reveal a little girl in a yellow calico print; two dolls in one; two perspectives to this story.

One

Away We Go

On the last night that we were together as a family, kitchen clean-up fell to me. The middle of three sisters, in a family of nine children, I alternated with my older sister, Ginger. Helen at nine had other chores.

We argued. "I did them last night," I said.

"No," she said, "that was to make up for me doing them the night before when it was your turn. Remember, you wanted to watch Mighty Joe Young?" This would be my last argument with Ginger for a while.

I hated scraping the dried macaroni and Velveeta cheese now hardened to concrete off the plates. On this last night together, we actually had a regular meal for a change. Uncle Bill left it up to my brothers to buy groceries for a couple of days. He gave them money for food, and they bought items for our usual fare: Elbow macaroni, Ragu sauce and spaghetti, fish sticks, and canned creamed corn.

Plunging my hands into the hot sudsy water was always relaxing until I got to the pots and cast iron skillet. Then it was Brillo and elbow grease all the way.

I wondered if the "cockaroaches" would follow us. The little beasts scurried in every direction whenever we opened a drawer or cupboard. We rarely had any Black Flag. We just squished them, but they kept on coming. I wouldn't miss the bugs, but I'd rather live with them if it meant we could stay together.

Tommy had taken out the trash and emptied the mousetraps that evening. We always had mice, too. As I sat at the kitchen table doing homework, I wondered if our lives were finally going to become normal again. A sudden movement flashed in my peripheral vision. By the time I turned my head, a brown blur disappeared behind an uplifted corner of the linoleum.

We usually had at least one cat, which helped hold down the mouse population. Our striped tabby, Tiger, had endless litters of kittens, which we loved. She'd just had another one. She would choose an open drawer or the bottom of a closet and make a nest in it. She blinked back at us with her brood of tiny mewing heads nursing at her belly. We couldn't use that drawer or closet floor till she moved her babies.

All of our pets foraged through the neighbors' alleys and trashcans for most of their food. Our dog Blackie was a large, short-haired, mixed breed of that color. Imaginative names, I know. We just let him out in the morning and at night. It never occurred to us to wonder where he went in between, or whether he would come back. He always did.

Then one day, we didn't. We just went away and left behind everything we knew.

This last apartment was the top floor of a three-story brownstone, a block in from the Grand Concourse. Our last move, but certainly not the first time we had to move suddenly.

Over the last four years, Mom found that landlords did not want to rent to widows with eight kids at home, regardless of how confirmed her finances were, so she would lie to them, saying there were only four kids. As she drank more and more, and her own depression enveloped her, life got increasingly unruly. We kids ran in the house, jumped off furniture, and took shortcuts out windows. We ran up and down the stairs, banged doors, and generally made a nuisance of ourselves. The landlords and neighbors saw Mom coming and going drunk, and felt she was neglecting us. We were running wild. Before long, we'd raise enough of a ruckus that the landlord would evict us and we had to move. Again.

The move when I was twelve had been the most painful to me personally. For the first time since our real home on Devoe burned down, I had finally put down some roots and made real friends. I could even have continued to take the ridicule from the neighbors who had begun to give us unsolicited Hefty bags full of clothes. I had loved living in that beautiful brownstone instead of an apartment with tenants above, below, and on either side who complained about how much noise we made. But we blew it, and we had to move again.

The move that had devastated our family had occurred four years earlier when I was nine. On February 12, 1961, our house on Devoe Terrace burned down on Ginger's twelfth birthday. We'd enjoyed a birthday cake after dinner. Ginger went off to her first Friday night dance at St. Peter's High School with our two older brothers, Jerry and Billy. The oldest, Gene, was in the Air Force by then. The rest of us kids were upstairs, jumping on the beds—one of our favorite activities. I think David, the youngest at four, enjoyed it the most. Because he was so small and light, he kept reaching to touch the ceiling. We were all laughing at our littlest brother when I heard a commotion downstairs and signaled David to be still. This took a bit of persuading.

I went to the top of the stairs and, leaning over as far as I could without being detected, I listened. I could hear my mother's voice, sort of hysterical, shouting to my brother Billy who had come home early. I crept down the front stairs a bit and could peep a little inside the living room where their voices came from. An eerie orange glow tinted the wall. They were rushing back and forth, carrying water from the kitchen, trying to put out a fire that began behind the cotton-filled couch and soon engulfed it. I could hear water splashing on the floor in the hall. Finally, Mom screamed over the increasing roar of the fire for Billy to go to the kitchen and call the fire department.

The smoke became thick and pained my throat to breathe. Tommy tried carrying water from the upstairs bathroom, sloshing it along the stairs, but it was like a gnat spitting on the fire for all the good it did. The stairs became slippery, and Tommy dragged a mattress off a nearby single bed and placed it on the top steps with the idea of forming an escape ramp—something he learned at school, I guess. It was all very frantic and sudden.

"Mom, what should we *do*?" I yelled down over the banister.

She had warned us to stay upstairs, but desperate now, she shrieked, "Get out! Go down the back stairs! Go outside!"

We tumbled down the slippery back staircase, narrow and dark, through the kitchen, and onto the porch. Mom and Billy met us there, and she counted heads.

"Oh my God, where's David?" she screamed.

I spun around as if she may have overlooked him, but he was missing.

Feeling that it was my responsibility to get everyone out, I ran back up the rear staircase, choking from the hot burning smoke I was swallowing. It billowed upwards, lifted on the draft from the open door. Desperately, I shouted David's name, tears streaming down my cheeks, a roaring in my

David at age 3

ears. I wanted to run back down to the fresh air. Where was he? I could not leave him here, no matter how much I wanted to get out. It was like drowning in smoke, instead of water. It hurt my lungs to breathe.

The second floor had several bedrooms, and there was another floor above. I prayed that he had not gone up there, or I might never find him. I screamed his name hysterically.

"David! David, we have to get outside," I pleaded. Miraculously, I found him hiding under one of my brothers' beds in the room at the top of the stairs. "Come on, we have to get out."

"No, no," he fought me. "I can't breathe."

He burrowed further under the second bed closest to the wall. I caught his ankle and dragged him out. He grabbed on to the leg of the bed, not wanting to go down into the smoke and fire. I pounded his little hands to get him to let go. Finally, he released his grip and grabbed onto me. I wrapped my arms around his waist and carried him down the dark narrow staircase. Once on the porch, I flung him into my mother's desperate arms.

"Oh my God, thank God," is all my mother could say as she cradled his head against her heart.

I bent over, sucking in deep gulps of fresh air. We all huddled together on the back porch landing. Billy had gone back in to Grandma's room next to the kitchen to get bankbooks and papers. He rushed back out as the firemen began arriving.

Our house stood on a little knoll, up and back from the street. Two external flights of stairs had to be mounted to reach the front door. As the neighbors stood anxiously down on the sidewalk, flames poured out the windows in great columns towards the black sky.

The firemen could not get their truck up the one-way street to our house. Double-parked cars blocked the narrow street, so the firemen came running on foot, dragging their equipment. One of them found us huddling on the back stairs, still believing that the fire would somehow be put out. He carried the smallest ones, David and Helen, out to the street where he set them down. Helen screwed up her courage and asked him if he could save her Thumbelina doll. He said he'd try, but he couldn't find it.

The neighbors draped blankets around us. We had only the clothes on our backs as we were whisked off to a neighbor's home. They gave us hot chocolate. A fireman came to question us. Apparently, one helpful neighbor suggested that David might have started the fire, as he was known to play with matches.

It was true that when he was three or four, he found a box of stick matches in the kitchen, sat on the bed, and struck them one after another, discarding them where he sat. The bedding and mattress caught fire. Someone called the fire department, and anxious neighbors stood in the street, even after they heard the fire was out. David was labeled a firebug after that. But the night of the house fire, he was with the rest of us upstairs, jumping on the bed. We knew with absolute certainty that he did not do it, and we said so, but it was as if they wanted to blame it on someone.

After much interrogation of the four-year-old, the fireman elicited a confession from David. I guess he thought that he must have done it, since this grown-up kept insisting it was so. As the night wore on, we were redistributed to relatives and friends.

The fire devastated our family, certainly, but I believe this false allegation and confession plagued David for the rest of his life. Kids can be very thoughtless in their taunts. "Remember when you burned the house down?" Or, "Well, if you hadn't burned the house down, this wouldn't be happening," ignoring the fact that it wasn't true.

That night, I was sent to stay with mom's cousin Aunt Rita Mary; Helen went to Mary Doyle's, my Mom's girlfriend who had worked with my dad; Ginger went with Aunt Mary. We were disseminated; a child here, a child there. The next day, the Red Cross brought us clothes and shoes.

Aunt Mary and Uncle Johnny heard the broadcast on the radio the next morning. "A widow and her eight children narrowly escaped a house fire in the Bronx last night." Incredulous when they heard the address, and getting no answer on the phone, they came on the run.

We lost everything.

Like Helen, I longed for my Christmas presents. I had a navy-blue baby buggy, and a pink-and-blue tin dollhouse with miniature kitchen utensils. They were still warm in my heart. Even in a household full of babies, little girls always played with dolls.

Before Christmas, I'd taken money I saved from doing odd jobs for a dime or a quarter and bought an Underwood typewriter—the kind with the big round keys that you have to press really hard to operate. It cost $40—a fortune to me. Perhaps I fancied myself writing *Nancy Drew* books. After the fire, it was just a melted hunk of metal with the keys welded together. Everything burned.

I was never able to go back into our house again, though I saw it once after the fire. It was so sad, so forlorn looking. The white paint was all smudged and charred. All the windows were gone, leaving holes with tracks where the flames had punched out the glass. The front door had a sign on it that said, "Condemned." Yellow tape was laced across the banister and the tiny yard strewn with charred hunks of what once had been our furniture. The Blue Spruce Christmas tree that grew on the lawn, which we decorated with blue outdoor Christmas lights each year, was stripped of green, its trunk blackened.

Gaping holes between the floors let the sun shine through. Even though the house was condemned, the big kids sneaked in with some of their friends a few times to see what they could pillage. They took a few mementos of the fire, but nothing seemed to be really worth saving.

The neighbors on either side had grown weary of how unruly we'd become over the past few years since Dad died. Not that they would wish anything like this on us, yet I couldn't help but think that they might be happy with us gone. No more kids jumping out the bathroom window onto their roof to retrieve stray balls, or climbing over their fence to steal the cherries from the big tree that spread unfortunately close to our fence. They were too sour to eat, but we used them as ammunition to fire at each other.

Undoubtedly, the neighbors were relieved and thankful for their own narrow escapes from the inferno. Our homes were just a narrow alleyway apart, about four feet. Like the luckiest of the three little pigs, they had built their homes out of brick. Ours was not of straw, but of wood. Same results.

The insurance company explored possible scenarios besides my little brother, the firebug. One was that a stray candle from Ginger's birthday cake had found its way behind the couch and may have caught fire. The fire was ultimately ruled an accident due to faulty wiring, perhaps related to recent renovations. Too late to tell the newspapers, and too late for David's reputation.

It was all gone, and nothing could ever be replaced—particularly our old lives. I longed for my home. For the rest of my life, I could mentally walk from room to room and describe the carpet patterns, the shade of the red paisley on the sofa, the kidney shape of the modern Formica coffee table. I still vividly recall the placement of the rooms, closets, and my secret hiding places, like under the stairs and behind the Lazy Susan. It had been difficult enough when the house was remodeled, and some of our nooks and crannies were replaced with paneling and cupboards. But we had been happy in that home. It was our final connection to Dad—to the old life—which was over.

At least we had money to find a place to live while we waited for the fire insurance money. It came from a lawsuit filed for my father's wrongful death four years earlier. One day a blood vessel burst in dad's nose. It started to bleed and wouldn't stop. I remember seeing him vomiting up blood, and he had to go to the hospital. After three weeks he was due to come home on his thirty-third birthday. The doctor decided that Dad had lost too much blood, and that he should have a transfusion before going home. We adored our dad and were so disappointed he would not be with us on his birthday. We'd missed him for weeks.

The next day, expectantly, we crowded around Mom and Grandma yelping like pups as they came through the front door. We'd been waiting all day for our daddy. But something was wrong. Mom wasn't smiling, and dad wasn't there. Uncle Bill and Aunt Mary were there instead. Everyone had been crying.

Mom and Grandma herded us kids into the biggest upstairs bedroom while our aunt and uncle waited downstairs. Mom looked dramatic, like Loretta Young. In a quiet voice, almost a whisper, she said, "Daddy's not coming home. He died today at the hospital."

Everyone started crying, looking from one to the other, trying to see a way out of this truth. I met up with my mother, and we both whispered at the same time, "Are you alright?" But we never would be again. I don't know if losing a dad is easier when you're older and have had him longer, but when you are a small child, there is still an invisible cord connecting you. You are still reaching towards them, not away to the outside world, as in the teen years.

Dad was given the blood transfusion the night before, and it was the wrong type. Blood was supposed to be checked for type when it was taken, and again before it was administered to double-check. But the nurse hadn't bothered rechecking it before she injected it into dad.

"It's always been right before," she later said.

But it wasn't this time. It had been mislabeled when it was drawn. Dad lapsed into a coma and died during the night. Not only did that nurse kill my father, she killed our whole family that day.

The *New York Times* obituary read:

John Canfield, Publishing Executive, Dies September 17, 1957

John Canfield, General Manager of McFadden publications, passed away last night at Midtown Hospital after an illness of approximately three weeks. Before joining McFadden earlier this year, he had been on the staff of LOOK for more than 15 years. Mr. Canfield passed away on his 33rd birthday. His wife, Rita, and nine children survive him. Also surviving him are a brother William, and a sister Mary. Mr. Canfield started his publishing career with LOOK while he was still in high school, working with the magazine on a part-time basis as an office boy. Following his graduation from Cardinal Hayes High School in 1942, he became a full-time LOOK employee while attending St. John's University, nights. His progress at LOOK was rapid. From his office-boy start, he progressed successively to Stockroom Manager, head of Accounts Payable, Assistant to the Manager of Budget & Sales Analysis, Chief Accountant in the Business Office, and head of Cost Control in the LOOK Production department. Becoming General Manager of McFadden Publication at the age of 32, he was one of the youngest executives to hold such a position at a major publishing company. The body is reposing at the Walter B. Cook Funeral Parlor, 1 W. 190th St., Bronx.

The *New York World Telegram* ran a similar piece with the inclusion that the Mass would be said at St. Peter's Church, University Avenue at Fordham Road—the church we attended every Sunday where our family members were married, baptized, confirmed, and where Gene was an altar boy—and finally, where we eulogized. Mom couldn't handle all the new responsibility on top of the loss of her childhood sweetheart.

The luckiest event of her life was when she met my father at Dominican Camp the summer after they graduated—she from St. Thomas Aquinas High School and he from Cardinal Hayes. It was a Catholic camp, and they were junior counselors. When summer ended, they couldn't bear to part. Dad turned eighteen in September, and mom was already eighteen. After his birthday, they were married in September at St. John's Church.

Mom was happier in the next fifteen years than she had been in all her life. They both wanted a large family, and nine children were born in rapid succession: the Canfield baseball team. Dad was disciplined, but

not inflexible. He made it all seem like fun, like in the book, *Cheaper by the Dozen*. He would line us all up from smallest to biggest, comb our hair, and inspect our nails. He knew what to do in every situation. He was organized and told Mom what she needed to do. She liked it that way. He made up a schedule for her to follow, bought all her clothes, even did the food shopping at A&P on Friday nights with the older kids in tow.

For the first time, Mom had her own home, and it improved weekly under the ceaseless hammer of Dad

John and Rita Canfield in 1945

and his father. Their six sons and three little girls were as robust and active as Michelangelo's mischievous cherubs. We were rambunctious, but not particularly troublesome. And grandma, dad's mom, took care of the others while Mom cared for the babies. We got along on simple meals like macaroni and cheese, hamburgers, and fish sticks. Dad pitched in here, too, because neither his mother nor his wife could cook well.

Dad's career growth progressed through hard work and personal sacrifice. He earned a finance degree while building the home and family of his dreams. In one photo of my parents, taken at an American Legion dinner, my mother looks happier than I'd ever seen her. Gleeful, even. Uncle Eddie, Aunt Rita, her parents, and spinster aunt sat around them, laughing and enjoying life.

Dad often worked late, brought people home, and entertained at fancy downtown restaurants in the evening. Sometimes Mom went with him, but she was shy—certainly no socialite—and usually stayed at home. Mom thought life would always be idyllic. She was wrong. My father was the center support beam of our lives. When he died, it all collapsed around her like a circus tent with its pole pulled out. It was up to the rest of the family to try to shore her up.

The day after the fire, the story appeared on the back cover of the Daily News with a picture of our house. Flames poured from windows upstairs and down. Firemen were visible where the glass had been. In contrast to the devastation on the back, the front cover featured John Kennedy sprinting from the ocean at Palm Beach, while Jacquie sat composed in the foreground with three-year-old Caroline and her dollies. What a mockery it seemed to me. Little John Jr. had just been born, and this family was the picture of contentment, beginning a new life. Our new life was to be one of chaos.

Jerry told us that when he and his friends were coming home from the dance that night, they heard from a few blocks away that there was a fire on their block. One of his friends remarked, "Hey, Canfield, wouldn't it be funny if it were your house?" My brother said, "If it is, I'll punch you in the mouth." I wonder if he ever did.

We moved away from that neighborhood to an apartment house near Aunt Rita Mary's. That was the first of our many moves, but we were happy to be together again with all new stuff. Over the next four years, our lives grew more chaotic. Besides all the moves, mom sought the antidote to her unbearable loss of my dad in alcohol. She drank more and more, and was gone more and more, as time went on.

In the four years that followed the house fire, while we moved from place to place, our standard of living decreased each time. We became outright shabby. Our shoes had holes the size of a quarter in the bottoms, which meant that our socks had matching holes. Calluses on our feet marked the spots. Like hoboes, we placed cardboard inside the shoe, over the hole. When it rained, the cardboard dissolved, and we replaced it. Socks came in actual sizes back then. Mom used to measure our size by wrapping the sock around our clenched fist. But increasingly, we wore whatever we could find. If they were too small, the cuff would slide down into the heel of our shoe. If they were too big, we bent them over at the toe and stuffed them in our shoes.

Safety pins replaced buttons. Hems were taped, stapled, glued—whatever we could find in the school's art supplies to make a repair. We never had belts, and it was not unusual for me to have a rip at the waist of my dress that tied with a sash, or a tear under an arm, that stayed that way forever. We just tucked it in. We had no boots, gloves, hats, or scarves in the last few years. If we did get them, we lost them soon afterward, and they were not replaced. Kids need parents to say, "Where's your scarf? Go back outside and get it."

We did not all bathe and brush our teeth regularly as there were never enough supplies or prompting. If no one makes young kids attend to these things, they are content to ignore their personal maintenance. The older kids were more fastidious, more self-motivated. We younger kids were not.

During the last couple of years, we had no holidays to speak of, except what one of us scraped together for another. When I went back to school after Christmas, and all the kids were telling about what presents they got, I would lie. Of course, I overdid it, saying I got tons of stuff, so I think they saw through it. How could I tell them my Mother forgot it was Christmas? Our last Christmas together we had no tree, no decorations, no meal, and no presents beyond the little remembrances from each other, like a pack of Juicy Fruit gum. There were little gifts from mom's parents, aunts, and uncles, but they never dreamed that what we got from them was all we would receive.

The same thing happened at Thanksgiving. My grandparents showed up for dinner, per Mom's invitation. Not only had Mom not been around for days, or told us they were coming, but there was no turkey with trimmings. Grandpa sent for take-out Chinese. Years earlier, after my Father died, my grandparents used to take us all to dinner at nice restaurants. But when Mom started getting drunk and embarrassing us, they stopped. We misbehaved too, leaping up, rattling china, and spilling things.

Every summer, we used to go down to Atlantic City for a week with Mom and Gram. The last time we went, Mom took us alone, and we stayed in a charming Victorian Inn. She got so drunk in the bar that they asked us to leave the first night. We had to take a cab all the way back to New York City without ever seeing the water. We never went again.

My brothers would go down to the neighborhood store and carry groceries to people's houses for them. "Box boys" they were called. They'd use the tip money to buy fish sticks or spaghetti or a watermelon. Sometimes, that's all we had to eat. We lived from meal to meal. My mother would go off, usually saying she was going to the store, and she may even have intended to come right back. Then she'd decide to have a drink, and she would be gone for days. When she did come back or call, she would defensively tell us that she had left money for us. It was hidden in the mop, or under the shelf paper in the cupboard, or under the linoleum in the corner beneath her bed.

We looked. It wasn't there.

I think she felt justified in her absence if she believed she'd left money in the house. She probably did leave money in the house, but conveniently "forgot" to tell us the correct location in order to have a little nest egg for herself when she came back. When she went out, Mom kept her money folded in her shoe. Maybe she was afraid of getting robbed, or losing her purse. It was another nest egg. If we found this stash at home, we didn't care that it was smashed, walked on, and smelly; we ran out to spend it.

Sometimes, she would come home and replenish her cash, then go right back out again, often taking a kid with her as a crutch. We'd sit around a bar for hours, play pool or pinball, and drink endless Cokes. I don't know why she brought us except to get her home. The littler kids were content just to be with her and put quarters in the jukebox. But the older we got, the more boredom took over, and the more likely we were to complain and whine about having homework and things to do.

She gave people money, or they ripped her off. She used to leave home with a gold cross around her neck, a ring, or charm bracelet—usually a gift from her mother for her birthday. She came back without any of it. Maybe she used them to buy drinks. Once she gave one of her friends our TV set. They came to the house and said, "Your mother said we could have this TV," and carted it right out from under us. After that, one by one, we refused to go with her anymore, and we worried when she took one of the little kids along.

Mom had checkbooks lying all over the house, in various stages of use, from Dollar Savings and Chase Manhattan Bank. She used the kind that had a stub between the book and the check. You filled out the check and the stub at the same time and kept a running balance. All of her stubs were blank. The partially used checkbooks were left curling and discarded, like decomposing apple peelings.

Before Dad died, Mom didn't even know how to write a check. I don't know how her accounting got done afterwards. I think as soon as she got her bi-weekly checks, one each from Social Security for herself and the kids, and another from my Father's estate, she'd write as few checks as she could get away with: rent, electricity, a big grocery order for food and incidentals, and the rest became pocket money until the next check came. It was a guaranteed, endless supply. If she could get out of writing those essential checks too, she did. We knew we had to hit her up on the first or the fifteenth of the month, or wait until the next check came. We were always there with our outstretched hands in a pent-up demand. She came to feel that we didn't care about or need her for anything, except to get money, and she resented giving it to us.

My mother lied to us all the time. She said she'd be right back when she went out, but we wouldn't see her for days. She lied about where she'd been. For example, she'd say she was at Gram's. Meanwhile, Gram had called looking for her. She told us she wouldn't drink if we stopped to get something to eat with her, then she'd get stinking drunk and embarrass us, and we'd be asked to leave the restaurant. It was just one lie after another. Sometimes I hated my mother. I couldn't understand what had happened to make her into this person she had become.

At forty-one, Mom still had baby soft pale skin and gentle dark brown eyes. She said she had bad acne while growing up, but I saw no sign of it. She dyed her hair chestnut-brown with auburn highlights to hide the premature gray she'd had since she was seventeen. She was Ginger's height, five feet seven inches—a little taller than I was at five feet three inches. Her weight varied between 125 to 145 pounds. Her narrow face was a little gaunt-looking, but she had a wonderful smile, rarely brightened by Max Factor's red lipstick that she used to wear. She'd peer into a little compact mirror and daub on the palest of face powder, then the lipstick, then wipe the excess off her teeth. She was really a very sweet, gentle person—when she wasn't drinking. That's when her hair showed an inch of gray roots, and her face became sallow and bare.

I thought about this person she had become: a mother who called one of her kids on the phone to come and get her. She'd either run out of money or forgotten how to get home in her drunken stupor. If one of the big kids answered those calls and tried to question her about where she was and when she was coming home, she would sidestep their questions and tell them to put one of the little kids on the phone. She usually asked for Tommy, sometimes David. Maybe she believed hauling her home through the dead of night was man's work, forgetting that they were only little boys—seven, eight, or nine years old. Like the boys, Ginger and I took our turns, too.

We younger kids had not started to refuse to go get her—yet. We were the kids; she was the adult. One by one, the others began to stand their ground, refuse to go, and insist on knowing when she was coming home.

It didn't matter what she said; she never kept her promises anyway. Or she'd just hang up and call back later.

Sometimes we went on foot to retrieve her; other times by cab if we could get a driver who would accept our promise that Mom would pay him when we reached her. Of course, then she'd say that they would get paid when we returned home to her hidden stash. The driver had no choice but to take us back or he'd lose the first half of the fare too. At all hours of the day and night, we were summoned to bring her home. Many times we had to walk fairly long distances.

We hated to go to these dives because of the scary neighborhoods. But we knew that if we didn't go get her, she wouldn't come home, especially if she had no more money. And we still wanted her. We didn't think of her as lost or lonely, grieving for our father. We only thought of ourselves, what we wanted and needed. So, we went to get her because we still loved her.

We knew she only came home to regroup, and then she'd leave us again, but we wanted whatever piece of her we could get. We often had to half carry her home through the Bronx neighborhoods, stopping to prop her against a building for awhile until she could walk again or to try to hail a cab that was sympathetic enough to take a chance on getting paid when we reached home. I really hated her then.

But there were moments in this last year when Mom enjoyed an occasional quiet moment with us kids, as if she'd surfaced from her private hell. We'd gather around her, hungry for attention. This usually took place on a Saturday or Sunday morning with sunbeams dancing in the shafts of light, streaming through the blinds. We would tell her our childish news, snitch on each other, poke and chide, and vie for her attention. Mom appeared relaxed. She smiled and chuckled, even kidded with us a little. She never said anything bad or negative to, or about, anyone. She would laugh good-naturedly at our antics.

These soirees would last about a half hour or an hour at most, then we'd start getting rowdy, competitive, or snide. She'd grow restless, and we'd struggle to keep her. She'd gingerly extricate herself from the pile without saying much of anything. It reminded me of the mother cats that we had often watched. She either finished or bored with nursing her brood, stood up unhurriedly, and strode away while the kittens dropped off in her wake. We regretted that we had given in to our pettiness and driven her away. I longed for those intimate times.

Things just seemed to be getting worse all the time. I knew we needed outside help, an adult that we could trust. I didn't want my mother to get into trouble; I just wanted my life to be normal. I don't know what the other kids were thinking. We never discussed "Mom, the problem." We just dealt with what was before us. Jackie and I would talk about it a little. One by one, each of us grew weary. We lost the optimism of the little kids that each episode of disappointment was isolated. And we began to rebel, one by one.

My oldest brother Gene and I had corresponded off and on in the three years since he went into the service. He was twenty-two now, married to a girl from Louisiana, had a little girl, and was stationed at Lackland Air force Base in Texas. Last year, he'd brought his young wife and baby home to meet the family.

Gene could help us without hurting our mom. I wrote to him, explaining how awful things were, begging him to come home and help us. Every day I willed my letter to hurry and get to him, as if wishing so hard could hurry him back. I needed Gene to come to our rescue before someone found out what I had done.

When I was little, Gene would put me on his shoulders and gallop around the neighborhood chanting, "To arms, to arms, the British are coming." I thought he was saying "two arms, two arms," while holding mine up and out to the sides. I didn't know what that meant, so I screamed, laughing because it was fun.

"To arms, to arms, the British are coming." Now I understood what that meant. Gene called to say he'd gotten the letter. He was coming. We were saved.

Gene got an emergency leave and flew home. As long as she had a man to lean on—especially one in uniform—Mom was happy. As the oldest, helping the family was ultimately Gene's responsibility, even though he had left at seventeen, leaving fourteen-year-old Jerry with all the responsibility.

Gene stayed for a week. This festive time pushed aside all of the madness that had happened since the house burned down. In my childish mind, I became convinced everything would change—that Mom would stop drinking, and we would be a family again. We would have a home instead of a caravan, moving from place to place. Mom would take care of us.

During Gene's stay, we all went out to dinner with Mom's parents and over to visit at their tiny apartment. We had dinner with Aunt Mary and Uncle Johnny, too. Sometimes Mom and Gene went out to a bar together, just the two of them, which Gene thought was so cool. Or they'd go to Uncle Bill's tavern, and Aunt Terry would join them there for a rollicking time. I guess my Mother behaved appropriately enough during those times and acted acceptably drunk.

They probably didn't realize Mom was an alcoholic, just celebrating the return of her eldest son. Maybe they thought it was an improvement

Mom, with Gene in the background

over the wallflower she'd always been. It was like Mardi Gras before Lent; I thought that everything would go back to the way it was before when we were happy and safe. I was partially right. Things did go back to normal when Gene returned to Texas, but not the old version of normal: the more recent one. Mom missed Gene terribly when he left and soon resumed her drinking.

One day I was supposed to babysit for Aunt Mary while she went to a Girl Scout or PTA Meeting. Uncle Johnny was working overtime. Ginger, their regular babysitter, was unavailable that day. Aunt Mary tried to call ahead to confirm that I'd be there, but a recording said that our phone was disconnected.

Always a great walker, though it was a couple of miles, she put her two girls in the carriage and hiked over to our house to confirm that I would be there that night. She was shocked to find Mom drunk in the early afternoon. I was so embarrassed. It was stunning to Aunt Mary that her sister-in-law—the meek person she'd known almost all her life—was this disheveled, staggering, incoherent wreck.

My aunt hastily carted her children out of there, sputtering about having to get home. She confirmed that I was still coming that night and then left. When I arrived that evening, Aunt Mary quizzed me about what was going on. At last, I told it all.

All day while she waited for me, Aunt Mary had been worrying about what to do. She wished she could avoid her meeting that night, but it was impossible. Growing up with an alcoholic father, she knew only too well what our lives must be like, but felt at a loss about what to do. Whom could she turn to for help without getting the authorities involved? Anyone who has lived with an abuser of any kind shares the unspoken rule: You don't let it out of the house. Otherwise, you may lose the control, and who knows what will happen then?

After a sleepless night, Aunt Mary found that the next day provided no answers. She went up to St. Peter's and met Ginger outside when school let out. She alternated between blasting Ginger for not confiding in her about our lifestyle, consoling her, and finally trying to come up with a solution.

Aunt Mary was reluctant to tell Uncle Johnny or her brother Bill that mom was not taking care of her children, that they were practically on their own, and that Rita was drunk most of the time and often gone. Though she had no workable solution, Aunt Mary knew she had to do something; she couldn't just leave her brother's children neglected. From her own experience, she knew that Mom would not listen to reason.

Burying her head in the sand was not an option either. She remembered all too clearly what it was like growing up with her father: the drinking, the beatings, and worst of all, the shame and humiliation. She would neither turn her back, nor air all the dirty laundry in public. There had to be another way.

She felt guilt when she wondered how all of this was happening without her knowing. And how could things have gone so far wrong without Uncle Bill, the Lents, and Gram knowing about it? These poor kids—they don't have enough to eat, don't have shoes, or money for lunch, or carfare. What would her brother Jack say if he were alive? What was he saying from heaven? These thoughts drummed over and over in her head in the days that followed.

Sure, there had been some hints that things might not be just right. Mom had slowly stopped coming to the family gatherings: Thanksgivings, birthdays, Christmases. For a while mom sent us to our cousins' birthday parties, sometimes without a gift. But even that had stopped a few years earlier.

And of course, Mom had put Grandma—Aunt Mary's mother—out of the house after Dad died. That was not so easily forgiven. My dad's mother was one of the old-fashioned grandmas who always looked old and wrinkly, probably from a hard life. She had her gray hair tightly permed and slept with silver rods in her hair every night. She wore her short-sleeved, calf-length flowered housedresses belted in the middle, and her slip was always showing. Her nylons wrinkled around her calves and ankles above sturdy black lace-up shoes with chunky heels like the nuns at school wore.

In 1945, Aunt Mary graduated from high school, took Grandma, and ran away from the abusive husband she'd tolerated for almost thirty years. They both got jobs and a small apartment. When Mary got married in 1949, our dad already had my brothers Gene, Jerry, and Billy, and my sister Ginger. Jackie was on the way. So, Grandma moved in to help Mom take care of the brood. When Dad died, the two grieving women argued about Mom's drinking, running around, and leaving her children home.

In a heated moment, Mom told Grandma to leave. She went to live with Uncle Bill and Aunt Terry, whose own family had started on the road to nine children.

Aunt Mary learned something very valuable from her mother's plight: how dependent a woman could become on a man for her very existence. Grandma had to rely exclusively on her children for her survival.

But the main reason Aunt Mary and Uncle Johnny had become estranged from us was that they had their own children, families, and jobs. They'd wanted to build a better life than they'd had and just got so busy that they lost touch. Mom had never been outgoing or easy to talk to. She was bashful and had nothing much to say beyond sharing her children's antics. All she did was smile, for the most part. Only Jack had been able to draw her out.

Aunt Mary swallowed her pride and went to see her parish priest of ten years. Instead of being compassionate and helpful, he was disdainful and turned away, coldly saying there was nothing he could do except to pray for her soul. That was a bitter blow to Aunt Mary, one she never quite recovered from. A devout Catholic, as was her mother, she had been actively involved in the church all of her life. They believed that when the chips were down, they could always find help at the church. This was the first time she had reached out a hand, and it had been slapped away.

It might have been tempting for Aunt Mary to follow the priest's advice: Just pray for our souls and hope for the best. But she could never live with herself if she abandoned her nephews and nieces. She knew what it was like to be one of those kids, living in fear and shame. She began by telling Johnny.

Of course, he was as dumbstruck as she had been. Together, they devised a plan. First, they had to establish the scope of the problem, to confirm that not only was Mom's drinking really as bad as reported, but that she was really neglecting her children. It wasn't that they didn't believe Ginger and me, they didn't want to believe us. They wanted it to somehow be a horrible mistake. After all, we were kids. Maybe we were somehow angry at our mother and exaggerating.

The next Saturday, about ten in the morning, Uncle Johnny came to our apartment. I don't think I'd ever seen him without a smile or without Aunt Mary. They were a set like salt-and-pepper shakers. But he was not jolly this time. He was built like a pit-bull, short and powerful after a lifetime as a swimmer and diver, and years of hard physical work with the phone company. He knew how to keep his temper in check, unlike his brother-in-law, Uncle Bill. He said he was working in the area and stopped by to say hi. The younger kids were up and watching Saturday morning cartoons. The older kids were still asleep.

Mom wasn't home, the little ones told him. Hadn't been home for a couple of days, in fact. They didn't actually remember when she left.

I knew Uncle Johnny was confirming with the other kids the things Ginger and I had said, so I kept quiet. They answered, a little unsure whether they were supposed to be truthful.

No, they didn't know where she was. Yes, sometimes she went out and didn't come back for a few days. They were used to it.

He was shocked.

Kids have mixed voices in their heads. Up until my talk with Aunt Mary, all our efforts had been to hide these things from outsiders. Perhaps our teachers had suspected something was wrong. We never got our papers signed. Without the money for bus trips, we'd had to remain behind at school. We falsified our bus passes because we had no money to buy new ones, but no one intervened. Now that Aunt Mary and Uncle Johnny knew, it was as if somehow there was no need to hold back.

When creditors first began coming to the door and calling on the phone, they asked for Mom. When we'd say she wasn't home, they'd say things sternly like, "Tell your mother that if this bill isn't paid, we'll shut off the lights," or, "We'll throw you all out in the street," in the case of the landlord.

So, instead of enduring the berating, we stood quietly peering through the peephole. We didn't want to deal with the lies. I think Mom paid the bills when there was no alternative, such as when needing to get the electricity or phone turned back on. She didn't see herself as dishonest, just disorganized and disinterested.

Uncle Johnny kept his cool, but our secret was out. Something would happen now. I didn't think that my mother would get into trouble, just that someone would intervene and help us. In spite of everything that had happened, we still loved our mother. We wanted her to stop drinking, to stop going away and leaving us, things like that, but we still loved the person underneath the problems.

This problem proved too big for Aunt Mary and Uncle Johnny to take on alone. They would have to consult Uncle Bill. He had a right, as Dad's brother and our uncle, and they needed his help. Uncle Bill reacted with shock and anger, and probably a little bit of guilt, too. The father of eight children himself, with another to come, Uncle Bill no doubt knew what life must be like for us kids. He knew Rita was weak. It was Uncle Bill who had fought the insurance company and won a quarter of a million dollars for his brother's widow and children to live on when they offered a $25,000 settlement. Now, it seemed, he had to protect the children from their own mother.

All combinations of what could be done quickly seemed to fall short. They thought about getting a housekeeper, considered which kids could go where, which family members could move to a bigger apartment or add on an addition to their home. These were impractical solutions for the short term, however. And they weren't even sure if Rita could be rehabilitated, or how long it would take. Jerry and Billy were just teenagers; they couldn't supervise these kids properly, yet they were surprised they had been shouldering the responsibilities for so long.

They decided to confer with Gram, Mom's mother. After all, they couldn't just take Rita's kids away without going to court, and that could be a real mess. Worse yet, the kids could get lost in the New York child welfare system, and outside of their influence of the family. The New York newspapers were full of horror stories about children being shuttled from one abusive government-run home to another, and now the city was bankrupt. They needed to take care of matters themselves, within the family.

Everyone knew Gram was of no use in a crisis. She was Mom's role model for helplessness. But her third husband Bill, a Civil Engineer who once worked on the Panama Canal, might be a good resource. He was slightly less shocked than the others, having observed evidence of his stepdaughter's drinking and neglect. How often had she invited them to dinner and then not been home when they arrived—even for holidays?

When Bill had complained to his wife, Gram resisted interfering, not wanting to do anything to alienate her daughter. There was always the unspoken issue of Gram's divorce from Mom's father John in 1936. Mom was twelve, and the Depression had deepened with each year.

John allegedly drank excessively and had trouble keeping a job, according to Gram. So, she left her only child with John's family, got a secretarial job, and moved in with her own sister. It is not clear why she did not reclaim Mom a few years later when she remarried. Perhaps Mom—a shy, only child—was comfortable living with her cousin same-aged cousin Rita Mary. Perhaps it was Gram's remarriage which brought a lifestyle that included travel, golf, nightclubs, and an active social life, but not children. She often picked up Mom from school, took her shopping and out to dinner, even away for weekends, and they loved each other. Mom loved her stepfather, too, and he was fond of her. Yet she remained with her father's family for five years until she graduated from high school.

Gram always dismissed her husband's concerns about Mom as exaggerated. So, he could only prohibit Mom's drunkenness in his own house. After a brief consideration, he recommended that Aunt Rita Mary and Uncle Eddie be consulted. He respected them and felt they would know what to do.

The rescue party kept resorting to bigger and bigger weapons to deal with the problem. Now it was time to get out the howitzer. My father's side of the family didn't exactly dislike my mother's side; it was probably more of a control issue. Mom was Rita Mary's cousin, and they had lived as sisters for five years. They were family, and they cared about us.

Aunt Rita Mary's mother and my mother's father were brother and sister, making the girls first cousins. They were raised as sisters, though they were opposites in temperament. Both were only children. Rita Mary was outgoing, self-confident, and assertive. Mom was timid, a follower, and presented no ideas of her own. She was sweet-natured and undemanding, content to follow. The girls became allies. Since they were both named Rita after their spinster great-aunt, they were called by their first and middle names. My aunt was Rita Mary, and my mother Rita Clare, though her step-dad nicknamed her Molly-O after the old Irish ballad of that name.

My mom's father John was a handsome, distinguished-looking Irish-French-Canadian—the darling of his sisters. After the divorce, he became the resident manager of the Whitney Mansion on Fifth Avenue, and saw his daughter as often as he could. Mom adored him.

Rita Mary was robust and energetic; Mom was frail. Rheumatic fever had left Mom with a heart murmur as a child, and she also suffered from chronic hay fever. Some resentment resulted from mom being an intruder who did not have to do chores because of her weak constitution.

The girls got along well enough, though. They went to school, church, Girl Scouts, and Catholic summer camp together. Shortly after high school graduation, Aunt Rita Mary married Uncle Eddie in 1941. He was on Shore Patrol in the Coast Guard throughout World War II. Afterwards, he became a New York State Trooper, an NYPD Detective, then Chief of Detectives. Surely he would know what to do about Rita and the kids. The two families formed a plan to get help for Mom and have her kids taken care of.

One day shortly after Uncle Johnny's visit, I came home from school to an eerie sense of doom as after a tornado. Uncle Bill, whom I hadn't seen in years, was there. He asked if I needed anything, and I said I needed shoes. He took out his wallet and gave me $25. I went right up to Beck's on Fordham Road and bought a pair of brown leather boots. All the while, I was wondering what was going on.

Uncle Bill drove us over to Aunt Mary's for dinner that night, but did not stay. Mom was out somewhere. After we ate, Uncle Johnny played the old eight-millimeter home movies that he had taken when we were little. As if from a long ago dream, the life that was all but faded from my memory projected on the screen. It was like looking into a crystal ball that saw into the past, instead of the future. There was my dad, back from heaven, standing tall and handsome in his gray suit and size twelve wingtips. All of us kids danced around his legs; him our Maypole, us carefree and happy.

We wore our new Easter outfits, and clutched baskets and stuffed bunnies. I saw our mother, radiant as Tinkerbelle. My aunts and uncles and all the grandmothers gathered around the Thanksgiving dinner table, everyone together. Uncle Bill carved the turkey while expectant faces eyed his handiwork greedily: a Norman Rockwell tableau.

It hadn't all been a dream. It was real. We had all been together once, happy and normal. I almost could not bear to watch and see that we once had it all when it was now so completely gone. Still, somehow it restored a little of our dignity after the escalating humiliation of the recent years. I wanted to climb back into that life. Perhaps, it could serve as a blueprint for the future.

Magically, there too were my cousins: Uncle Bill's bunch and Aunt Mary's little girls. All of us, such cute little kids in red plaid nighties on Christmas morning, surveying the cornucopia of Santa's leavings. Uncle Johnny played Santa every year. Finger to his lips, he "Shhh-ed" into the camera and distributed toys like an elf. Birthdays clicked past, frame-by-frame, with candles for wishes you believed would really come true. Endless games of pin the tale on the donkey, which we'd played at every birthday party. I saw my younger self, racing for a seat in musical chairs, wearing a frilly party hat and new Sunday clothes.

We mugged for the camera as we splashed in the lake at Uncle Bill's summerhouse in Woodstock. Aunt Mary and Uncle Johnny had swimming races in the water or pushed us kids around in inner tubes. Grandma waved from atop a boulder at the shore, still wearing her printed housedress. Mom sat sprawled beside her in a remarkably similar outfit. Mom never owned a pair of shorts or slacks while Dad was alive and in charge of buying her clothes.

No one was crabby or ill behaved. The camera captured the cloth diapers hanging down off the babies, fastened with big safety pins, or covered in rubber pants that looked like parachutes. They sucked on rubber nipples pulled over glass baby bottles, like Swee'pea in the Popeye cartoons. The kids were having fun while the adults relaxed and enjoyed their young families—all together.

Funny how everyone dressed up for every occasion: dinner, vacations to Gettysburg, shopping at Alexander's Department Store. Pearls and high heels were essential to see the polar bears at the Bronx Zoo. I watched scenes of a New Year's Eve party at my uncle's tavern with ladies dancing the Lindy together. Outside, coats boasted fur collars, and Uncle Johnny's two-tone green Ford shined with newness reflecting the incredible post-wartime prosperity. Our families marched forward together.

It was painfully joyous to see my father perpetually young, the way I remembered him, one of the men in a gray flannel suit. Like Mona Lisa, an enigmatic smile was fixed forever on his face as he rode the seesaw up and down. One child sat in front of him, a couple opposite, and two in the middle for balance; Gulliver with Lilliputians climbing all over him.

I was fascinated to see my mother—young, pretty, and thin as a willow. Despite bearing and raising nine children, she looked like a teenager in love. She, too, seemed to be enjoying the melee of kids. In one picture, two-year-old Tommy sits on her lap and she beams down at him. Gently, she lifts a golden lock of hair from his forehead and smiles tenderly into his adoring, upturned face. Mom had always done what she was told, played by the rules, complied, and never defied. In return, she was happy; someone always took care of her.

Some of these pictures of Dad were taken in 1957, shortly before he died, not even eight years ago. How strange that life could change so much in eight years. People had shoes that were older than that. Finally, I truly understood what Mom was so unhappy about. I could see how much she had lost though never hoped to recapture.

There continued to be photos of us after Dad died as life marched on. I saw myself, three months later, making my First Holy Communion on December 6, 1958, in a billowy white dress. I remembered the stiff crinoline slip, soft white cotton gloves, and the bride-like veil. Then, my

Seven Canfields: (back row) Ginger, Nancy, Jack, Jerry; (front row) Helen, David, Tommy; (Billy is taking the picture)

confirmation on May 18, 1960. I looked more grown-up in a simple white graduate's robe, removable red collar, and matching beanie. Suddenly, I recalled both days vividly. For just a moment, I was the star in our sea of kids, the center of attention.

The last picture I saw of my mother on that fold-up screen was at my cousin Karen's first birthday party in December 1960, two months before our house burned down. The fire, like Dad's death, was another major turning point in our lives.

Mom—the girl, and her smile—had vanished for good by then. A lovely, tragic woman replaced her. She looked like a 1940's film star: inscrutable, unable to smile. Her deep chestnut hair was cut and styled fashionably. She wore chic clothing: a black silk sleeveless blouse and gray wool skirt. In this instant, mom had the elegant, haunted look of the widowed Jackie Kennedy.

After that, Mom's animated eyes became dull, polite, and expression-less. In every photo she appeared preoccupied, a little anxious. Perhaps waiting to get away and have a drink. As the end of the film slap-slap-slapped in the dark, we sat silently in mourning for our old lives. No one spoke. In that instant, I realized that there truly was no way back.

Because Aunt Rita Mary had been active in her parish since her own childhood, she was able to extract referrals for childcare options from her parish priest. Meanwhile, Uncle Eddie made inquiries at the police department and at the courthouse. He received a referral to a lawyer, and once all of the alternatives had been examined, they devised a plan and presented this to the Surrogate Judge.

My mother stood mute before Judge McGrath while he told her that since she was not willing or able to take care of her children, they were now wards of the court. Uncle Eddie and Uncle Bill were our guardians, and we would be cared for while she sought treatment for her drinking. End of discussion. These were the only conditions under which she could get her children back.

A few nights later, Uncle Eddie and Aunt Rita Mary assembled us in the living room of our apartment. He stood with his huge hands spread wide, shoulders and eyebrows raised, and an expression that said, "Here's a thought," like it just occurred to him.

In a measured voice he spoke. "We're going to take you kids." Uncle Eddie pointed at each of us sitting on the couch, and said our names in a sing-song voice, "Jackie. . .Tommy. . .Helen. . .David. . .and Nancy," paus-ing between each name as if to prove he knew them, "to see a school tomor-row—a boarding school—to see how you like it." This was said in a voice that implied that it was temporary, like we'd have a choice about attending.

He continued, "Jerry and Billy will come and stay with Aunt Rita Mary and me, and Ginger will go stay with Aunt Mary." He let the distri-bution of the older kids sink in. I summoned the courage to ask the obvi-ous, "What about Mom?"

He adopted a concerned, pensive look, as if to say, "Oh yes, your mother." I think he'd hoped no one would ask. "Your mother is sick. She needs to go to a hospital for a little while," is all he said.

Sick? Since when? We lived with her, and she was never sick. Drunk, yes, but not sick. Did he think drunk was sick? Was this all a big mistake? My mind raced. But Uncle Eddie and Aunt Rita Mary had a way of driving a nail through a statement, leaving no wiggle room for discussion. He walked us away from that conversation and back to the image of what a nice place the school was.

Abruptly, the meeting ended. Uncle Eddie and Aunt Rita Mary went home. We got ready for bed, each lost in our own contemplation about our future. Without any input from us regarding our feelings or preferences, we'd been told our fates.

I mentally replayed Uncle Eddie's talk. He resembled the actor Cesar Romero: six-feet-four, premature silver hair, and a perpetually tanned complexion. He sported the nickname at the precinct of "The Silver Fox." Soft-spoken and pleasant-looking, he did not seem capable of raising his voice, much less muscling criminals into handcuffs. But he didn't need to. He commanded respect with his smile, and acquiescence by his mere presence. He was an intimidating man.

Uncle Eddie did not mince words. He was gentle, but absolute. Over the years, whenever he spoke to us, it felt a little like an interrogation. Or like he might be recording the conversation for cross-examination later. I don't know if this was because we knew he was a cop and figured he could see through our lies, or because we had guilty consciences. He intimidated us the way the nuns at school did: They were always right.

Aunt Rita Mary could take him, though. They seemed so similar to me; it was more like they were brother and sister—in temperament, if not in stature. She was about five-feet-five, chunky, had light brown hair and eyes, and had a smile that came and went. But when you had it, it was full of delight. She was blunt, spoke softly, and listened intently—always pausing to make sure you were done speaking before she replied. She said things like, "I'm hysterical," without actually laughing. She didn't need to raise her voice, either. Her weapon was Uncle Eddie, though she rarely needed to wield it; the fear was sufficient. And even that was actually dread of his disapproval, rather than of any physical harm.

I never heard them raise their voices to anyone, but we wanted them to approve of us. I don't know why, but it felt like there could be no returning once you got outside of their good graces. I suppose, deep down, we assumed that they cared about us. They were strong people who did what was right. They believed that splitting up our family was very difficult, but right for us.

My younger brothers and sisters would take their cues from me in the next few days of change. I was the unofficial "leader of the little kids." This was the reason, the relatives said, why I was going to the school: to be with the other kids because I was like their "little mother."

Aunt Terry said she and Uncle Bill would have taken me home with them after the court refused to give them all five of us kids because they had eight of their own. It was deemed best that I stay with the other kids. I liked Aunt Terry's house, but I did not want to be separated from the others, no matter what.

Jerry, Billy, and Ginger were considered the three "big kids." Jackie and I, in the middle, had no real classification. But now we were being treated like little kids too, not asked for our opinions or advice, just given our marching orders.

Mom signed herself into the Hudson River State Hospital in Poughkeepsie for alcohol treatment while we stayed overnight with the relatives. There was no big goodbye scene with Mom the day we went to see the school for a weekend. We were used to her disappearing for indeterminate periods of time and figured we'd see her when we got home on Sunday.

When I told my friends about these weekend plans, hoping for some insight about boarding schools, they were mixed in their reactions. Some said we were lucky to be going away to a private school. A few warned that we were being shipped off, never to return. I chose to believe that it would be as we'd been promised. How could they just rip us up by the roots and send us away permanently? We wouldn't even have our stuff with us.

A bevy of activities followed Uncle Eddie's speech to us about the boarding school. Suddenly, we were having dinner at each of our three relatives' homes and shopping for outfits to wear to check out the boarding school.

Then Jerry and Billy went to Uncle Eddie's, Ginger to Aunt Mary's, and we took the hour-long drive to the school. When Mom came out of the hospital, she would stay with Gram until she was deemed fit to take care of her family. Naively, I thought that's all it would take. Once the plan was executed, everything would be all right. I kept thinking that this would be a sort of brief interim step towards having a home again, like the one we'd had before. Instead of Dad, Mom would carve the turkey and preside over all of us at the holiday table, like in the home movies. By Monday, everything would be okay.

Uncle Eddie drove the lead car. I wondered if this boarding school would be like the British ones I'd read about where resources were so meager that residents "ate the bread and smelled the cheese," according to Jane Austen, and a cup of hot water was listed on the menu for those who'd brought along a tea bag.

The car's heater tranquilized us. Its hot blast warmed the furthest corner of the sleek black station wagon, despite the faux-fur ski jackets we wore against the March cold. I appeased the gods of motion sickness by skipping breakfast, but with Uncle Bill's chain smoking, the heat, and my own apprehension, I still felt nauseous. It felt like all the gears had seized up inside my chest.

Somewhere in that hour-long drive north from the Bronx to Rockland County, we'd crossed over into another world. Through my window, everything looked so different. I half expected people to be speaking French when we arrived. I smiled secretly, thinking about Uncle Bill, the man of action. How he must be dying inside, poking along behind Uncle Eddie's car, clinging to the slow lane. Uncle Eddie never drove faster than forty-five miles per hour. He was a New York City

Detective, and I think he was perpetually scanning for criminal activity. Uncle Bill's style was more like leaping out of a speeding car.

I glanced around. The wagon was roomy enough for all of us kids to ride together, but then Uncle Eddie and Aunt Rita Mary would be riding alone, so the three boys went with them. My little sister Helen sat silently behind me. At nine, she was four years younger than I. Quiet, like Mom, despite the blonde hair and blue eyes like mine. Jack, at fifteen, looked the most like Mom, with nearly black hair and pale skin, minus the widow's peak above our father's deep blue eyes. He was the only one of the children who was left-handed like Mom. Tommy, eleven, was blond, but he had Mom's velvety brown eyes. David, the youngest at seven, had Dad's brown hair, but Mom's dark eyes. The nine of us were like a litter of Dalmatians with different variations of spots.

Uncle Eddie drove his unmarked, light-blue sedan through the morning traffic across the George Washington Bridge. Overhead, the dull gray metal of the bridge looked as if it had been built with a giant Erector set, blending bleakly with the overcast sky. Like a funeral procession, our cars plodded on. We kids peered absently through the closed windows, our minds wandering. I recoiled when I remembered the family scenes revealed by those home movies Aunt Mary showed the other night. The years before Dad died were fluttering behind like clothes off the line in a stiff wind.

As houses slid by my window, I glanced at Uncle Bill's face. His profile was tense. He resembled the actor Gene Kelly. Usually, he was animated, laughing or telling a funny story—a typical, boisterous Irishman. Now, his jaw was set, the deep dimples that came with his smile were erased, and his eyes stared, fixed somewhere beyond the road—in the future, or maybe in the past.

I was always somewhat afraid of Uncle Bill. When Grandma watched us while our mom went out at night, we often got wild and raced around, uncontrollably. Grandma, trying to regain order, would threaten us. "Do you want me to get Uncle Bill on the phone?" We actually had a square red desk phone, just like the President. Sometimes she would have to call, and then he would say in a low menacing voice, "Do you want me to come up there and take my belt off to you?" I never knew of him actually doing this, but it put the fear of God into us so that we settled right down—for a little while, at least.

Although I'd never seen it, Uncle Bill's reputation for fisticuffs was legendary. He'd been a boxer with the Golden Gloves before World War II, and then boxed exhibitions during his years as a foot soldier fighting for his country. When his service ended, he boxed lightweight at clubs like Joe Dempsey's. Now he owned a tavern in Astoria, Queens called Canfield's Tavern. No doubt he had occasion to pitch a few drunks into the street on a Friday night. He'd been a fighter all his life like his father—because of his father.

When I saw him again after several years' absence, I was shocked. In my mind he stood six feet tall like my dad, but actually was about half a foot shorter. Instead of an ogre, he was fun-loving like the Lucky Charms leprechaun, and very handsome.

Uncle Bill's white knuckles gripped the steering wheel now. He wore a dark-blue suit, starched white shirt, red silk tie, and matching handkerchief sprouting from his breast pocket. Freshly shaven, he always dressed like that, whether he was going to a nightclub or to church. And he always smelled of Old Spice like my dad.

Uncle Bill had an infectious laugh, a machine-gun rat-a-tat-tat kind of a laugh, and his sister Mary had it too. It kept going long after you expected it to stop, until your lips lost the struggle and drew up over your teeth into an involuntary smile. He squeezed the laugh out of you. It bubbled up from inside like ginger ale. It didn't matter what was said. Once he began, you followed.

I tried to think of something to say to brighten the bleak atmosphere in the car and provoke that dimpled smile. But he was empty of humor—and still, like after a gun has gone off. From his expression, I wondered if he were reflecting on Aunt Mary's plea to him a few days ago. I was on the other side of the wall when she said, "If Jack were alive today, this would break his heart. How can we do this to our brother's children?"

Her words brought my dad back to life for a moment, and grim resolution seemed to be carved into Uncle Bill's granite profile.

As we drove down the Main Street of Nanuet, I noticed the old-fashioned candy store, bank, and flower shop. It looked like horses should be hitched up outside. Inside the car, I squirmed, remembering how I had betrayed my mother after Aunt Mary's surprise visit to our apartment. It set events in motion that impacted our lives like a nuclear explosion. For several days afterwards, we had to wait and worry about what would happen. The atmosphere felt like the time when

"Life had become so miserable that I had to do something before it was too late."

the world held its collective breath in suspense over the Cuban Missile Crisis. This was the dread that fell over our home.

I felt guilty about all that was happening, as if it all were my fault. For years, we had survived mom's drinking and disappearing and the lifestyle that went with it. But life had become so miserable that I had to do something before it was too late. This time I had started events in motion, and now we were all being launched into the unknown.

Two

We're Here

The car slowed down, interrupting my reverie. Apprehensively, I stared through the passenger window, trying to understand this place. We passed a statue of the Blessed Mother on the right, standing sentry atop a pedestal in a glass enclosure. Along the other side of the road, a long field-stone wall ended abruptly in an open field with six newish, split-level ranch houses plunked down in a little semi-circle. I noted every detail, trying to translate it in my brain into something I understood.

When Dad was alive, we used to go out to Uncle Bill's summerhouse in Woodstock's countryside. We knew we were almost there as we passed fields like this. Everything about New York City had seemed old, brown, or gray. Everything here seemed modern: light-red brick houses bathed in sunshine with pale-gray roofs, white trim, and black shutters. I liked the exterior, at least.

Next, three more brick homes all in a row, but much larger. I wondered whether this was part of the school. No one ever said, "We're here," but we seemed to be looking for some place to pull in. Inside, I filled with dread—not that this looked like a scary place, but more like the time I learned to dive at camp the first time and had to actually release my toes' grips on the diving board and plunge in.

There was no one around. In New York, the streets teemed with people day and night, always noisy and electric. Here, it was empty: a landscape painting with no life in it: a stage with scenery, but no actors.

The tall leafless sugar maples lined Convent Road, alternating with stately old evergreens. White split-rail fences bordered both sides of Convent Road, which conveyed travelers east and west between Nanuet and Spring Valley.

I knew the school must be near and looked out my side window again. I couldn't see it. We passed driveways that led to old farmhouses on the right, some two and three stories high, painted white with yellow or forest-green trim, and occasionally with screened-in porches.

Convent Road gently sloped downhill to a shallow valley where we turned left between two stone pillars. A wooden sign with black cursive writing that looked like it should read, "Sleepy Hollow," instead read, "St. Agatha Home for Children." This must be a Catholic School, I thought.

I had attended Catholic School for my first four school years where the nuns were knuckle-wrapping strict. I wondered what the difference was between a boarding school and a Home for Children. No kid wants to go back to the strictness of Catholic school after they've tasted the freedom of public school. I remembered my awe at the transition from fourth grade in Catholic school to fifth grade in public school. It seemed like I learned nothing new the whole year, and very little the following year.

As we entered the driveway, I was amazed to see a three-story, dark-red brick Gothic-looking building. I'd seen many similar buildings in the city. I fancied that this one had hiked up its skirts and escaped to the country, so out of place did it seem. Its façade had a graceful entrance with evenly spaced tall, white columns around a wooden porch, supporting another porch above it. White ladder-back rocking chairs stood at attention, empty and still.

On the two sides of the building, arched windows nearly twelve feet high reached for the sky. Some of those on the second story held tall, narrow stained glass like church windows. Several tilted outward to admit air. Dormer windows along the roof suggested attics above. A white cross

"As we entered the driveway, I was amazed to see a three-story, dark-red brick Gothic-looking building"

that must have been ten feet tall topped a belfry. Here would be the church bell, if this were a church.

A circular driveway led past the front of the building, but we parked at the left side entrance. As we unfolded ourselves from the cars, I drank in the first drafts of cool, fresh air, and felt somewhat revived. Alongside this paved area lay a lawn the size of a football field, its grass winter-brown. Two white temples—each the size of a two-car garage—stood apart on the lawn. White benches offered a quiet spot to think or even picnic. A life-size statue of Jesus gazed down peacefully from a pedestal.

Bordering the field along Convent Road, tall forsythia bushes offered the only color. Brilliant yellow flowers dotted the length of the dark brown, whip-like branches, which grew up tall, then bent over from their own weight.

My attention snapped back abruptly when a nun dressed in a habit slipped out from the side door to greet us. She wore silver wire-rimmed glasses beneath a black silk bonnet that was tied with a large bow under her chin. It looked like a fluted paper plate. Draped over her shoulders, a black cape hung to the belted waist of a long-sleeved black dress. Minute traces of white collar and cuffs peeked from beneath the hems.

Except for the cape and the cap in place of a veil, her outfit was similar to what I'd seen on the nuns in the city, yet softer and not so severe. The site of the nun, the designation of Home instead of Boarding School, and the fact that it was Catholic came as one surprise after another. I wondered what else they had left out of the telling.

The building seemed antique, but not at all dilapidated with age. Uncle Eddie and Aunt Rita Mary greeted Sister Maureen who stood at the top of three steps. She smiled in a friendly way and said a gentle, "Hello." Uncle Eddie was genuinely reverent around nuns; he always referred to them as "the Good Sisters."

Conversely, Aunt Rita Mary acted like they were all girlfriends she'd gone to high school with and with whom she shared confidences. It made the nuns seem more like people than saints. I guess her ease came from a lifetime of Catholic school, camp, clubs, and volunteer work in her parish. The nuns and priests even came to their home for dinners.

Uncle Bill was respectful, but not submissive. He had been raised in the church, of course, and his mother and sister were devout. He'd been married there, and had his children baptized. He even attended mass when he could. But he also knew its flaws, like declining to help his sister when she came to them in need. Skeptical of the whole arrangement, he was cordial rather than reverent.

It seemed that the adults had met before. Probably Uncle Eddie and Aunt Rita Mary had scoped out the place in advance, maybe with Uncle Bill and Aunt Mary. They would never just send us somewhere without being confident that we would be well cared for, particularly since we'd been tossed around so much. Uncle Eddie introduced each of us by name, and we shyly said hello, stepping right back into our Catholic School demeanor of submission.

Sister Maureen led us into a vast old-fashioned hallway—immaculate and uncluttered save for a simple, large glass lantern that hung at the end of a long tether from the ceiling, warmly illuminating the central hall.

A wide, black border edged the checkerboard floors of large, red and black tiles trimmed in narrow gold stripes. Chair rails of the same black enamel contrasted with white walls. My first thought was, "This must really hide the dirt." The floors twinkled like marble. No rats or roaches here.

Sister Maureen indicated the two curved staircases with the wave of a hand. "Those lead to the chapel on the second floor, and the Sisters' convent above." We did not go up, but we could see at the landing a triangle of deep blue sky through a tall window veiled in sheer white curtains that hung slightly parted. It was an oasis of tranquility amid the unfamiliar. The black baseboard and chair rail marched up the stairs to the landing and beyond—no doubt a self-defense against the onslaught of young parishioners on their way to mass.

Our little group turned left through open double doors and faced a long corridor lined with what I believed to be classrooms on either side. This place was surprisingly quiet, the way I remembered Catholic school to be, but without the smells of chalk dust, pencil shavings, or discarded half-eaten lunches. Those familiar scents would have been a comfort in these strange, sterile surroundings. But here, I felt a mixture of dread and anticipation.

Instead of proceeding down that hall, we kids were seated in a reception room just inside on the left and asked to wait. I looked at the adults' faces, and everyone seemed somber behind brave smiles, like in a hospital waiting room—or at a wake.

I felt like we were puppies, being left at the pound, watching the backs of our retreating owners. We sat quietly, expectantly, while they re-crossed the entry hall to Sister Maureen's office at the front of the building. All was silent except for the noisy, irregular clicking and whirring from a big gray metal cabinet in the telephone room across the hall. It sounded like a giant robot, gears churning, tick-tick-ticking. The quiet was absolute, except for that box.

After lunchtime, but before school got out at three o'clock, I wondered where all the kids could be. My past schools were never so silent, even during classes when the halls were empty. A woman sat in profile in the narrow office, attending to an antique switchboard like the Telephone Company had. She seemed near my mother's age, I guessed. Maybe forty. Her short, dark hair topped her heavyset frame, and her belt cinched her dress patterned with tiny flowers.

She smiled at us as she spoke into her headset. "Saint Agatha Home, good afternoon, how can I help you?" She paused. "One moment, please."

Since there was nothing else to do, I stared across the chasm at her in silence. It was as though we were stranded on neighboring islands and could only wave and smile. The woman was penned in by the switchboard and a red cabinet with a paper tape cascading from an apparatus on top. The latter looked like a Teletype machine I'd seen on Movietone News. This seemed to be a command center of sorts.

"Hello. My name is Mrs. Mauro," the woman said to us, removing her headset when the switchboard finally quieted. She half turned towards us, interrupting the silence with her soft voice and gentle smile. We each mumbled hello, but did not offer our names or get up to approach her. She was friendly and chatted a little when not taking calls. She indicated the children's books on the bottom shelf of the coffee table and the water fountain under the stairs in the hall. No doubt she'd attended this dropping-off ceremony many times before and knew we were apprehensive. Her warmth brightened the austere surroundings.

We began to relax a little. David fidgeted. He got up and began touching things, rifling through the books, wanting to go for a drink. I grabbed his shirt and pulled him down next to me. He was so special to us, this handsome boy—long-legged like a colt, and always restless. He had a light olive complexion like my Mother's father in a photo I'd seen of him. We all spoiled David. He was our baby, but we all got to boss him around, too, because we were older. Maybe that contributed to his low frustration level. He was always the most ready to laugh, make a joke, and crack a smile. A wise guy, some said.

While Mrs. Mauro answered a call, I stood to stretch and peeked down the long hall. A series of wooden doors interrupted the bare white walls. In the narrow, windowless room where we waited, vinyl sofas and matching chairs seemed strikingly modern. On two walls hung paintings of rustic scenes with the caption, "Hudson Valley." On the third wall hung a round mirror with etched flowers around the rim, into which David now peered. Like me, he was probably wondering if he'd changed visibly since we fell down the rabbit hole.

Sister Maureen appeared and asked us to follow her to her spacious office with its big wooden desk and comfortable chairs, which became slightly cramped with five adults and five children. She looked serious as she told us that she was happy we would be staying at St. Agatha and assigned cottages and Sisters.

I stifled the panic rising in my chest again. This sounded rather permanent. Sure, we had to sleep somewhere, but I thought the whole boarding school was in this building, that we would sleep upstairs and go to school downstairs. It seemed plenty big.

I knew that everyone expected me to set an example, remain calm like the "little mother" they had christened me. Sister Jane joined us briefly. She was introduced as our social worker and another red flag popped up. I never even heard of a social worker and didn't know what she was supposed to do with us now that she was in charge of our "case." Clearly, Sister Jane and the relatives had met before, and they nodded gravely.

"I won't keep you," she said, raising her hands in front of her chest. "I just wanted to say hello and welcome. My office is down the hall. We'll get together later."

As we began to retrace our steps towards the exit, we stopped in Sister Joanne's office next door to Sister Maureen. She looked up from her work and smiled, then stood to shake hands with the adults and peer into our faces to see how it was all going. Dressed identically, even to the glasses, she was tall and thin, and seemed to be Sister Maureen's boss. None of these nuns were particularly effusive, like The Flying Nun, but rather serious as I'd always experienced nuns.

As the adults exchanged pleasantries, I hung back and examined the surroundings. I looked across a large reception area into a huge conference room, now unused and dim.

The dark, heavy oak doors I'd seen from outside were inlaid with tall, shimmering, leaded stained glass that looked like cathedral windows. On either side of the door were triple panels of glass, and above, more of the same. I could see that these doors led to a vestibule, then outside through a second set of matching doors. The sun pierced the layers of glass, spilling brilliant multi-colored blocks on the floor before them. I wanted to go stand in their psychedelic warmth. However, the chitchat was over, and we headed back out the way we came in, mumbling goodbyes to Sister Joanne and Sister Jane, meekly following Sister Maureen.

Three

Home Sweet Home

Outside in the crisp cool air, I stood briefly at the top of the steps while Sister Maureen indicated the distant tree-fringed boundaries beyond the fields, insulating St. Agatha from its neighbors. The buildings seemed to be resting, waiting for their inhabitants to return. I kept reminding myself that it was just for the weekend, sort of like squeezing your eyes shut until a scary movie ends.

"The children are still in school," Sister Maureen broke into my thoughts as she stopped alongside Uncle Eddie's car. As if she'd read my mind, she pointed across Convent Road, opposite the entrance, to a two-story white building standing well back from the road.

"The big building in the middle is the upper school. To the left is Sacred Heart cottage for kindergarten-aged children. And in the front, the lower school, for first through third grade."

"It's so big," I whispered to Jackie rather incredulously.

He nodded slightly. My brother had believed all along that we were staying, but did not press it when I insisted it was for the week-end—probably trying to spare me.

Uncle Eddie held the door and Sister Maureen climbed into the back seat to escort us to our temporary homes. We kids all rode with Uncle Bill. He said nothing; none of that adult, "Won't this be nice?" stuff. He didn't seem to like it any better than we did.

The upper school

I reminded myself that this was just an adventure, which we would all laugh about on Sunday when we got back to the Bronx. My friends would forever say, "Remember the time you got shipped off to that Catholic Boarding School?" and we would roll our eyes at the memory like we were talking about Uncle Joe's farm in Iowa.

At Catholic school, we'd considered nuns holy, but we came to fear their strictness. Not all of them, of course. Most were nice, but when someone strikes you angrily with a ruler for chatting, you fear them all for safety's sake. The boys laughed about it, showing off their wounds to each other, but the girls were afraid and dreaded their disapproval as much as the harsher rebukes.

My siblings and I were generally respectful kids, just somewhat unruly left on our own. We had fallen away from the rules of the Church the way most kids do when no adult makes them tend to their religious duties. For the previous four years, we'd attended public school, and the younger kids attended religious instruction once a week at a nearby Catholic school. Jackie and I had made our First Holy Communion and Confirmation. When we lived on Devoe, Gene was an alter boy at St. Peter's—the honor of every Catholic family dreaming that the priesthood could not be far beyond, and providing an "in" with God. Instead, more in keeping with his mischievous personality, Gene was expelled from school for fooling around. After graduating from Dewitt Clinton High

School, he joined the Air Force. Mom and Gram adored Gene, the first-born, and missed him terribly after he left.

I didn't want to think the unimaginable, that we'd have to live with nuns taking care of us. Jackie had to be wrong about this. But what if after our weekend visit to St. Agatha things went back to the way they were? Why couldn't Gene come back and keep us all together? Why couldn't Jerry continue to be in charge until Mom got better?

Jerry, eighteen, would begin attending City College while staying with Uncle Eddie. Our mother's increasing absenteeism forced Jerry into the role of "man of the family" left vacant by Gene. He tried to get us to do chores, play nicely, go to bed on time, do our homework, go to church, and was not averse to muscling us when we were uncooperative. Of course, when Mom was around, we undermined him and got his decisions reversed, much to his frustration. All of the responsibility without the rights. Ours was a reactionary household without any plan. All Jerry could do was try to handle each situation and crisis as it arose, a lot to ask of a teenager. But now that I saw the alternative, I knew we could be better behaved, help out more.

And why take the big kids to the relatives when the two boys, Jerry and Billy, could be out on their own soon? Let the younger boys go with the relatives.

Billy at seventeen was finishing his last year at St. Peter's. He was quiet, intelligent, witty, handsome. He took after both my mother's father with his fine features and blond hair, and my dad with his bright blue eyes. He was a Johnny Carson imitator, with that same dry wit and easy, charming delivery, but he could also grow quiet and become reclusive. He remained focused on school and succeeded there. He let Jerry run the younger kids, for the most part. But if we get another chance at staying together, that role would be easier because things would be different.

Or why not take Helen and me to live at Aunt Mary's with Ginger, or Aunt Terry's? Two or three girls together in a bedroom didn't matter much more than one. I thought Ginger was the lucky one.

She turned sixteen the month before, and was a sophomore at St. Peter's. It had been a real challenge for her and Billy, concealing our home life from the school, the nuns, and most of all, their friends. Ginger had babysat Aunt Mary's kids for a couple of years, and used her earnings for the never-ending expenses of Catholic school and her expanding social life of proms, parties, and school activities. Often she had to dip into her funds to buy us dinner, or donuts and milk in the morning before school when Mom was gone and there was nothing to eat. Sending her to stay with Aunt Mary did seem natural. It didn't occur to me that she would be lonely and want to be with the rest of us, as it apparently turned out.

I kept reshuffling the deck of options in my mind. Why couldn't someone get a bigger house, or add on to the one they had?

Aunt Mary and Uncle Johnny waited eight years for the first of their two little girls, now six and eight at the time we went to St. Agatha's. They lived in a nice basement apartment, just spacious enough for their little family. Aunt Mary was home-economically gifted and could make any place comfy. Shoe-horning any more of us in would have been a hardship to her family.

Uncle Bill and Aunt Terry had a newer, tri-level ranch-style home in Westchester. Its rooms were spacious, but they also had eight kids and another on the way. They were persuaded that, while their desire to take the rest of us was well-intentioned, the arrangement would not be best for anyone: their kids, them, or us. Uncle Bill didn't think his brother would agree, and always regretted going along with the St. Agatha alternative.

As a kid, I couldn't see that the options were impractical, and didn't consider the other families at all. It seemed wiser to them to keep the five of us together until mom got well. We wondered how long that would take.

We backtracked up Convent Road to the boys' cottages. Three large brick houses in a row were named Loyola, De Paul, and Seton Hall, according to the painted wooden plaques mounted beside each entry door. At the third one we got out of the car and met Sister Alexander, dressed in the snow-white version of Sister Maureen's outfit that the Group Mothers wore. Sister Alexander—a big, powerful-looking woman—filled the doorway to Seton Hall. Her size might be essential in dealing with thirty or so high school boys. Though her voice was soft and

somewhat high-pitched, she spoke in an authoritative, no-nonsense way like Aunt Rita Mary. Both were accustomed to co-operation.

I turned my back to look at the surroundings while the adults chatted. Athletic fields stretched in all directions. I could see the Administration building off to the

Seton Hall

right. And in between, a running track and baseball diamond. Behind it, a green water tower as tall as an apartment building mounted atop four spindly legs.

The interior of Seton Hall felt like the rectory of a church—dark, cool, and silent. The long hallway ended in a "T" at the entrance to the dining room. Sister Alexander pointed out the bedrooms, TV room, and bathrooms.

"This will be your room, Jackie. Here's your bed, and you can put your things in this locker," Sister said at the entrance to a room with six beds. Jackie, still a resentful look on his sullen face, took his assignment in silence. He opened the locker and put his small bag of belongings inside without a word or a glance around.

"It's hard to believe any boys live here," Aunt Rita Mary kidded, prob-ably trying to break the tension. "Everything is so clean. I have two sons and three daughters who are not this tidy. No towels on the floors, no unmade beds," she trailed off. "Certainly none of the disinterested house-keeping I had long since grown accustomed to."

"The boys do chores; they even buff the floors," Sister said, "to earn their allowance. But we have a housekeeper that comes in each day, too."

In the brightly lit dining room, blue-and-white-checkered cloths cov-ered ten tables which seated four boys each. Drapes of royal blue flanked white metal blinds matched the tablecloths. The walls held paintings—some religious, some like Ansel Adams' prints of mountains—and a crucifix.

From the dining room, we went next door to the recreation room. Comfy chairs for observers waiting a turn surrounded two competition-sized pool tables. I looked at Jackie and raised my eyebrows in the universal "this is nice" expression. But he was stoical, and I felt a little like a traitor, finding something good about our situation.

"That piano gets a surprising amount of use," Sister Alexander said as Aunt Rita Mary commented about what a nice home this was, or something similar. I hoped our cottage had these amenities. I had been wondering what we would do all day Saturday and Sunday. Now, at least we can play pool and pound on the piano.

With no one around except Sister Alexander, it felt like a model home we were viewing to buy. Without further ceremony, we left Jackie with Sister Alexander. He and I exchanged looks as I moved outside. I figured once we were all settled I'd come and see him later. In my head I heard the snap-snap-snapping of when you pull up a plant up by its roots—a sort of permanent severing of ties.

We could have walked over to 12 Hayden Circle beyond Seton Hall. The six houses we'd passed earlier formed a cul de sac. Tommy and David were handed over to Sister Robert, a pleasant looking and smaller version of Sister Alexander. Her smile was friendly, and she chatted more. I was glad that the younger boys would stay together. Tommy could look out for David, who often needed rescuing when he put his foot in his mouth. Besides a short temper, David had a habit of arguing everything to the death—like which was a better baseball team: the Yankees or the Dodgers. On top of that, he would always choose the team that was winning the season instead of staying loyal to one team. This drove Tommy crazy. But Tommy's diplomacy could either get David under control, or help to defend him when he put his foot in his mouth.

Sister Robert's face was sweet with a ready, broad smile. She was young and slightly plump, friendly-looking. But while she smiled, her eyes watched us. She had been at St. Agatha long enough to have formed the opinion that a swift separation was best. After brief pleasantries outside, she placed a hand on the shoulder of each boy and decisively steered them through the front door. I wanted to go in and look around, but Sister Robert knew best, so we got back into the car.

At the end of the service road, we turned left and looped back down Convent Road again like mailmen on a delivery route, dropping off kids instead of packages. We entered the first driveway on the girls' side, almost directly across from Seton Hall into the older farmhouses we'd passed earlier.

The car stopped at the first of two buildings connected by a long glass hallway called, "St. Agnes Cottage." Helen and I would be staying here.

Sister Lucy met us at the first door. Brief goodbyes accompanied glances at watches as our Uncles hastened to avoid the Friday night commuter traffic; back to the City for Uncle Eddie, and over the Tappan Zee Bridge to Westchester for Uncle Bill. I was tired and hungry, but snapped alert at the realization that this was what I had dreaded all along: the actual moment of being left behind.

I felt like screaming. But like our mom, we didn't make a fuss. We allowed ourselves to be led away. My aunt and uncles would have been

St. Agnes cottage 1935; it still looked the same in 1965

disappointed if I, of all the kids, began protesting and bargaining. This would frighten Helen, too. So I kept silent and reminded myself, "It's only for the weekend, it's only for the weekend."

I believed me.

Four

Going Home, Going Home . . .

Sister Lucy was courteous and crisp. She seemed kind of annoyed as she began to show us around in a hurried clip, as if we'd kept her waiting. "This is the living room," she said, her arm sweeping in an arc.

The setting was like a painting, each item of furniture placed just so. I wouldn't have been surprised if there were outlines on the floor for where each piece should be placed. The sun streamed in through three walls of windows with Seton Hall and Hayden Circle visible across the road.

"In this half of the room," Sister gestured, "we watch television from eight 'til nine P.M. The older girls are allowed to stay up until nine-thirty, then it's lights out for everyone. Television is never on during the day."

Yipes! At home there were no restrictions on the television besides first come, first served. The big kids usually won control of the TV, except for Saturday morning cartoons while they slept in. At home, I spent most of my time outside with my friends, though I enjoyed hanging around on a rainy afternoon, watching The Little Rascals or the East Side Kids on Saturday or Sunday afternoon.

Waist-high bookcases divided the room. On the other side were small round tables and chairs. As we passed through, Sister said, "This area is for reading, games, and homework." It looked like the little kids' section of the library. The low tables covered even lower chairs tucked neatly underneath. I loved to read and was eager to drop down and scan the rows of cloth spines that covered the shelves, but Sister Lucy strode briskly through like she had somewhere else to go.

She said only that which was necessary as she showed us around. She never joked or said anything kindly like Sister Alexander and Sister Robert had. Kids never really get to know nuns, only their habits. She seemed older than the other Sisters we'd met, but at thirteen, everyone over twenty seemed old to me. More polite than friendly—she says it, you do it, and everyone gets along just fine. Too often, however, I did not. My chattiness in Catholic school earned me rapped knuckles from a ruler. I was pro-moted from third grade to fourth on a trial basis because of my "visiting."

We passed through open pocket doors, which slid into the wall. I looked at Helen, and she blinked back. We didn't speak as we scurried behind Sister Lucy who seemed to be in a hurry as her black, tightly laced, chunky heels echoed through the abandoned rooms. A naturally brisk walker, Sister took long, purposeful strides—snowy skirts swirling about her black cotton stockings. I followed with my arm draped loosely around Helen's shoulder.

Sister gestured with a sweep of her white-linened arm along the way, tidying, adjusting shades, and snapping closed cupboard doors left slightly ajar. The smell of furniture polish hung in the air.

Straight ahead, six-feet-high wardrobes partitioned a small dormitory for four girls each. Pearl-gray iron-framed beds supported mattresses on springs, neatly made up with tight hospital corners. Snowy white chenille spreads hung several inches above the floor. Matching chairs sat on the left side of the bed, and a two-drawer nightstand sporting a ginger jar lamp on the right. At the foot of each bed, a neatly folded towel and washcloth hung over an aluminum rack. I could see under all the beds, chairs, and tables—there was not a dust bunny or a rogue slipper anywhere.

At the end of this wing, through an open door, I glimpsed a tiny bed-room where the resident counselor slept, who oversaw the girls when Sis-ter was away. We backtracked and turned down a corridor leading to other bedrooms.

Down a short hallway we passed another bedroom for six more girls before crossing the biggest dorm, similarly partitioned for twenty girls. We stopped before the entrance to the communal bathroom. All of the rooms were painted white. Those with windows had white curtains and pull-down shades. Except for the bathroom, the floors throughout were black with flecks of multi-colors. Shafts of mid-afternoon sunlight pierced the windows and splashed onto the floor, warming the room.

I was tired.

Sister indicated the two beds where Helen and I would sleep, just across from her own room, with the entrance to the bathroom in between us. She pivoted and unlocked her room with one of a large cache of keys extracted from the mysterious folds of her habit. She handed us each a towel, a washcloth, and a brown paper bag from her room. Inside was a new toothbrush, toothpaste, pink sponge rollers, night gown, slippers, and a night robe—as Sister called it—which we stored in our assigned lockers.

This welcoming gift was no trivial acquisition to us, coming from a household where everything was in short supply. We stole from each other, then fought the battle of justification later.

"I didn't know it was yours," followed by the inevitable reply, "You knew it wasn't yours." This included sheets for the beds, cosmetics, toothpaste, clothes, one of the three forks in the kitchen—everything.

The entrance to the bathroom near the foot of our beds was actually a thruway to everywhere else. Everyone who went to the bathroom, shower, kitchen, dining room, or play yard—and returned—would have to pass by our beds. We would have no privacy at all. The bathroom held a row of three toilets in white enameled stalls, eight white sinks, and a concrete floor painted gray with a drain in it. A windowless shower room joined the bathroom. Between the two rooms, a doorway led down a glass hallway that connected this building to the dining hall.

We peered into the darkened shower room, which surprisingly didn't smell musty. Five curtained shower stalls stood opposite curtained dressing stalls, like at a public pool.

"Here," Sister said drawing back the curtain of the dressing room, "you remove your clothes and leave them on the hook. Wrap yourself in a towel and step into the stall and draw the curtain. You can hang your towel on the hook outside the shower, and retrieve it when you're done, and get dressed in the alcove."

In a house with six boys, three girls, and one bathroom, we had learned to be modest from a very early age. This bordered on exhibitionism, by comparison.

We stepped into the breezeway's enveloping warmth. It felt cozy, like a car left out in the sun with its windows rolled up. The entire length on both sides had windows up to the ceiling with no curtains or shades. One of two side doors led to the parking lot and a large, concrete play area for bike riding and basketball.

We stepped through the second door into a typical play yard with swings, slides, and a couple of seesaws—landscaped half in sand, half in blacktop. The idea of the play yard seemed incredibly confining to me—to think of playing in a designated area, after I had shepherded the little kids on daylong outings to the Bronx Zoo since I was eight years old.

This was only for the weekend, I reminded myself.

"You see that field," Sister Lucy pointed behind the dining building towards a dense stand of trees around a meadow. "At dusk, and early in the morning, deer sneak out to graze," she said, smiling a little at us. "On weekends, the counselors take the girls for hikes back there, and in the summertime, there's a day camp. There are barbecues set up to roast marshmallows and hot dogs."

Back in the breezeway, we stepped up a few stairs and opened a door into the adjoining building. The dining room looked like it could have seated a hundred at its long banquet-style tables covered with red-and-white-checkered tablecloths. Windows around the whole room offered a panoramic view. One door led to the kitchen where we found the first person we'd encountered, besides the Sisters: Anna, the housekeeper for St. Agnes.

She looked up from preparing snacks for the children, who would soon be arriving home from school. I thought she looked like Ella Fitzgerald. Perhaps it was her huge, friendly smile. She didn't say much after a brief hello. She just stood with her arms folded over her ample, white-aproned bosom as Sister explained us to her. She too had witnessed this scene, repeatedly.

A scar snagged my curiosity. It appeared as if someone had slit Anna's throat from ear to ear. I tried not to stare, but I imagined her head just flopping backwards like in some horror movie.

Back in the dining room, Sister cautioned us, "The upper two stories of this building are not in use, and are off-limits." This piqued my curiosity. I could tell she was a person who got her way, because she didn't need to threaten. She simply said it like it was the law. Still, I wondered what was up there.

As we returned to the big dorm, kids began pouring in from school. Several doors banged repeatedly. Girls of all shapes, shades, and sizes flooded in. The bigger girls wore forest green jumpers with S.A.S. embroidered in gold on a crest sewn to the breast. White blouses with short sleeves and a large Peter Pan collar, green bow tie, black-and-white saddle shoes, and white bobby socks completed the uniform.

The younger girls were more disheveled with partially untucked white blouses atop pleated blue and gray plaid skirts. Without being told to, each girl pulled off her jacket and changed into play clothes. A small group encircled us. After a brief general introduction by Sister Lucy, Helen and I were left alone with the curious girls while she hustled everyone off to change clothes and head outside for snacks.

Riveted to the spot like moths to a board, I answered the usual questions that bore down on us. Helen stood anchored at my side. I imagined Tommy and David were going through a similar routine, except Tommy would only answer the question while David would run his mouth.

"Where'd you come from?"

"Bronx."

"How old are you?"

"I'm thirteen, she's nine."

"What grade are you in?"

"I'm in eighth, she's in fifth."

I noticed most of the girls looked Puerto Rican, with a few white, and an equal number of black. Having moved and changed schools so often, we knew the routine. Helen provided one-word answers when asked. Like our mother, she was very reserved. There was a brief period a few years earlier when I came home from summer camp and found she'd become quite the chatterbox. I thought her personality had changed over the summer while she recuperated from a bout of rheumatic fever. It made her the center of attention for a little while, maybe loosened her tongue. She was the only one in the family, besides our mother, who ever got any kind of illness besides colds and cuts. Helen slowly drifted back into her usual quiet self.

The girls boasted that they were from either the Bronx or Brooklyn, and a short segue led to a debate about which was better. All were from either New York City or Puerto Rico. Everyone had seen *West Side Story*.

Some of the girls seemed pretty tough, but I didn't think anything was going to happen to us with Sister around all the time. Most of these girls were younger than me. I answered only the questions put to me by my short-term interrogators, and offered no opinions.

"Do you know how to dance?"

"Yes."

"Jump double Dutch?"

"A little."

"Play basketball, jacks, hearts?"

"Yep."

"Ride bikes?"

"Yes."

No one asked what happened to our family. Off limits, I guess. Maybe they didn't want to be asked in return.

I couldn't formulate a single question. My mind was stuck in the "receive" mode while I looked at all these curious faces staring at me. I can

Gazebo

still see them, almost forty years later, with their skeptical expressions, puzzled by my insistence that we were here for only the weekend.

They soon dispersed, changed now into play clothes to go outside and get snacks. One little girl with a solemn face and a husky voice said her name was Norma. She was a few years younger than Helen, one of the two six-year-olds in the group. Wordlessly, she slipped her hand into Helen's and led her off to the yard where Helen could push her on a swing, a freebie from the new kid. This, Helen recognized. She smiled over her shoulder for the first time that day.

Another girl named Ellen, now wearing jeans and a faded red sweatshirt emblazoned "Columbia," said authoritatively, "We have to go outside to the yard," and led the way. She was claiming me, apparently. Ellen was a tallish girl, about five-feet-five, neither skinny nor fat, but still somewhat gangly. Her nondescript hair had no highlights, no gloss.

Outside, Ellen said she'd been at St. Agatha for a long time and proprietarily pointed out all of the neighboring buildings, describing their purposes and who lived there. Other girls interrupted and corrected her, and little disagreements cartwheeled off from every sentence. I could see that Ellen was not popular, but sort of the Barney Fife of the crowd. Even so, she took the opportunity to snag the new kids for as long as she could before they figured out what made all the other kids dislike her.

The day was so clear, the sky so blue, and you could see so much of it. In the city, the tall buildings blocked out much of the sky, but here it seemed to go on forever. Huge, white, cottony columns of clouds warned that snow was still possible. The air felt a little cool and very dry. It would get dark soon, and we would have to move inside. But for the moment, it was sunny and bright.

I looked up the hill between St. Agnes and another cottage to find a glass-enclosed gazebo. "Is that part of St. Agatha?" I asked Ellen.

"That's a playhouse," Ellen said, "for the little kids in Mt. Carmel, when it's too hot or too cold." Midway, a hedge of twisted, thorny branches stood without any roses. In spring, summer, and fall, it would provide some privacy from cars passing along Convent Road. Mt. Carmel housed the toddlers, I learned.

Some of them laughed and skipped rope in the concrete portion of the yard while a small, tanned nun named Sister Mary Christine turned the rope at one end and smiled back at them. The little scene reminded me of one of those nun stories, like The Bells of St. Mary's.

Ellen liked being the tour guide. She pointed across Convent Road from Mt. Carmel to the six cottages in Hayden Circle, then to Seton Hall for the oldest boys. How I wished I could just run over there, away from these strangers, and be with my brothers. Instead, I broke my silence and told the girls I had brothers over there.

To my surprise, a ripple began. Gossip was currency here, I quickly learned. Being in the know, even briefly, gave you an advantage. The word spread rapidly with varying degrees of accuracy. Having siblings in other cottages seemed to be some kind of status. Everyone who had brothers and sisters in the older cottages boasted of them, like kids in elementary or middle school who boast about their siblings in the upper grades.

We wandered around the back of the dining building to find pavement for ball playing and bike riding. There were a couple of basketball hoops set on polls at regulation height. We climbed up on one of the stoops outside the dining room to hang around until dinnertime. Besides Ellen, some of the other older girls tagged along.

Danite, a stocky black girl about my height, five-feet-three, had eyes like two little chips of coal and short, kinky hair. She cracked her knuckles more often than she spoke. As one of the eldest, she shared the private room next to Sister Lucy's with one other girl—a privilege, apparently.

Miriam was in seventh grade. Ellen, Danite, and I were the only eighth-graders. Miriam slept in one of the three beds out in the open. They were unified in their curiosity about me. Some of the younger girls had a sort of predatory look about them, as if sizing us up. Kids do this when someone new comes to class or moves to the neighborhood. They wonder how the new kid will relate to them. Clearly they could dismiss Helen with her placid expression; there was nothing aggressive about her. Or maybe they cold bully her. They didn't trust strangers, for sure. The older girls seemed curious. It was all about, "What does she mean to me? Does she get more privileges? A better room? Will she be more popular than me?"

I wasn't nervous about them; I was too tired. The idea never occurred to me to wonder why they were there, or ask about their families. I just thought of them as part of the Home, like the little people that come with a dollhouse.

Ellen was one of the few other white kids. Perhaps they worried that she'd gain some strength in racial numbers.

Ellen had lots of freckles across her nose and cheeks, speckling other-wise clear, translucent skin. Her sharp features—a birdlike nose; and beady, close, deep-set eyes—kept her from being pretty. She had a nice smile when she was pleased, and straight, white teeth that made her look prettier. My own neglected teeth made me especially observant of others, and I always held my hand over my mouth when I laughed.

Unfortunately, Ellen was often scowling about something or in an argument with someone, and then her expression was screwed up like a spoiled child. Her voice had a high, hysterical quality. I heard later that she had no memory of her family, having been in Homes all of her life. I noticed the girls made fun of her and teased her, even while she was tell-ing me about St. Agatha, though I didn't know why. It seemed more like a habit to pick on her. But she'd evidently had enough of being pushed around, and now she was pushing back.

Danite's skin was the color of the purplest plum. Her inscrutable expression reminded me of a guard at Buckingham Palace. Silent and watchful, her eyes crinkled at the corners when she was amused. Robust—not fat, but blocky—Danite sported an athletic build. She wore a metal comb stuck in the back of her closely cropped kinky hair.

Miriam had the most quirks. She seemed to genuinely dislike Ellen and often punctuated Ellen's statements with a sneer and, "Nuh-uh. You lie, girl." They both fidgeted, had nervous energy, and interrupted each other continuously—Miriam even more so. Maybe they were competing for attention. Though not the aggressor, Ellen defended herself from the smallest criticism. Both girls had quick and jerky movements, same build, gangly limbs, and the energy of Tigger. But Miriam could strike some remarkably slack-jawed expressions that simply conveyed, "Huh?"

Miriam had enormous brown eyes, Sophia Loren's pouty lips, toffee-colored skin, and thick, shoulder-length hair, jet-black and glossy. Her hair looked like she just yanked the sponge rollers off her head in the morning, and didn't bother to follow up with a comb. Curls boinged all over the place. Like Danite, she had perfect, brilliant-white teeth.

Miriam either shouted Ellen down or stood toe-to-toe with her fists clenched and chest puffed out like a fighter, usually with an offer to bust her in the mouth in order to settle even the simplest matter. Alternately, she had a constant nervous laugh. Sometimes it was more of a reckless, hysterical guffaw. She often goaded and liked to nudge people with her elbow, and then she'd laugh and laugh. She actually slapped her knee at times. Childish things struck her as inordinately funny, like seeing someone slip on a banana peel, or bang their funny bone. Certainly not malicious, she merely lacked compassion.

When not laughing, Miriam spoke, and foamy spit collected on the outside corners of her mouth. She had a goofy yuk-yuk-yuk kind of laugh—surprisingly uncool for someone who perpetually pointed out the flaws in others. Her arms and legs were disjointed, like the scarecrow in *The Wizard of Oz*. She angered easily, and soared from good-natured to maniacal within minutes.

"She always makes stuff up like she saw it happen. Don't say you don't, girl, or I'll bust you in the mouth," Miriam threatened. Danite stoically watched for the fireworks. Instead of moving her head to look from face to face, she slid her eyes back and forth like Felix the Cat.

Miriam's little sister Norma had adopted Helen as her friend. At six, her features were like Miriam's, except she was wide-eyed and serious with a husky voice that didn't seem to fit a little girl.

"Miriam," she whined now in that throaty voice, "it's my turn on the swing, and Patty won't get off." Depending on how she felt at the moment, Miriam could either do battle with the offender, or give her sister's shoulder a slight shove and tell her to quit being a baby. Right now, her interest lay in challenging Ellen, and therefore told the little one to get lost.

Norma pursed her pouty lips, then she broke out in a rippling laugh like Tinkerbelle. What a strange bunch. Maybe they were hungry.

The girls had words and expressions I never heard, like, "Don't get wacky," for losing your temper. Age determined the pecking order, and privileges came with advancing a grade and staying out of trouble. And then I waltzed in—the oldest, on top— with Helen gaining status by association. I became curious what it all meant to them and to their places within the order. This would account for Danite's caution. Miriam seemed to have the self-confidence to deal with whatever came her way. I just wanted to sail along until I could go home on Sunday.

The day grew dark and cold. My family hadn't eaten regularly for years, so I was always gleeful at mealtime. Today I had abstained from eating before my car ride this morning, and had only eaten the two Oreos and milk at snack time. My stomach growled.

In the dining room, I let the kids sweep me towards a seat. There wasn't any assigned seating.   Ellen sat opposite me—then Helen, with Norma on her other side.

"They cook the food down in the kitchen, then the driver brings it to the cottages," Ellen volunteered as we filed in one kitchen door and out the other. Anna served from a stainless steel covered pan of fish sticks, tall pots of mashed potatoes with melted butter, and pans of vegetables. At the sight of that food, I could hardly wait to sit down to eat.

That Friday night dinner struck a familiar note: fish sticks and spinach, a Friday night staple for as long as I could remember. Catholics did not eat meat on Fridays; it was a sin. Once everyone was seated, we folded our hands and said Grace out loud together. We hadn't eaten a meal as a family for a long time, much less said Grace, but the words came back immediately.

"God is great, God is good, and we thank Him for our food. Amen."

The girls were not exactly pious, but didn't fool around either. Catholics had a bunch of rules, but if you followed them, they were considered a sort of recipe for getting into Heaven.

At one time, I thought everyone was Catholic. It was as definitive in our world as your gender, or being Irish. But a funny thing happens when you see your parents slack off on the rules. I noticed that my mother was not stricken down for skipping mass, as one might expect. Some people summon the courage to skip Mass and pocket the money for the collection basket on Sunday to go buy candy—or alcohol—instead. But at St. Agatha, under the watchful eyes of the Sisters, they seemed to actually live by the rules of a Catholic without giving it a second thought.

After grace, the mood during our meal was lighthearted, and everyone behaved. I gagged at the smell of the spinach glopped onto my plate, and was relieved that we were not forced to eat anything. In fact, there were others happy to have my portion while I ate Miriam's tapioca pudding.

Anna presided over the group of thirty or forty girls. She did not hesitate to step up to someone who became a little rambunctious, and bark out a girl's name in her high-pitched, Butterfly McQueen voice. She followed first warnings to "knock it off" with the wave of her wooden spoon. The kids responded—not out of fear, but out of genuinely liking Anna. She was cool and did them special favors, according to Ellen.

After dinner, we carried our dishes into the kitchen. The pace remained casual and relaxed. Being new, I wasn't on KP duties yet, but I didn't know what else to do, so I helped out Ellen. We loaded the green melamine plates and cups, along with the silverware, into a rolling plastic drainer that slid in and out of the dishwasher. When full, the domed, stainless steel top lowered, and the washer started automatically. It was mounted on a stainless steel counter over the sink, which lined two walls, like in a hospital cafeteria.

Clouds of soapy-smelling steam billowed up every time the lid rolled back, and it sounded like those dishes were flying from side to side under the heavy water pressure; it made such a racket inside. When the drainer was lifted out, the dishes were warm and squeaky clean.

Once every item in the kitchen was put away, we went back to the dorms. Ellen said we could go down to the canteen later—a concept I remembered from camp. Only the eighth graders were allowed to go, and only Friday nights.

Helen had gone off with Norma to do her Friday night duties. Ellen explained that we had to wait until Sister Lucy returned from prayers and dinner in the main building to check duties. Then she would give out the weekly allowances: thirty-five cents for Ellen.

I helped Ellen dust and tidy the playroom. This gave me an opportunity to peruse the book titles. They included my favorite classics: *Nancy Drew, The Hardy Boys, Bobbsey Twins, The Red Pony, National Velvet, Red Badge of Courage,* and so on.

When she returned, Sister asked how we got along. I told her the usual: Fine. She inspected everyone's chores closely, and then compared it with her chart to see if Ellen passed inspection each day. Ellen had, so she received her full allowance. If she had skipped one night, or slacked even halfway in her duties, Sister docked a day's allowance. This usually led to rebellion by an angry girl, whose only retaliation was to refuse to do her duties.

"At the canteen you can buy soda and candy," Ellen instructed as we headed out. "Pedro brings all his forty-fives. He has every record: The Four Tops, The Temptations, Marvin Gaye, Diana Ross and the Supremes. Some people dance. It's a good place to find out who's going with whom. You know, that sort of stuff. No nuns," Ellen said.

Danite snorted sarcastically.

At seven o'clock, we stepped out into the cold, unexpectedly black night. I had left Helen with the younger girls, who wanted to get done taking their showers before TV time. Sister would not turn it on until everyone assembled, which put pressure on the stragglers.

It seemed colder here than in the City. There were no tall buildings to act as barriers from the wind. Either way, I burrowed down into my ski jacket and jammed my hands into my pockets. I had no hat or gloves.

All around, the cottages glowed like campfires under a moonless sky. They looked like those lighted snow globes, each with its own tableau unfolding inside. As we passed between the cottages, Ellen mentioned that the high school girls were all mean and tough—that they would beat you up as soon as look at you—so steer clear.

The Big House, as they called the first high school girls' building, had tall white columns at the front entryway like an old plantation mansion. "The Little House has the oldest girls," Danite piped in quietly.

I suddenly remembered our Catholic School and the "Trip to Blauvelt" carnival each year, and told Ellen and Danite the story.

"We took a bus and stayed for the day. You could do ring toss or throw beanbags at bottles to knock them down and win prizes. Someone said that orphans lived at Blauvelt—that the carnival was held to raise money for them."

Before I could finish, Ellen said that St. Dominic's Home was in Blauvelt.

I continued. "Me and my friends had a bunch of little prizes we won, so we went to look for the orphans. We figured orphans wouldn't have any money to play the games. We were scared of getting caught, but we sneaked behind the fair and came to a house with one of those French patio doors and peeked in. Suddenly, a couple of girls came around from the back and we jumped back. They didn't look all raggedy like we expected, just regular. We held out our prizes to them, and they took them and said thanks. Before we could say anything else, one of the nuns found us and said to stay at the fair, not to wander off. We waved to the girls and went back."

I wondered about these girls at St. Agatha and whether they were orphans. No, because orphans had no parents, and some of these girls spoke of their mother or father. Maybe this was a place for kids who were not orphans, but their parents couldn't take care of them.

We kept our distance from a few of the high school girls—brutes according to Ellen—barely visible in the darkness on the path ahead of us. Their laughter and voices drifted cheerfully back to us as they rambled down the hill to the canteen and the high school boys.

We passed the barn with cars parked outside.

"The chauffeur and night watchman drive these cars," Ellen said.

"Chauffeur?" I asked incredulously, thinking of rich people and mansions.

"And the nuns," put in Danite.

"Kids don't usually come here with their family; they come with a nun or a Social Worker in one of the Home cars with Joe Flynn. He drives kids into the City, too, like if someone has to go to St. Vincent Hospital to get their tonsils out or something. He picks up people and brings them here, too," Ellen said.

We crossed Convent Road and passed the Administration building. There was no moon or stars, only lights beckoning from the buildings. But the girls knew their way around without any problems and seemed to have nothing to fear in the utter blackness. I couldn't believe we had arrived here only a few hours ago. It seemed like days, so much had happened.

We passed through an archway that connected the Administration building to the Bandroom. "Recreation building," Danite said.

We stopped at a sign over the door that said "Canteen" in white letters. Music, bright lights, and noisy kids tumbled out every time the door opened. Some kids milled around the lighted area outside in relaxed, small groups—snacking, talking, flirting, and laughing.

"For Halloween, we had a party with decorations, and there was a cauldron with smoke. Jim and Mary wore scary costumes. It was cool," Ellen said.

"Sometimes, we have regular dances," added Danite.

"Yeah, some people dance; others just stand against the walls, watching and waiting for their friends," Ellen said.

"Who are Jim and Mary?" I asked.

"Jim and Mary Bryant are counselors for the little kids. He has Savio group; she has Little Flower. They do other stuff, too. Like, he teaches the drill team, and they do canteen," Danite said. I later learned that the groups were usually named after saints.

Ellen whispered about who liked whom, who was going steady, and who had broken up, while Danite corrected her inaccuracies here and there.

The canteen looked like a soda fountain with things like potato chips, candy, gum and soda for sale. Inside, we met Danite's brother, Ben. He acted and looked liker her— cracking his knuckles continuously, looking down at the floor, sliding his eyes sideways. The only difference I could see, besides gender, was that he had a slighter build. I asked if they were twins, but Danite said he was a year older.

Outside—oblivious to the declining temperature—kids lounged on the low white wall, so long that it ran down past the Priest's residence.

"It's called St. Roche, but we call it St. Rocks. Father Traube lives there with Tuffy, and he always comes to hang out with us," said Ellen.

A Jesuit priest with a gray crewcut, long black cassock, and friendly manner bounced among the kids. He had a big German shepherd at his side.

Ellen introduced me proprietarily, like her new pet. Father Traube reminded me of the priests at St. Peter's who played stickball and basketball with the boys in the street behind the school during lunch and recess.

St. Roche, a.k.a. St. Rocks

"I try to get to know all of the kids by name. I go to a different cottage every night at snack time to get better acquainted, and recruit kids to join the C.Y.O.," he winked at Danite. We had C.Y.O., Catholic Youth Organization, in the City. It's a club with activities like sports and leadership. Father moved on to another group.

The low white wall beckoned kids to flop down on it. Though nothing more than a fieldstone wall, it was the spot. It was easy to be seen here by the opposite sex and to check out who's going off "talking" with whom. This was both the gossip wall and the Wailing Wall.

If there were any real secrets to be told, a couple would meander off for privacy. Naturally, there was a fair amount of sneaking a smoke and making out beyond the circle of spotlights around the canteen.

Lots of girls my age spilled down from a string of buildings on the hill, a place called Duryea Lane, barely visible in the dark. Girls went here from St. Agnes after they graduated from eighth grade.

We stayed for about an hour in and around the canteen, and Ellen treated me to a box of Junior Mints since I had no money. I was surprised and delighted to see the familiar face of my brother Jackie. He seemed shell-shocked and didn't even smile when I introduced him to Ellen and Danite who both nodded then slid away to leave us alone.

"I saw Tommy before," said Jackie. "He was ok, and said David was getting along as usual." This meant he was already arguing with people.

I reminded Jackie, "Just hang on, get through the weekend, and be glad we're going home on Sunday." A couple of guys stopped and clapped Jackie on the shoulder in a familiar way, and I was introduced to Julio and Jose. It was time to head back up to St. Agnes, so we parted.

With the faint strains of "My Girl" trailing behind us, we crossed Convent Road. A girl ran up behind us out of the blackness. The idea of a high-school girl ready to beat me up startled me and my heart quickened a little.

"Are you Tommy Buzzard's girlfriend?" she asked me.

"Uh, no, I don't know Tommy Buzzard," was my startled response.

"Oh yes, you do. Don't lie, girl," she said. She seemed mad, but heard someone calling to her, then turned and ran back towards the canteen. "White honky," she spat over her shoulder as she trotted away.

"What was that about?" I asked.

Neither of my companions had a clue. From Miriam I learned that Tommy Buzzard was an "outside" boy from Nanuet High School. I don't know how she knew. That girl Carmen liked him, but he had a girlfriend, whom she apparently thought was me. I was puzzled by the "white honky" remark since she was as light as I was, but apparently she was Puerto Rican. She also had two brothers in the Seton Hall with Jackie. Maybe that would keep her from hunting me down later.

Back at St. Agnes, the girls were showered and in their pajamas, robes, and slippers. They had a routine. I gathered my "nightclothes," as they called them, and went in to take a shower. Miriam was just getting out of the shower. She had a reputation for swiping towels from girls in the shower so that when they came out, they had nothing to put on. It drove them nuts, but most were afraid to put up too much of a fuss, lest Miriam's merriment turn combative. A couple of girls, like Patty and Ellen, wouldn't back down out of sheer orneriness. Others , like Danite, were exempt from Miriam's pranks. Miriam didn't bother to shroud herself for the few steps between dressing room and shower. It simply didn't bother her to be seen naked, and she thought it was hilarious that the other girls were so modest. Besides, she was developing, and probably wanted to show off a bit. This upset Sister Lucy, though. Miriam said Sister once took the shower curtain and wrapped it around her until someone brought a towel. Miriam struggled with Sister saying, "Get off me." This recollection brought peals of laughter.

But it shocked me, too. I was not used to seeing anyone naked.

"You shouldn't hang around with Ellen," Miriam told me on the way to the TV room. "She's Rockland."

"She's what?" I never heard that word before.

"You know, mental. She goes crazy. She says that at the Home she was in before here, the kids used to pick on her all the time, and it made her crazy. They pushed her head in the toilet, and flushed it a couple of times, I heard." Unsympathetic cackles erupted along with this confidence. But there seemed to be a subtle warning there, too, like, "Don't ally yourself with her, if it comes down to taking sides."

"They send crazy kids to Rockland State Mental Hospital if they can't control you with the psychiatrist or drugs. But if you beat up the nuns and counselors, that's pretty much it. No one wants to go to Rockland because we heard they dope you up, tie you down, and lock you in." Foamy spit had gathered in the corners of Miriam's mouth.

When I was a little kid, we were threatened with the truant officer or reform school to get us to behave—even the orphan asylum. No kidding. There used to be one right in our neighborhood on Kingsbridge Road. Of course, we did not know that it had closed in the twenties.

I could see that Ellen was quirky and jerky, the way she made broad, sweeping, generalized statements about the high school girls, for example. Or the way she became moody all of a sudden, flinging something on the floor or clapping her long arms against her sides as she whirled and fled the room over something trivial, like her hairbrush missing. But I was in no position to alienate anyone, even her. I just had to get through the next couple of days of this scene from *Little Orphan Annie*.

Besides, Ellen had befriended me. She took me under her broken wing, and I felt obligated to at least be nice to her. If not loyal, at least I was diplomatic. Either way, I could never deliberately hurt anyone's feelings.

Ellen reminded me of a girl named Hope in fifth grade. She was fat, unkempt, and she smelled. Hope rarely showered, so her hair was a greasy mop. She had tons of pimples, and wore a fake fur leopard coat throughout the whole school year. The sleeve was ripped under the arm, but the coat was obviously her armor. She could have been naked under there, for all we knew.

In those days, we still sang songs like "God Bless America," and recited the Pledge of Allegiance in class each morning. The lines of one song went, "Walk on, walk on with hope in your heart and you'll never walk alone." The boys changed it to, "Walk on, walk on with Hope in your heart and you'll never walk again."

At first I thought that was pretty funny, but then I saw the impact it had on Hope, day after day. As a new kid, I didn't dare stick up for her, but at least I refused to chant the revision. I made an effort to be friendly to her at other times, which she received with suspicion. But then we moved again.

On Saturday morning, I awoke to the sound of dozens of slippers scuffing along the floors. Window shades snapped up, sunlight flooded in, and Sister Lucy—like a Border Collie after sheep—prodded everyone to get dressed and go over to breakfast. The dormitory felt toasty warm without the stifling feeling.

We were not allowed to dine in our pajamas, and I was not about to dress right there in the dorm by the door through which everyone passed, especially since I now wore a bra. Helen and I took our clothes into the toilet stalls and dressed there. I don't know what the other girls did.

After swiftly making our beds and storing our nightclothes, we went to the dining room. There seemed to be a magnetic force pulling everyone along, scurrying towards the next activity like on a cruise ship—until we got out into the yard and the boat was set adrift, aimlessly.

In the dining room, we sat in the same places we'd occupied the night before. Green Melamine bowls of hot oatmeal steamed before each place, set by kids serving on KP. Matching cups and saucers awaited the lukewarm, watery cocoa from battered stainless steel pitchers. It tasted like it was made with powdered skim milk. Empty clear blue plastic tumblers matched pitchers of cold milk. Slices of toast, already buttered in the kitchen, were placed on individual bread plates. This likely prevented spats over who received more than her share and who received none. Instead of the warm, golden, soggy toast topped with yellow rivulets of melted butter I hoped for, this toast was slightly charred, cold, and hard, and the butter sat on top like bits of plastic.

Everyone chatted, relaxed because they did not have to rush off to school. The din in the room was a little noisy, though no one yelled from table to table or shrieked with laughter. The girls talked about the usual stuff: clothes, boys, music, school, recent injustices.

"God, you're such a slob," Miriam chided Ellen for dragging her sleeve through the butter on her toast. Ellen took most of it in stride, but once she'd had enough, she stood abruptly—knocking her chair over backwards—and took her plates to the kitchen. Miriam just laughed all the more, and her groupies followed suit. No one stuck up for her. No one wanted to be the next target. Miriam was in the limelight today, giddy and hyperactive.

In the group of nearly thirty-five kids, I could see who was suspicious, hostile, or moody, and who was good-natured. There were a few sleeping volcanoes, though I wasn't yet sure what would cause them to erupt.

The girls all seemed a lot younger than me, but coming from a large family, I was pretty relaxed within the crowd. I finally felt comfortable to begin asking questions.

What do we do after we eat? Duties. And then? Play outside until lunch. After lunch? Play outside until dinner. Except today, the counselor Diane would take some kids into town to the movies. You could go only if you did your duties consistently during the week and had money to pay for yourself. Allowance for eighth-grade girls was sixty-five cents. The following year, in high school, it shot up to a dollar thirty-five.

Diane could fit just a few kids in the Home's station wagon, so you had to really be in good standing to go. As new kids, Helen and I were not eligible. I didn't care about that because in the City I could go to the movies anytime I had the money. Besides, I was developing a plan for when Sister Lucy returned, to see if Helen and I could go over to visit our brothers.

On Saturday, each kid stripped and remade her bed with clean sheets. A few girls wet the bed and had a rubber sheet under the regular one. Miriam was one who wet her bed, so this was something she never teased others about. Everyone knew there was a good chance of getting busted in the mouth by Miriam for that bit of teasing.

Hospital corners on a smooth, tight bed were required every day. Otherwise, Sister yanked the sheets out, and you had to start over. The girls consulted the newly posted list of chores in the dining room, then set about their duties: kitchen chores; scrubbing showers; dusting and sweeping bedrooms, playroom, or the TV room; and picking up bits of trash in the yards. This was in addition to alternating turns at KP. No duties, no allowance. No exceptions. Partially done jobs, like sweeping without mopping, went unpaid. Helen and I helped the other girls with their chores, rather than stand outside by ourselves. Besides, as new kids, we needed to ingratiate ourselves and not look like special characters.

I kept watching all the girls and listening to them. It seemed easy to say the wrong thing and start a spat because everything would be going along calmly, then suddenly someone erupted. I guess it was the same at home between David and Tommy, or Jackie and one of the older boys. I thought about this and concluded that maybe this is just something kids do: tease each other, make fun, or take sides. I never thought about that before, but it was the same even in my crowd of friends. God, how I wanted to go home.

After duties, we all went outside until lunch. We spent a lot of time standing around. The play equipment was too juvenile for me to be interested. There were only a few bikes, and I didn't play basketball. So, once again, we clustered around the steps and chatted. This was dull too, because I couldn't relate to these girls who seemed so sheltered, so unworldly. I told them about my plan to ask Sister Lucy to go see my brothers, but they said she'd never let me go since visiting was on Sundays.

Skirmishes popped up here and there about trivial things, like whether someone was lying about how big her room was at home in the Bronx, or what pets she had. A lot of the stuff did sound exaggerated, but how could anyone know? It was like my brothers squabbling over who was a better player: Roger Marris or Mickey Mantle. They just squabbled for the fun of it.

Diane was the only adult there on Saturday and Sunday when Anna was off. Sister Lucy went back and forth to the main building for meals and prayers, same as the weekdays, but stayed longer. Diane was very tall, and the girls made fun of her behind her back because she looked like Olive Oyl, but they liked her because she was gentle and easy going. She was new to this cottage, and did not rule with a raised wooden spoon like Anna, but with favors.

Patty told me about the last counselor they had, Gabby, who had lived-in for a long time. "She got fired for beating up the girls, even though she was sweet as pie to Sister," said Miriam. "She got so mad at

Ava, she locked her outside. Ava kept pounding on the door and getting madder. Finally, she took a rock and broke the window, then reached in and opened the door. Gabby was so furious, she grabbed Ava's arm, and whacked her over and over with the steel-bristled radiator brush. Really cut up her legs. When Sister came back and saw what Gabby did, she asked Gabby what happened, then asked the girls. She fired Gabby right on the spot. We all cheered." Not only were they getting rid of Gabby after all of her injustices, but Sister took their sides and believed them for a change.

Diane was easy-going, though; a social worker in training, Miriam told me. Diane handled kids in a firm, yet friendly, way. She went around to each little group and asked how we were doing, trying to show an interest. I noticed she did not do most of the talking, just asked questions to get the kids talking. That always led to interrupting each other to get their own version of how the school week went. They really didn't have that much going on in their lives besides what they did as a group: school, mass, cottage life, and siblings in other cottages, if they had them.

None mentioned playing any sports, and they were not old enough to go to dances. You had to be in high school for that. They went to school on the grounds, and saw the same kids at every event. Some kids went home on weekends, which afforded all kinds of boasting rights about where they went, what they did, what they ate, and how late they got to stay up.

Being new, Diane got them to tell what it was like around here in the summertime when school was out. They went swimming and had lessons every day up at the pool, did craft classes, went on trips, like picnicking at Rockland Lake, and had Olympics, of all things. Each cottage represented a different country. They had costumes and they competed in sports, like softball, swimming events—and games for the sedentary, like chess, checkers, and cards. This surprised me. It sounded like camp.

I became bored from sitting around, listening to people talk about stuff I didn't really care about. At first I was interested, but it was so confining, just waiting all the time.

If I was back home, I'd be hanging around outside with my friends, too, but we would not be confined. We'd play King and Queen, a game like handball against a building. We'd go in and out of the candy store, or pick a destination to walk to, like the park. In warm weather, we'd plan an outing to the beach. But since I had no friends here, and nowhere to go, it was more like waiting around. We sure couldn't plan anything to take ourselves off to. I felt powerless.

When Sister Lucy returned, I was going to ask her if Helen and I could walk across the street to see our brothers. It seemed like such a simple request, I couldn't imagine why she would say no. Then, since we had nowhere to go, we'd walk up to that long wall near the entrance, sit up there together, and compare notes about how things were going. We'd decide what time we'd meet tomorrow, and just savor the idea of going home.

There were a couple of bikes in the yard for general use, and the girls took turns riding—some less generously than others. Kids shared rollerskates with their particular pals. A few balls were available for dodge ball and basketball. The swings and seesaws were always occupied. Some of the kids sat halfway in and halfway out of the entrances to the breezeway, on the ground, or on the stairs to the kitchen. They played hearts and jacks like we did back home. There were the usual squabbles about sharing, who was taking too long, or who had taken too many turns. Everything had to be negotiated among the girls, or the bullying began.

After Sister Lucy came back from breakfast and prayers, she came over to see how everyone was getting along.

"Sister, could Helen and I go see our brothers?"

My request surprised her. "I'll have to check with the other Group Mothers. I'll let you know," she said.

I thought we could just go over there, but apparently, they had their own routines in different cottages, and we were not welcome to just come knock on the door and call for the boys like we would back home.

Sister Lucy worked out the arrangements, and I was allowed to take Helen for an hour and meet Jackie, Tommy, and David on their side of Convent Road, midway between the buildings. I didn't have to knock on their doors; they came walking out and we all met at once, like actors on a stage. It was funny. Together, we walked up to sit on the stone wall, but it was too high to jump up on, so we stood around talking. We just wanted to be off by ourselves, together, but we couldn't leave the grounds. We didn't know where to go, anyway.

"How's it going?" I asked Jackie.

"Oh, great," he said, looking away.

"What's the matter?" I asked, thinking something in particular had happened. But he just looked at me as if to say, "Everything."

"How about you, Tommy?" But before he could say his usual, "Okay," David piped in.

"These kids all want to pick fights. Everything I say, they argue about," David said.

"Just do what I always tell you: Keep your mouth shut," Tommy said, a little exasperated.

"What time are we going home tomorrow?" David asked me, ignoring their usual debate.

"After lunch. Uncle Eddie said two o'clock. I guess we can meet down at the main building and go inside together, okay?" Everyone agreed, except Jack who just looked away. We chatted about nothing, and took each other's picture with the camera I'd brought along. We compared notes about the cottages, nuns, kids, food; lots of eye rolling. We all liked the food and agreed the rest was kind of strange.

We talked about what we wanted to do when we got home: watch TV, stay up late, eat in the living room. Jack and I would go out at night. Freedom.

Tommy wondered aloud for all of us. "I wonder how Mom's doing."

Our collective hope was that she went to the hospital, got cured, and was back home waiting for us. Maybe that's how all these other kids felt.

We were not used to "visiting" with each other; we just sort of co-existed, reacting to life. So this little gathering with no place to roost felt strange. Like when we went to camp, the boys and girls stayed at opposite sides of the lake from each other. We met on one side or the other for the Olympics or Sunday visiting. It felt strange until Mom came up. She was the glue, now absent.

Our hour was up. We repeated our plan to meet outside the Administration building at two o'clock, the next afternoon.

We were all incredulous at this world that was so different from our own, but Jackie was angry because he told me that he was sure that we were being tricked, that we were not going anywhere. And this boring place was going to be where we stayed; we were not going home.

He was not encouraged by my saying things like, "We should consider it a big adventure." None of us seemed the worse for wear, just anxious to go home. We wondered what mom would be like all cured, as if she were getting a new hairdo.

We hugged awkwardly, then the boys headed off towards their cottages. Jackie dropped off David and Tommy before heading slowly back to Seton Hall. Helen and I crossed the street and met up with a few of the girls coming back from confession at the chapel. Some went as a habit; a few from genuine concern that they might die with a sin on their soul. Others just wanted an outing with a destination to break up the routine. Given their lack of freedom, most of their sins were probably confined to their minds.

Saturday evening, since it was dark and cold, we didn't stay outside for long after dinner. Once we scrubbed up and put on our nightclothes, we gathered in the game room. Sister was a stickler that night. I don't know if it was because of modesty or drafts, but everything came to a halt until our robes were all buttoned up and we had slippers on. The recreation room and the breezeway were drafty, and we were not allowed to sit on the bare floor, which was as cold as concrete. Sister Lucy controlled the thermostat.

In front of the TV cabinet, which stood in the corner by the front door, was a huge, oval, multi-colored, braided rug covering most of the shiny black linoleum floor. Around the perimeter of the room sat easy chairs, a couple of Colonial-style rockers with cane seats, and a hassock or two. All of the furniture throughout the building, except the bed frames, was made of the same light blond wood.

A couple of the smallest girls had dolls, whose hair they brushed and braided, or whose clothes they changed. During the week, kids did homework at the tables in the game room after dinner, with no horsing around allowed during that hour. The counselor was available to help with homework problems. If you finished early, you could leave the playroom, play a board game quietly, or read a book. You couldn't do anything to distract the others still at work. Usually, the Sisters did not assign homework on the weekends.

The wide range of books thrilled me. I loved books. Sister disdained comic books, and wouldn't allow them in the cottage. Several puzzles and board games like Scrabble, Life, Monopoly, checkers, and chess stacked on top of each other. Kids read and played card games like Rummy, Spades, and Hearts. Everyone seemed to know how to play chess, even the littlest kids—perhaps because of the annual Olympics.

After dinner, showers, and tidying up, Sister switched off the lights in the dorms. At eight o'clock we assembled on the braided rug in the living room, and Sister selected a channel, then turned on the TV. She told us *The Wizard of Oz* was coming on, but we would not be able to see the whole thing because it ended after our bedtimes. There were a few moans of exasperation, which had no effect on Sister Lucy, and then the movie began.

Some girls brushed each other's hair, made braids, or twisted sponge rollers over their own strands. During commercials, girls took bathroom breaks or went to their lockers for a hairbrush, but Sister wanted everyone where she could see them and sent someone to fetch the dawdlers. Reading, writing a letter, or playing a game across the room was okay if there were no squabbles or clowning around.

Sister Lucy sat in one of two straight-backed, stuffed green leather easy chairs. A small matching hassock at her feet held her knitting supplies. We sat splayed out like a peacock fan in front of her on the rug.

During a commercial, Miriam said, "She always picks such corny shows, like *Ozzie and Harriet,* or *The Donna Reed Show,* or *Father Knows Best.* I like *Ed Sullivan.* They have that little mouse, Topo Gigio," and she cracked up laughing as she imitated the mouse.

The girls chimed in with other shows, all wholesome and entertaining. Maybe they were meant to show how normal families lived. When Rickie Nelson sang *Travelin' Man*, I bet even Sister secretly swooned.

I watched all these shows at home, too. I never thought about it before, but they showed how people in families should behave and treat each other. Moms wore dresses, high heels, and beads—even at home. They seemed happy to be homemakers, cooking, cleaning, sewing, and caring for their home and family.

Not my mom.

Dads wore a suit or a cardigan sweater, and cheerfully set off for work each day. I remember my dad used to wear a suit, white shirt, and tie when he left for work every day. Mostly, I remembered his shiny black shoes with skinny string laces. Wingtips, he called them.

The TV dads carried brown bag lunches in briefcases or lunch pails that their wives prepared. Families ate dinner together. The kids joined clubs, played sports, and went to the beach with friends. They got into wholesome mischief, like putting a frog on the teacher's chair; not shooting up heroin in the lunchroom. As remote as these TV shows seemed from our lives, I vaguely thought this is the way it should be, and maybe the way we wanted it to be. It was that way at Aunt Rita Mary's. Out loud, the kids boisterously recorded their disdain: "Cornyyyyyyyy."

While we watched TV, Sister Lucy knitted slowly and methodically, blue metal needles click-click-clicking. She glanced up—sometimes at the TV, sometimes at her flock—between knits and pearls. The girls vied to hold her skein of yarn across outstretched hands while Sister wound it into a ball. They always seemed to compete for some little individual attention. Sister said to me, "I'll teach anyone who's interested in learning, how to knit and crochet. I think all of the girls should know how to, the same with sewing. Many of the girls have made hats, long scarves to wind around their necks, and booties—for themselves and as gifts. Would you like to learn?"

I said, "Yes, Sister." On the commercial, she retrieved from her room a pair of knitting needles and a ball of yarn. She demonstrated how to cast on stitches, made sure I saw it all, then pulled them all out and had me do it. She was very patient, and went over it until I got it. Then she showed me how to knit, and had me do row after row. I liked this because I could see the results like making a cake.

When I was little, I remember my grandma crocheting white cotton doilies all the time. I was fascinated to watch the thin cotton string go into her hands, swiftly wind around her crochet hook like abracadabra, and then out came lace that she draped over the back and arms of the sofa.

Several kids worked on projects while watching TV. Most wore knitted booties on their feet. Sister gave Helen and I each a pair, multi-colored with cuffs and drawstrings. I started immediately with my lessons so I would know how to do it when I got home.

At the appointed time each evening, two girls were selected to "go across" to the kitchen to get the snacks. I was allowed to go with Miriam that night—a real privilege because it was one of the few times kids were out from under the watchful eye of an adult. With Miriam's encouragement, we ran and skated in our slippers along the drafty breezeway. Miriam laughed loudly her yuk-yuk laugh, for which she knew there would be a reprimand later.

"The dining building is haunted upstairs," Miriam told me. "This used to be the infirmary, and kids died here. Now they haunt the place." I wondered where she got that story. While the kettle boiled for Sister's tea, Miriam opened the door from the dining room, and we crept up a wide staircase to the empty second floor. There were little, gray, iron beds, chairs, dolls, and even a couple of old-fashioned dollhouses on tables. Miriam's story must be true, I thought.

The room was neither tidy nor dusty, but appeared as if it were still in use, still cleaned periodically. One large, two-story dollhouse, open on one side, displayed chairs pushed away from the dining table. It was as if the mama had just departed to the kitchen while the kids went outside to play, and Papa retired to the drawing room to read his newspaper. I could envision a little girl, interrupted from playing there, who left abruptly. I had an active imagination, and here was the equivalent of the grandma's attic I'd always longed for.

We could stay only briefly, but I could see why the girls who were not terrified snuck up there every chance they got, and why they said these rooms were haunted. It had the feeling of someone lingering. I thought that my hand placed on a bed would find it still warm.

From Miriam, I soon learned another secret about the upstairs habitat. Anna had a young daughter, about twelve. She came to work with her mother sometimes, probably when she was sick or when school was out. But the girls mused that she lived up there all the time because that was more interesting. Her name was Elizabeth. From time to time, she would sneak down to the dining room when the girls were at school and twirl around the posts that held up the ceiling. She'd croon in her quiet, baby-soft voice like her mother's. It was she who played alone with the doll family for company and left abruptly when her mama called.

Sometimes—Miriam told me—someone would happen across her, like when they came to the dining room to collect the snacks in an afternoon, and Elizabeth had sneaked out of her confines. Or they crept upstairs to see her. You didn't dare do this when Anna was around, as she was very strict. Probably Anna had made a deal with Sister Lucy that she could have Elizabeth there, as long as she did not disrupt the regular activities.

That night, Miriam foraged through everything that wasn't locked up. Mostly it was the thrill of spending some unsupervised energy. We twirled around the posts in the middle of the room, laughing and goofing off in the cavernous dining room, while the teapot gathered steam. Everything was so controlled that this private time offered a brief opportunity to let our hair down.

Snack was all made up on a tray: a few cookies at lunch, or peanut butter and jelly sandwiches in the evening, milk or juice. A porcelain cup sat inverted on a saucer, ready for Sister Lucy's tea. A clean white cloth lay over all. Once in a while, there were ice pops or watermelon in the afternoon, but these were eaten outside. I didn't care what it was; I loved snack time. "Sometimes, Sister comes over, or sends someone to check up on us. She just says, 'You've been here long enough, now get back. She's probably worried we'll burn the place down.'" Snorts of yuk-yuks followed.

Miriam scuffed along in her slippers. She carried the snack tray and I carried Sister's tea on a separate tray. Everyone carefully selecting their cookies with a napkin. Later, the tray was handed around to collect dirty napkins full of crumbs. When retiring for the evening, each made sure that she left no crumbs or napkins, because Sister was faithful about taking away snack privileges when messes were left behind.

On Sunday morning, Sister Lucy awakened everyone by calling us to get up for Mass. Without moving, I watched her progress. In each cottage, the Sister had her own room with a bathroom, so we didn't see her without her full habit. The night before, however, a ruckus caused Sister Lucy to come out and investigate. She wore a nightgown and robe with a small clip-on veil over her head that looked like her habit, except for the hat. I don't know why kids are so fascinated with the nuns' habits, as if they might have angel wings underneath.

No breakfast before mass on Sunday morning. We dressed in our better clothes, and with Sister Lucy in the lead—like Miss Clavel of the *Madeline* stories—we trooped down the path in something less than two straight lines and in silence. She wore a black crocheted cape over her usual outfit, and black knit gloves.

We entered the side door of the Administration building, through the front entry hall, and up the winding stairs to the Chapel. A statue of Jesus greeted us on the spacious landing above. The staircases continued on to the next floor where the Sisters ate their meals. Everything was hushed.

Through the double doors to the chapel, we passed through a vestibule, awash at one end in brilliant colors from the stained glass windows that anointed those entering the chapel. It was much larger inside than I expected. Surprisingly beautiful, with frescoes on the ceiling trimmed in gold, there were three altars ornately decorated. In the choir loft above the entrance, a large organ stood. This reminded me of a mini St. Patrick's Cathedral, where grandma took us on one of our outings. It was not for Mass, but to see the beauty of the church.

Under Sister Lucy's sternest gaze, we filed in as silently as forty girls could. Woe to anyone who spoke, we'd been warned. The chapel was somber and cool, with beautiful dark wooden pews, great columns, and archways. On the walls down each side aisle sat carved white marble Stations of the Cross, depicting the stages from the time Jesus was condemned to die, carried the cross, and was finally laid in his tomb. Each tablet, a masterful work of art.

Father Traube stood patiently at the center altar, hands folded across his chest, watching the congregation stumble quietly in. In his gold-trimmed white robes, he looked different: pious, not the easy-going man who played soccer with the kids and roughhoused with his German shepherd outside the canteen. As I waited for Mass to begin, I glanced around for my brothers. Heads turned, Tommy and David smiled back at Helen and me from the other side of the chapel. We mouthed, "See you after Mass," before a stern reminder from Sister Robert directed their attention back to the service.

The Mass felt warm and familiar. Father's Latin sounded like every other Mass, and I remembered when to answer, when to kneel, when to sit and stand. My mind wandered as I peeked at the girls around me. I could see Miriam in the row in front of me at the end. She would say something to Danite, who never took her eyes from the altar, and giggle periodically. She whispered, gazed around, and fidgeted like a captive bird. She told me that her mother was dead, and her father could not take care of her and Norma in addition to working. She said he was very strict, so they were glad to get away from him, but wished they could go back to the Bronx.

As young kids, we had been sent off to camp for eight weeks at a time during the four years after my father died. So, we were somewhat used to being away from home. And when the house burned down, we were all scattered about. At these times, we were distracted, but they were lonely times. Yet, we knew it would end and we would go home.

After Mass, Jackie, Tommy, and David clustered briefly with Helen and me before we headed back up the paths to change clothes, eat lunch, and get ready to go home. The boys looked really fine in their new suit jackets. The sun was strong and full of promise. Kids in their Sunday best let off steam after sitting quietly through Mass. They shrieked and ran and called to each other. No one stopped them. Some kids passing by said hello to one or the other of us. A couple of boys from Seton Hall stopped to check out Jackie's family.

I felt apprehensive now that our freedom was near, like it might be snatched away by a passing crow. I wouldn't relax until we were in Uncle Eddie's car, passing that stone wall and the statue of the Blessed Mother, heading towards New York. For now, we parted to wait in our different holding pens.

High-school girls raced up the path past Helen and me. They had a special breakfast ritual on Sunday. According to Miriam, the Home rewarded the older kids by giving them privileges for being mature and showing self-discipline. So, on Sundays, they were allowed to cook their own bacon and eggs. This was such a sought-after privilege that the girls sprinted past us in order to be first in the kitchen. They hoped to avoid having to wash another dirty frying pan left in the sink or chasing after the prior user to wash it. Some cottages allowed kids to invite their brothers and sisters from other cottages to Sunday lunch or small birthday celebrations.

Since I'd told everyone that we were there for only a weekend, they were interested in seeing what would happen. Ours had been a unique experience and went fairly smoothly. Or so it seemed, now that it was drawing to a close. I liked some things about St. Agatha, but was eager to rejoin my life. This had been like a field trip.

Once we changed out of church clothes and ate, Helen and I assembled our meager belongings. We wanted to be ready to leave at two o'clock on the dot—earlier, if they let us. Apprehensive and expectant, we went outside to ride one of the cottage bikes, play ball, anything that kept us busy until it was time to go.

I snagged one of the bikes and rode carefree around and around the buildings with the breeze blowing through my hair. I felt a great sense of relief after the constraint of the weekend, the way you feel when daylight savings time ends and the days are suddenly longer and lighter. I was getting out, going home. Now that leaving time was at hand, I thought that I rather enjoyed being out in the country.

Sunday lunch, which they called dinner, was a hot meal. They served egg noodles topped by Swedish meatballs with puddles of brown gravy, and peas and carrots.

Sister Lucy was not there to say goodbye. She was down at prayers with the other Sisters. Helen and I went to our lockers, collected our bags, said our goodbyes, and headed down the path to the main building so we would be there promptly at two o'clock when Uncle Eddie said he would be here. Diane hadn't heard about any of this from Sister Lucy, but she let us go because we were going to the main building where Sister was.

I clutched our new possessions and headed for the finish line, happy to have gotten through the weekend. My brothers were out front and we entered the same waiting room. Mrs. Mauro did not work weekends, so there was a nun dressed all in black, and the name plaque read "Sister Jude" on the divided door that was now closed. We told her why we were there. Puzzled, she called for Sister Jane, our social worker.

We were all atwitter at being so close to leaving. Even Jackie looked a little hopeful. Nearly half an hour later, Sister Jane appeared and asked why we were there.

"We're going home; we just came for the weekend. Uncle Eddie is picking us up at two," I told her, though my confidence waned a bit.

"I was not aware of this. When did all of this come about?" She looked skeptically from Jackie, to me, and back—as if to see if we really believed what we were telling her.

"That's what Uncle Eddie told us. We were coming for a weekend, to see how we liked it. He said he would see us on Sunday at two," I rushed on. I was pushing back the wave of doubt and dread creeping forward, threatening to wash over me. I was the spokesman for the group, but the others began to chime in and back me up. Uncle Eddie wouldn't lie.

Sister Jane, a seasoned veteran, was non-committal as she held up a hand to silence us. She said she would look into it, and went back down

We thought our "weekend" visit to the home was coming to an end

the hall towards her office. We were so convinced that I think she actually doubted herself, whether she had gotten it all right.

She came back soon and said, "I called your Uncle Eddie. He did not mean that you were going home today. He meant he would see you next Sunday at the regular visiting hour: two o'clock."

I protested. "No, that's not what he said. He said we were coming for the weekend to see if we liked it here, and that he would come and take us home at two." I looked at Jackie for backup, but he looked away, furious. He told me later that he never believed that we were going home until we were really assembled there. Then he thought, "Maybe." David echoed everything I said. Even Tommy was mad. Helen remained silent.

Sister Jane told us that we were mistaken and to go back to our cottages. Stunned by what I believed was a deliberate deception, and feeling foolish, I was speechless. We shuffled, all of us furious, back out to the front of the Administration building where visiting hour was in progress. Finally, I knew I had to shake off my own despair and convince them to settle down. I said I would straighten it all out. I don't think they believed me, but no one had any other ideas about what to do. I said I would call Uncle Eddie and tell him we did not want to stay.

Other kids bounded about with family and friends who had arrived on the Red and Tan bus lines from New York. In the two pavilions on the lawn, visitors sat on benches, laughing and sharing stories. Kids lumbered around. Brown bags full of picnic lunches were spread out here and there. Many of the kids were Puerto Rican, and their families brought delicious rice and beans, chicken, and plantains: fried bananas dusted with powdered sugar. Visitors typically did not go to the cottages. After all, most of the kids received no visitors. This happy activity was confined to the band room and the grounds around the Administration building.

I had never been so disappointed in my life. And my mother was the queen of disappointers. I felt trapped and betrayed. At first, I was griping, too. But when my brothers started threatening to run away, I changed my tune. I had to calm down for their sakes—had to put a positive face on it.

"They must have meant next Sunday, and we misunderstood," I said, struggling to sound calm at their protests. Jackie snorted. I can still see David's face: angry, rebellious, tricked, and mistrusting. I felt the same way, but couldn't let on. Helen and Tommy took it quietly. One more disappointment. Jackie was furious and he muttered and shook his head in disbelief and looked away. I'm sure he wondered why I was taking their side, and probably wondered what he would face when he went back to Seton Hall.

We had lives back in the Bronx. We had friends. We had stuff. What about the kittens we left behind? And Blackie, our dog? What about the humiliation of slinking back to the cottages?

"I promise, I'll call Uncle Eddie and find out what's happening. Then I'll call you." Even as I said it, I wondered where I would find a phone to use. We all trooped back to our cottages and what were to be our new lives. Deep down, I feared we would never leave. This was all just another lie, like when Mom said she was going to get her hair done and didn't come back for days.

"Are you coming back after that? When will you be back? I'll come with you." But she'd get mad and say we were the children and she was the mother, and that we were not to check up on her.

Then we'd kick ourselves because, once again, we trusted her. And the big kids would say, "You should have gone with her," even though she wouldn't let us. I don't know why we believed her and trusted her over and over.

In the cottage, the kids had filtered back outside. Of course, there was no end of teasing from Miriam when we returned; she just flat out found it funny that I was tricked so thoroughly. The kids had their own word for this humiliation: Busted. Miriam shouted this while pointing in our faces.

I had to laugh, or I would cry. She was making jokes about it for the rest of the afternoon. I don't think it ever occurred to her that it was mean, though the other kids seemed to have some innate sensitivity.

Outwardly, I shrugged it off. But inside, I felt cut adrift and completely powerless. I could only imagine what my brothers were going through in their cottages if the girls could be this mean. I stayed very quiet for the rest of the day and evening. I didn't know what to say; I didn't know what to think. I was at a complete loss as to what was going to happen to us. I felt like I would never be happy again.

After supper, it was time to start thinking about the new week—showers, hair setting. Freshly cleaned uniforms appeared, and school supplies were reassembled. Sister Lucy required that everyone's hair be curled for Mass and school. Pink sponge rollers were distributed to all newcomers, and even the smallest children learned to roll their hair. Some kids lost their rollers, and some had such thick or long hair that they used paper bags to curl it.

Some wound strips of cloth, or fan-folded pieces of brown grocery bags, around the hair of those without rollers. I don't know how this originated, but it was funny to see Miriam and other girls in these makeshift curlers. They called each other "ragheads." At home we used big rollers that we called "beer cans."

That evening we all spread out on the rugs, pristine after showers in our nightclothes. The fun and excitement of the weekend was over; time to quiet down and get back into the routine.

A new routine for Helen and me. A new life. No going home.

When Sister Lucy came back after dinner and prayers, she brought school uniforms for Helen and me. Naturally, she had heard about what happened to us. She knew all along that we were not leaving, but never suspected that we didn't know. She couldn't imagine how or where we got the idea that we were just coming for the weekend. She was very nice to Helen and me. If she had not been away from the cottage, this would not have happened. Diane should not have been persuaded to let us go, but she was new, unfamiliar with procedures, and thought it was an oversight.

That night, I lay in my bed and tried to sort it all out. My head began to throb from suppressing the tears and outrage. My stomach knotted. I fast-forwarded through the tape that was my life, everything that had happened to bring me here. I was a prisoner, and I had just let it happen. I didn't even know where we were or how to get home. I had no money and no access to a phone. All I could do was wait.

Helen asked me once, "What's going to happen?"

All I could say is, "I don't know." She accepted that in her usual stoic way.

At last, I felt so sorry for myself, tears ran down my cheeks. So that Helen would not hear me and become frightened, I buried my face in my pillow and sobbed silently.

Part 2

*St. Agatha Home
for Children*

Five

Fire!

A swirling ashcan lid smacked against a brick wall, then slid silently into the snow. The blizzard blasted mountains of white powder on New York City, hushed for just a moment, then drew another deep breath for further onslaught.

The lamplighter had hurried by hours earlier, amongst the first falling flakes. He left behind soft golden circles of light on the whitening ground. In the night, the snow glowed pearlescent. The final gasps of evening fires sent wisps of smoke dreamily up chimneys to be snatched away by another gust.

In the silence of the frosty Brooklyn neighborhood surrounding the Roman Catholic Orphan Asylum, everyone slept. Torrents of rain began to fall. It froze on impact with the snow, forming a glazed shell, trapping the powder beneath. At 2:30 that Sunday morning of November 9, 1862, a tiny, solitary soul groped along the darkened halls of the Asylum. A seven-year-old inmate, sick with an intermittent fever, left his bed to rouse one of the nuns. He couldn't sleep.

"The smoke is making me cough," he said, startling Sister Theresa as he touched her lightly on the shoulder. Thinking him feverish, she sent him promptly back to bed. Unable to return to sleep, and thinking that now she smelled smoke, she rose quietly. She crept into the hall to investigate, then peeked over the banister and saw tongues of flames licking the wall below.

She ran back to awaken the other Sisters. "There's a fire! We must get the children out," she urged them. They fanned out without any specific plan, except to guide the children to safety outside. Through the rooms they flew, nightdresses eerily swirling about their bent figures like leftover spirits from Halloween.

The Sisters sped from floor to floor, down row after row of tiny beds, shaking the heavier sleepers. They screamed over the mounting confusion, "Children, get up! There's a fire! Go outside! Hurry!" Silently, they prayed, "Jesus help us." The lives of two hundred fifty little boys rested in their hands. They pleaded for deliverance through the inferno.

As tiny startled eyes comprehended, the sleepyheads bolted from their beds. Some pulled their nightshirts up over their mouths and noses like bandits to block the acrid smoke. Squinting through tears, they choked and tumbled down the stairs. Their naked feet barely touched the steps. Now the fire was no secret; it had fully declared its takeover.

All of their young lives, these children had been warned against the perils of fire—to both their bodies and their souls. They clawed through the darkness, knocking over chairs or anything in the way. They scurried past other ghostly little figures in nightshirts—wailing, reaching out, and groping for help—with only flames to light their way. "Mama," some cried instinctively.

Stinging tears wept from Sister Theresa's eyes as she held her elongated sleeve over her mouth and nose. She fought the instinct to flee. Waving her arms like demented semaphores, she propelled the children through the thickening smoke. Down the wide staircase they fled, guided by the flailing arms of another Sister. She urged them past the flames that burned the wood paneling on the wall. Beyond the cavernous entry hall, they found the relief of fresh air and freezing rain. "Hurry, children, hurry!" No pretense of decorum or self-confidence now; there was no time.

Like frogs evacuating their holes in a downpour, the children scampered off in different directions. Icy gusts rushed in through the gaping doors, fueling the flames now crab-walking across the ceiling. As rain cascaded down towards the front door, the children hopped over treacherous potholes. Ankles twisted and gave way as they sprinted. Some youngsters clutched fallen comrades under the arms or by the back of their nightshirts and hauled them to their feet.

With her head turned away, shoulder into the blinding curtain of wind and water, another shrouded figure guided the shivering youngsters away from the blaze. She herded them behind the Asylum to the barn that served as a playhouse that stood alone. It would suffice to shelter them temporarily.

Few neighbors ventured out to check the source of the commotion. That decision would condemn them in the morning's press. But volunteer firefighters and policemen who yielded to no impediments came on the run. Bareheaded, pulling on jackets, they shouted the universal alarm, "Fire! Fire!"

Once the nuns agreed that everyone appeared accounted for, they informed the rescuers. Only then did the Sisters retreat, smoky and singed.

The fifteen-thousand-square-feet building, constructed in 1856, had undergone renovations over the previous year. It sprawled over fourteen city lots. The brick exterior was impervious, but the floors and woodwork of pitch pine burned like a trail of lighter fluid. Up from the basement, through the communal rooms on the ground floor, the fire raced to the bedrooms above. Assured that everyone escaped, the fire crew had little choice against the firestorm. They fell back and let the blaze burn itself out.

Two hours later, James Gill of Hose Company #13 began his inspection. Anguished, he found the small charred remains of a child on one of the upper floors. A search party set out. The men scoured the rest of the building; no niche went unchecked. Another tiny body appeared.

New furnaces had been installed during the recent renovations—two each in the basement of the north and south wings. That night, they'd been lit for the first time. The inquest identified a faulty flue in one of the furnaces as the cause of the fire. The wide entry hall and staircase permitted so many to evacuate safely. The coroner found no evidence of wrongdoing. He determined that the children who perished had become disoriented during the evacuation and ran up instead of down, doubtless to escape the acrid smoke. Though most of the books and papers in the building burned, a roster materialized, and names were called. All but two stepped forward: Michael Carrick and Daniel McMann.

Finding new homes for the orphans in the overcrowded city began that night. Three quarters of the city's most impoverished residents already existed in dilapidated tenements—nearly twenty percent of them ragged immigrant children. Many of the boys in the orphanage had been rescued from those very tenements and given a home at the Orphan Asylum.

Newspapers regularly condemned landlords as caring only for ways to squeeze ever more people into flats meant to house one-tenth their population. They installed shelves around the rooms three tiers high as sleeping platforms and rented them out individually. Intended for one person, landlords soon saw that small families would pay more for the same space, just to have a roof over their heads. In the center of the room, rows of cloth slings tied between two horizontal rails like hammocks rented for pennies a night. Fifty or sixty people shared a single outdoor privy—still, an improvement over the poorhouses. At least here, the inmates had their freedom.

Politicians indifferent to these conditions delighted in having a place to shepherd the ever-increasing hoards of immigrants for whom no other housing could be found. Happy, too, because these dregs would not disturb the more than one thousand new millionaires attracted to the increasingly fashionable New York City. Only when health epidemics of smallpox and cholera, or rampant crime, threatened the wellbeing of those taxpayers in their mansions did the constables become involved. Their solutions smacked of a corporal, not a charitable, nature—clubbing offenders back into their hellholes.

By 1845, two million Irish fleeing famine in Ireland came to the already overcrowded city with no place for them to live, and few resources to sustain them. Some fifty thousand became prostitutes and produced twenty thousand illegitimate babies who often ended up fending for themselves. The overall death rate in the city reached three percent. And for the Irish, fifty percent. Homeless children, dubbed "Street Arabs" in the newspapers, estimated ten thousand strong in 1848 and kept growing in population. According to a newspaper clipping from the late 1800's, these children gained a precarious subsistence for themselves or their parents by pilfering and begging. They swept the crossings; picked over the ash boxes; gathered rags, bones, and refuse paper; or sold matches, toothpicks, or other small articles. They peddled apples, oranges, and flowers.

"The Irish are of a low order of intelligence and very many of them have imperfectly developed brains," said the Superintendent of the insane asylum at Blackwell Island. This attitude typified the Protestant contempt toward Irish Catholics who numbered twenty-five percent of the immigrants pouring into the US. The great resentment against them that existed in Protestant Great Britain sailed to America. When asylums became popular, an insidious condition evolved within their populations. A disproportionate majority of the children incarcerated by protestants in authority were Irish (about fifty percent) and Catholic (about forty percent). Orphaned and abandoned, these ragamuffins slept on the ground, on fire escapes, under staircases, or in doorways. They banded together in small groups and used the leg or arm of one another as pillows and for warmth. Sometimes, they could find no place to lie down. Medical care and education did not exist, and abandoned babies died from exposure as often as from measles. Children formed gangs to survive. Their fathers died or disappeared some time after their conception.

Some older children cared for younger siblings twelve to fifteen hours a day. They struggled to keep the family together. Mothers worked in sweat shops, if they could get a job at all, or did piecework at home, often enlisting their children's help. Usually, the only food the tykes ate all day consisted of what they could forage for themselves. Sometimes, mama brought a little something home to them at night, but they dare not rely on it. They took what they could find.

A cholera epidemic in 1866 led to the Tenement-House Act of 1867 in which remedial legislation required such changes as, "Tenements must have windows." Landlords avoided improvements until 1869, using excuses such as the smallpox epidemic. One loophole after another delayed compliance until 1884 when "The Tenement House Commission" came into being. Its ultimate goal: To place the value of human life above the landlords' profits. Expert witnesses testified that providing decent housing to the poor could still be profitable without squeezing the very breath out of them.

Later, Police Commissioner Theodore Roosevelt abolished police lodging-houses, which had sprung up all over the city. Well-intentioned at first, they had become flophouses that bred vice and crime. Likewise went the makeshift "rear houses"— unlighted, airless shanties—little more than packing crates, really. They tacked nondescript shacks haphazardly onto the backs of once respectable brick homes, then piggybacked onto those. They spread like parasites that dwarfed their hosts. Landlords packed as many as three hundred thousand people into a square mile, resulting in frequent fires, epidemics, and death. Conditions grew so desperate that once each year, the Superintendent of Outdoor Poor distributed $20,000 among the blind destitute in Blind Man's Alley because the city could not provide shelter for them.

Contempt and prejudice against immigrants fleeing revolutions and famine at home labeled them "dangerous elements." This relieved the conscience of the real estate agents and landlords who exploited them. In one instance, one hundred ninety-two people lived in one house, including ninety-one children—numbers merely noted in the report of one Sanitary Policeman. No action resulted. By 1890, the population of children under five in the more than thirty-two thousand tenements equaled about one hundred sixty-five thousand. Census-takers counted children over age five as adults. Many worked on the wharf, shucking clams, by the age of four.

The alternative: incarcerating them in the poorhouses, or paupers' prisons, alongside desperate adults. These institutions copied England's solution of locking up families when they fell into debt. Charles Dickens' own bitter experiences are credited as contributing to his bleakest works, like *Nicholas Nickleby* and *Oliver Twist*. As an adult appalled by childcare facilities in England and America, he wrote exposés about the abominable conditions of the poor.

Equally aghast at the conditions he found upon arrival in New York City, was Reverend Charles Loring Brace. A young protestant minister from England, Brace walked the streets and studied the plight of its children. Reverend Brace admired their entrepreneurial spirit. They did not give up and die. They worked hard to survive, and often with compassion for their fellow sufferers. Brace believed that with guidance and resources these heroic qualities would enable the waifs to be recast as useful citizens.

Reverend Brace began fundraising among wealthy protestants, disgusted by the impoverished conditions that increasingly encroached on their upper-class society. They particularly abhorred the Irish Catholics pouring into the city, escaping the potato famine at home. He opened "Newsboys Shelters" for thousands of boys who sold periodicals and lived on the streets. Here, they could find a hot meal and a bed each night. In 1853, Brace founded the Children's Aid Society. His Shelters proved so successful that their numbers grew rapidly. They expanded to include rooms for reading, classes, and prayers.

Facilities for girls came next, then industrial schools to teach the children a trade and enable them to become self-sufficient. Brace did not believe in orphan asylums or long-term care of any kind where children could be forgotten. He had visited them and disdained the austere conditions and their dismal results. The children experienced no love, and did not learn how to get along in life. Outside the gates, they were fit only for the next institution: usually a prison.

Getting real homes for destitute children with loving families became Brace's lifelong dream. He truly believed in the basic goodness of people and their genuine desire to be charitable. He imitated the Mercy Trains for orphans employed in England, and briefly in Boston. In a program generally called "placing out," they distributed tens of thousands of children from the streets by railcar to new homes with farm families in the west.

Each week, wherever the train stopped, signs appeared in advance—advertising its arrival date, time, and purpose: the need for good homes for children. Groups of ten to thirty youngsters sent by train from Grand Central Station were accompanied by an Agent of the Society. For days, the little bands traveled from one town to another along the railroad lines. Children could be adopted, legally or not, and treated as members of the family rather than servants. Or they could be indentured: a contract whereby children performed the normal chores of a farm child in exchange for their care and schooling. (See appendix for sample agreements.)

Indenturing did not mean slavery, only a contract of expectations on both sides. Over the years, Children's Aid received letters from some of the children and their adoptive parents. One mother wrote:

> You wanted to know if John Reyer is with me. He is with me and always will be. If he were our own son, we could not love him more than we do. We have given him our name. We call him Charlie Highland. He thinks we are his parents and we want him to. I love him so much that it would break my heart to part with him.

Letters like this encouraged other orphanages to follow the Society's plan. They too had found that children had not just come to the orphan asylums for short periods of time. Often, they remained for many years, sometimes their whole childhood. This left no place for the ever-increasing population of the newly destitute to receive shelter. More and more orphanages had to be built and funded—an expensive, prohibitive solution. The train distribution seemed an ideal remedy and new variations of "placing out" developed. From 1854 to 1929, an estimated quarter of a million children found homes at the end of a train ride.

The Sisters of Charity at first disdained the notion of parceling children out this way. But with the shortage of alternatives, fires, epidemics, and an excess of children, they reconsidered. By 1873, they embraced the idea, with a few modifications. Foremost, they required that their children—whom the Sisters baptized, regardless of the child's origin—must be raised as Catholics. Unlike the Children's Aid Society, they would not allow the children to be indentured at first. Also, children did not go out unless a specific "order" came from a particular family requesting a child with specific characteristics. The Sisters believed that with advanced advertising, people would solicit children of a specific gender, age, coloring, and temperament. A child so selected, they reasoned, would be cherished and treated as the parents' very own. Confirmations like the following notified the expectant couple.

SISTERS OF CHARITY
No. 175 East 68th Street, New York City
NOTICE OF ARRIVAL No. 26
Mr. Jesse Bell
Mason City, Iowa

We take pleasure in notifying you that the little girl which you so kindly ordered will arrive at Manley, Rock Is. Train on Thurs., June 24, due to arrive at 5:15 A.M., and ask that you kindly be at the Railway Station to receive the child 30 minutes before the train is due to avoid any possibility of missing the connection, as trains will not wait should you not be there.

The name of the child, date of birth, and name and address of party to whom child is assigned will be found sewn in the Coat of boys and in the hem of the Dress of girls.

This receipt must be signed in ink by both husband and wife, and is to be given up in exchange for the child who will have a corresponding number.

Yours very truly,
SISTERS OF CHARITY

RECEIPT FOR CHILD

We beg to acknowledge receipt of the little orphan as numbered above and promise faithfully to raise said child in the Roman Catholic faith and to send h… to school and give h… all the advantages that we would give to a child of our own, and report to Sisters of Charity as to health and general condition when requested, notifying them of any change in address.

Alternately, older children could agree to leave the city for a new lease on life as an apprentice to one of the farm families served by the Orphan Trains. Following is the agreement they signed, which details the child's name, location, date, and what the responsibilities of the child would be, but not what (s)he would be given in return. They presumed a home, food, clothes, and similar basic needs.

APPRENTICE AGREEMENT

On date, Apprentice's Agreement showing name indentured himself willingly through the New York Juvenile Asylum. A copy of _____'s agreement is also at the new OTHSA (Orphan Train Historical Society) office.

I, name   , the person described, will apprentice myself to name   for the period and on the terms described in the foregoing instrument, and the sections of the Chapter of the "New York Juvenile Asylum," thereunto annexed, and do agree with name   the party of the second part to the foregoing Indenture: To well and truly serve him and his lawful commands, do no damage to the said party of the second part, nor see it done by others, without preventing the same, as far as I lawfully may, nor will I waste the said party's goods, nor lend them unlawfully to any, nor will I absence myself day or night from said party's service without the said party's leave, nor frequent porter houses, taverns, drinking saloons, playhouses, or gaming houses, but will in all things behave myself as a faithful apprentice.

IN WITNESS WHEREOF, I have hereunto set my hand and seal this date , in the year of our Lord year.

Signed, Sealed, and Delivered in presence of

Witness name

Like many programs, the "placing out" program was imperfect. But compared to the conditions these children left behind—life on the streets, starvation, and exploitation—it succeeded. Over the years, many children wrote touching letters to the agents who transported them. One such letter to a member of Brace's family, enlisted as a trusted agent, said:

> Dear Mr. Brace: When I lived in New York, I had no bonnet and now I have more bonnets than I can wear. And I get no whippings and I have a father and mother and brothers and sisters here and they are kinder to me than my own ever were. I think I will never be happier than I am now.

In the long term, the goal of restoring destitute children to happy, healthy, and productive citizens proved as monumental a chasm as the Grand Canyon. On the street, many of the children had grown too rough and coarse to be dropped into decent, God-fearing homes. Calloused like the hooves of unshod horses, some swore, smoke, and drank like full-grown men. Some learned how to protect themselves fiercely; others merely cowered. Many experienced much more of adult life than any sheltered child ever should.

The value of routine washing, clean clothes, prayers, and Sunday School seemed as alien to them as the opportunity for it. Truth and honesty worked for chumps; one had to eat, they felt. Many of the youngsters left on their own for very long became too damaged to be rendered suitable through a bath, haircut, clean clothes, table manners, and a little fattening up. Not all brackish water can be made potable. These children remained incarcerated indefinitely. Still better off than those living on the streets, their childhoods were lost forever.

These vagabonds, rounded up like mustangs, sometimes filled vacancies left in orphanages by the more fortunate kids who rode the trains.

Others made a stop to first get polished up and trained on farms set up for that purpose, like Brace Memorial Farm in Valhalla NY, where children learned to do farm chores as well as learn manners, hygiene, religious training, and education. Those who thrived found new homes in the west. Others, unable to adapt, either ran back to the city streets or went to Homes for Children until deemed capable of providing for themselves, usually at age fourteen.

Human nature does not change much. Not all of the families opening their homes to these waifs turned out to be the good, God-fearing folks Brace had anticipated. Many children testified to happy and loving families. But stories of exploitation, brutality, runaways, and child slavery trickled back to New York with some of the children.

May 28, 1865
Dear Friend: The place where I lived I did not like. They whipped me till I was all black and blue. I told the lady I did not like to stay there, so she told me I might leave. I have a good place now. I hope you will write to me and let me know if you see any of my folks in New York. I would give 100 worlds like this if I could see my mother, Katie Murphy.

For nearly seventy-five years, the "placing out" program continued, until 1929 and the Great Depression. People could not provide for themselves, much less take in additional mouths to feed. Hoboes took the place of babies on the trains.

Then, as now, inspectors to ensure the children's health and happiness were in short supply. Frequent revisions occurred to the program, alternatives constantly sought. When reuniting the family or adoption of the child proved impossible, the new goal became constructing smaller Group Homes. A German plan came into favor called the "Cottage Plan." Cottages were not what we think of today, like at the beach. They were large homes, usually in the country, smaller than the mansions and in-town homes of many families with resident servants. Set up for thirty to fifty children, each had a Cottage Mother—or, ideally, a couple—to oversee them. They could be established on a few acres of land. Even a series of cottages could serve as dormitories with a central kitchen, dining room, laundry, prayer room, and other communal functions, similar to a boarding school.

But this design would take time and capital to construct. The politicians asked what would become of the orphanages already in existence. And what about the economies of scale of having a thousand children under one roof rather than under fifty separate roofs, with only one Warden, plus the expense of additional overseers? And what of the many powerful jobs of the Wardens, Directors, and Managers of those orphanages, and their cohorts in Tammany Hall? Much resistance to change resulted, particularly when the economy fluctuated wildly and fell into a depression after a meteoric rise.

By 1873, the New York Stock Exchange closed amid thousands of business failures. Tens of thousands of people sought charity for the first time. Few politicians wanted to improve the existing orphanages, much less discard them for new construction.

In 1875, the American Society for Prevention of Cruelty to Children (ASPCC) formed. They strove to protect the swelling ranks of children, many of whom were left to fend for themselves by overwrought parents. They distributed children like playing cards among more than five hundred agencies such as the Gerry Society, missions, and various religious organizations, until consolidated under the ASPCC. This new society acquired the sole *legal* authority to distribute children, though many organizations provided the care for them. The ASPCC also had the legal right to prosecute negligent parents and hold them accountable for the care of their own children. The foundation of modern Juvenile Courts and Child Welfare System resulted.

Six

In Search of a Home

The quality of life in New York City had significantly degraded throughout the Civil War and its aftermath. Increased number of noisy, horse-drawn buses and trucks with their stinking oil lanterns fouled the air as they clattered across the cobblestones. Overcrowded tenements never got cleaned; sanitation services became nearly non-existent. Animal carcasses lay steaming and rotting in streets already clogged with month-old garbage from the ever-increasing populace. Smoke and smells resulting from the industrial revolution polluted the water and air. Dreaded epidemics of influenza, yellow fever, cholera, typhoid, polio, and other diseases broke out regularly. The air became so contaminated that it drove the wealthy class out of the city during summer to their country estates, jeopardizing the city's tax base. All of it demanded political attention.

Amid these wretched conditions, Mrs. John Reid—a Brooklyn woman—struggled to breathe. The only expectation for her recovery, according to her doctor, lay in a move toward clear country air. Away from the city, her lungs could be cleansed and renewed. Her husband had become a prosperous businessman after they emigrated from Scotland in the first half of the nineteenth century. Despite the dire economic conditions, John Reid began his search for a country home in the rural regions surrounding the city. He must have held high hopes for his wife's recovery, for at a time when a Dr. West advertised "a stylish cottage for rent in Nanuet, $120 per year," Mr. Reid chose to build his own home, instead.

The rustic Hudson Valley, nearly thirty miles north of the city, was described as a "triangle of mountain, valley, and river edge." People built country homes in neighboring Nyack and Spring Valley to escape the oppression of summer in the city. Mr. Reid learned of a piece of land within easy access to the bustling commerce along the Hudson River that would be ideal for convalescing. The hamlet of Nanuet was a straightforward commute by train into the city. John Reid bought nearly seventeen acres.

Historians believe that Nanuet derived its name from the local Leni-Lenape Indian Chief Nanwitt, from whom Dutch settlers of the 1600's acquired the land. After the King of England drove the Dutch out, he bestowed several patents, or land grants, as rewards to encourage rapid settlement. There are many documented encampments by George Washington during the Revolutionary War. Not far from Nanuet is the town of Tappan, where General Andre was tried and hung for plotting treason against America with Benedict Arnold. Ancient artifacts have been unearthed, including bones dating back to the last ice age. Glaciers left behind artesian wells and a sandstone foundation, highly suitable for farming. Underground springs crisscrossed John Reid's new property.

The brusque steamboat trade along the Hudson had been superseded by the swifter "iron horse" of the Erie Railroad in 1856, and accounted for the rapid growth of the County. Boarding a train at Grand Central Station, Mr. Reid would have savored the delights of the local mountains along the way. Named with another Indian word that meant "sweet water," the Ramapo peaks cradled Rockland County. Besides the land's inherent beauty, many reputable Medical Doctors made their homes in Rockland County, so Mrs. Reid's health could be properly attended to. Fresh dairy products, eggs, and meat appeared daily from neighboring farms.

In November 1874, a hired carriage from the train station carried Mr. Reid the single mile to his building site. He clopped along hard-packed dirt roads, through the bustling hamlet's Main Street, past the lumber-yard, grocer, mercantile, church, hotel, and out of the village. In contrast

Main Street, Nanuet

to the city, no crowds assembled here. No crime in the street, no pick-pockets or beggars, no urchins; none of the heartwrenching poverty that plagued the metropolis.

Without teams of horse-drawn buses spewing smoke from their oil lanterns, the incessant throbbing and clanging of vehicles gave way to chirping birds. On foot or by carriage, country folks went unhurriedly about their business among home, shops, church, work, and school.

The countryside might have still been ablaze in autumn colors, the air crisp and cool, leaves heaped beneath the semi-naked trees. Halfway to the building site, the horses turned onto the well-worn path past Nanuet's Old Red Schoolhouse. Neighboring farmers had plots of about fifty acres surrounded by woods teeming with game: just the place where Mrs. Reid could redeem her health.

On November 2, 1874, Mr. Reid purchased the land and ordered the building of a two-story home with an attic, barn, and outbuildings. The construction concluded rapidly since the effects of the Depression that began with the market crash in 1873 had not crept into the self-contained hamlet of Nanuet—or anywhere in Rockland County, for that matter.

The simple, yet well-built, two-story home had tall, white Grecian columns on both front and side porches. Broad windows flanked the

Original Little Flower House

double oak front doors, and five more brightened the bedrooms above. Houses sported whitewash of lime mined in the nearby mountains.

An upper floor sunroom seemed ideal as a sitting room where Mrs. Reid might enjoy the sunshine and outdoors, safe from the cold and damp. At last, all was ready. The new cottage lay close to the northern portion of the land, parallel to—and set back slightly from—the road later named Convent Road. It linked the hamlet of Nanuet in the east with its western neighbors in Spring Valley and the town of Pearl River to the south. In bygone years, stagecoaches reputed to have traversed this road stopped at the Ross home across the way when it was a tavern and inn.

In February of 1875, the Reids settled into their new home. The surrounding fields of blackberry bushes, apple, plum and pear trees—barren twigs then—promised fragrant blooms in upcoming months. Wildlife and game abounded, even in winter. Honking ducks and pheasant wafted up from the fields at the crack of a gun or the sound of a footfall.

The mountain air—which earned the area a pseudo name, "the Denver of the east"—suggested short walks around the property, or a rocker

on the porch in the noonday sun. Curative carriage rides could be anticipated with the coming of spring.

Across the road, the Pascack Brook, fed by the Hackensack River,
filled to its banks with snow each year. The Reid property sat at a low
point in a shallow valley, and crisscrossed by meandering creeks, which
filled the artesian well, then wandered off to join the brook.

Beneath the pristine blanket of snow, the untilled land was clogged
with fieldstones, used locally for foundations in buildings—hence the
name, Rockland County. Industrious farmers cleared them to plant crops.
Cattle, which grazed in verdant pastures during warmer weather, now
stuck close to the barn for shelter from the wind. Corrals penned horses
vacationing from the plow to pull wagons, sleighs, and carts all winter.
Surely, Mr. Reid thought his wife would revive amid this tranquility.

But she did not. In May, as buds began to appear, Mrs. Reid caught a
cold, then pneumonia made her critically ill. Mr. Reid urgently summoned his son, the Reverend Thomas A. Reid, teaching at Fordham
University. The young Jesuit, recently returned from studying theology
abroad, came at once. The morning after their reunion, he hurried off to
Spring Valley to offer Mass for his dying mother in a tiny mission chapel,
but she died.

The next morning, while Mr. Reid arranged to return to Brooklyn, a
small group visited. They implored the Priest to stay on as Chaplain to
the community. Currently, they enjoyed only an annual Mass offered by
the Priest from St. Ann's Church in Nyack. Reverend Reid, recently
ordained and far from master of his own fate, could not accept. The chapel, like the little house, stood empty and forlorn for many years.

Seven

Abandoned Babies

T homas Reid was born in Brooklyn on July 21, 1842. He became an ordained a Roman Catholic Priest on June 10, 1865, a Jesuit in 1870, and took first vows two years later. Assigned a teaching position at Fordham University in 1874, Reverend Reid preached at various parish missions. Once it became clear that his grieving father had no heart for returning to Nanuet, Father Reid recommended that it be offered to the Sisters of Charity as a refuge outside the city to care for orphans. He had been ministering to the Sisters at St. Joseph Home for the Aged on 16th Street, just a block from St. Francis Xavier College, where he preached and provided religious services.

In Baltimore, 1809, the Sisters of Charity scratched out an existence under the leadership of Elizabeth Seton. Legendary in New York City for their extraordinary work during the cholera epidemic of 1832, they also nursed thousands of wounded soldiers from both sides during the Civil War. Not long after her death in 1821, proceedings began to canonize Mother Seton as the first American-born Saint.

About that time, John Joseph Hughes—an Irish immigrant who fought his way up from gardener and stonemason—became a priest, then the most powerful man in New York City. Hughes molded the Archdiocese of New York from nothing into America's Rome with himself as its first Archbishop in 1838.

Reverend Hughes, with the help of the Sisters of Charity, founded the Society for the Protection of Destitute Catholic Children known as the Catholic Protectory. They purchased a 114-acre farm near Westchester and installed as its President the famous protestant convert, Levi Ives. He vowed, "By proper religious instruction and the teaching of useful trades, the Protectory could raise the children above their slum environment."

Next, Reverend Hughes formed church societies to assist people in dealing with personal, family, and neighborhood problems. He helped form the Irish Emigrant Society to secure jobs, with nuns in his diocese as employment agents for Irish domestics. Rich families knew that a maid or cook so recommended would be honest and reliable. The nuns encouraged Irish women to run boardinghouses for new immigrants, and they came to dominate the city's produce business.

In 1846, over half of the population of sixty Sisters of Charity formed a separate community and called themselves the Sisters of Charity of St. Vincent de Paul. Under the leadership of Reverend Hughes's sister, Angela Hughes, they established the Academy of Mount St. Vincent in 1847. Mother Angela became a role model for the city's Irish women.

Archbishop Hughes set up Catholic schools and hospitals; brought nuns and priests from Ireland, Italy, and France; opened orphanages; and empowered the downtrodden Irish of New York. He founded Fordham University and installed Jesuit Priests to run it. In the 1850s, he began to dream of a Cathedral, which would reflect the growing strength of the Irish in New York City and represent their expanding wealth and power. He built the first St. Patrick's, on Mott Street. Later he handpicked the architect to construct the largest Gothic cathedral in the western Hemisphere: the new St. Patrick's Cathedral at 5th Avenue and 50th Street. The Archbishop attended the installation of its cornerstone in 1863. Meanwhile, the original St. Patrick's caught fire, but Hughes ordered it rebuilt. Archbishop John Hughes died January 3, 1864 without seeing his dream accomplished. Completion came in May of 1879 at the unprecedented cost of $4,000,000. By then, Irish Catholics comprised half the city's population, had forty churches, and owned property valued at approximately $2,000,000.

Under the leadership of Mother Superior Angela Hughes, the Sisters of Charity opened St. Vincent's Hospital in 1849, the Roman Catholic Orphan Asylum, the New York Catholic Protectory in 1863, and the New York Foundling Asylum in 1869. Infants abandoned all over the city dead and alive had no alternative facilities in orphanages. They simply did not exist.

Discarded infants taken to missions received care from paupers. Families with too many mouths to feed believed that an unwanted newborn might be better off left at a church, on a doorstep, or even put out of its misery. Infanticide became a growing epidemic. Sick abandoned babies, 150 to 200 per *month*—for whom no money for doctors or burials could be found—usually died. Police found them strewn around in empty crates, vacant lots, or floating in barrels along the Hudson River. They needed immediate rescue and long-term care.

The New York Foundling Asylum, established by Sister Irene Fitzgibbon in October of 1869, aimed to save the lives of these tots. Sister Irene was one of the many thousands of women influenced by the charitable works of Mother Seton. Born Catherine Fitzgibbon in England, 1823, she was nine when her family came to Brooklyn. When Catherine finished school in 1850, she became a Sister of Charity and adopted the name Sister Mary Irene. She taught school at St. Peter's parish school. After ten years of administration and leadership in education, Sister Irene turned her attention to the ever-increasing number of abandoned children. She shared her concerns with Archbishop McCloskey, the first Cardinal of New York, who approved her plan to open an asylum.

After studying existing establishments with similar goals, Sister Irene organized a group of charitable women to help acquire the resources necessary to start receiving children. She placed a "lady of charity"—a society woman called Mrs. Paul Thebaud—as its Committee Director, and rented a house at 17 East 12th Street. They intended to begin receiving children on January 1, 1870.

During the night of October 11, 1869, in the entryway of the house on 12th Street, an infant appeared, mewling weakly. Later that same night, a second cry was heard during a torrential downpour, and The New York Foundling Asylum was in operation three months early. By the end of the month, they housed forty-five foundlings, some with pitiful little notes or identifiers:

Brooklyn   November 23, 1869
Dear Sister,

I now sit down to write to you a few lines but I hardly know what to say, for when I inform you that I am the mother of the child left on Thanksgiving night between the hours of 8 and 9 o'clock, without even a slip of paper to tell you the name of the child left in your care, my heart aches so much I cannot tell, but I knew that I was leaving her in good hands.

Although I have been unfortunate, I am neither low nor degraded and am in hopes of one day claiming my child. Her name is Jone G, born on 5 of October 1869 between the hours of three and four o'clock in the morning...she had a piece of canton flannel tied around her head and little red and white socks on her feet—and if the prayers of an unfortunate creature like myself will do any good, offered to the mercy of God in heaven—for you know that every night on my bended knees I pray for you.

I am very sorry that I have nothing to send you at this time but I am in hopes there will be a day when I shall be able to pay you for all your trouble.

Word spread of the small wicker crib placed in the vestibule of the Asylum, where children could be safely left, no questions asked. Available writing materials offered mothers the opportunity to leave the child's birthday, time of birth, name, and other notes. The children came from parents, neighbors, police, or parish priests, and left with only brief explanations of their origin—sometimes without a word. The one hundred and fifty babies typically found strewn around the city each month swindled by ninety percent immediately after the Foundling opened.

Some of the mothers' touching letters contained mementoes, now on display at the Foundling in New York City. A piece of fabric torn from a dress, a ribbon, or trinkets would uniquely identify the child if the mother returned to reclaim it. Not all of these desperate women were illiterate or of ill repute. Some had husbands who'd left them; others had been seduced by a landlord or a boss, became pregnant, and had nowhere else to turn.

By the end of one year, the Asylum moved to 3 Washington Square North to accommodate the more than one thousand children brought to them—two-thirds in such poor health, they died anyway.

Not everyone approved of the foundling program. Some believed that it encouraged immoral behavior, or families to shirk their responsibilities to their own children. But the work went on. Sister Irene sought first to nurse the unwanted babies of the city, then—once well enough—to find them permanent homes. She began offering services to distraught parents and, whenever possible, to reunite the family.

By 1870, New York City recognized the valuable services the New York Foundling Asylum provided. It donated the block from 3rd and Lexington Avenues, 68th and 69th Streets, as a site for a new facility, along with $100,000 seed money for the building, if the charity could match the funds. In the following year, they held a fair, which raised three-quarters of the required amount. The remaining balance came from three private citizens. The new building opened in October of 1873 at 175 East 68th Street.

The Foundling sought homes and families for the babies. Sometimes failing, they sent children to other institutions or to the Orphan Trains. St. Ann's Maternity Hospital opened for pregnant, homeless, and indigent mothers in 1880. Prenatal care and delivery endeavored to ensure the safety of mother and child. A wet-nurse program began whereby mothers who nursed one other baby along with her own could remain at the hospital free of charge. For other infants, women from as far away as

New Jersey received a small stipend to nurse babies until the child turned two years old. They had to bring the tots in for inspection once a month.

In 1875, the New York State Child Welfare Laws added a clause, requiring religious training for all children in institutions. Catholics hailed this as an opportunity to ensure that their children would be raised within their own faith, thus ending the practice of placing Catholic children into protestant facilities.

The New York Foundling Asylum incorporated in 1889 and renamed itself The New York Foundling Hospital in 1891. Like Mother Seton, Sister Irene championed children. Before her death in 1896, recognition came for her great strides in medical and maternity care, foster homes, and adoption services. Sister Irene dedicated her life to the care of foundlings, and just before her death, she added to her accomplishments the establishment of the Seton Hospital for incurable consumptives, all at a cost of $350,000. She collected the money herself.

By the end of the century, well established Catholics in New York were founding most orphanages in the east. Some cared for as many as a thousand children at a time. As these vast institutions became too unwieldy, and public attitudes changed, actual plans for smaller,

Girls from the NewYork Foundling Hospital were welcomed at St. Agatha

congregate care establishments began to replace the dreams. Towards this scheme, Reverend Reid proposed to his father that he donate the vacant home in Nanuet. The senior Reid assented. On December 3, 1875, he transferred ownership of his property—legally described as "sixteen and 38/100 acres, more or less"—to the Sisters of Charity of Saint Vincent de Paul "for the consideration of one dollar."

Eight

The Mustard Seed Takes Root

In January of 1876, the transaction was documented at Mount St. Vincent de Paul, the Motherhouse for the Sisters of Charity, in Riverdale, New York.

Sister Mary Lewis, Superior of St. Joseph's Asylum in Brooklyn, rejoiced at the opportunity to build a new asylum for children. It took eight years to gather the necessary funds to open the new Home. Sister Lewis's successor, Sister Mary Ulrica O'Reilly, accepted the challenge from Mother Mary Jerome, now Superior of the Sisters of Charity. She intended to duplicate her past successes—instituting places like St. Joseph's Military Hospital for Civil War casualties, the Catholic Protectory, and a training institution for children, among similar undertakings—by bringing to life the dream of a new Home for Children.

Three other nuns joined Sister Mary Ulrica, and with five little orphaned sisters from the Gerry Society, they followed the path traveled a decade earlier by John Reid. Imagine the apprehension, the excitement, the anticipation on the part of the children leaving the city they had known all of their young lives.

Like the orphan train riders, they would be dressed in new outfits purchased for the occasion. Similarly, on their laps they would clutch little cardboard suitcases stenciled with their last name and containing their meager belongings: a little tooth powder, a slate and chalk for lessons, an extra dress for chapel, a nightdress, a change of stockings, an extra under-garment. More possessions of their very own than they may ever have had.

Once the raucous clatter of the train ceased—wheels against tracks, the toot-toot of the whistle, and the asthmatic wheeze of the engine climbing towards their future ceased—a profound silence ensued. At the Nanuet train station, people disembarked, climbed into horse-drawn carriages or rough farm wagons, or set out on foot. Doubtless, Sister Ulrica had telegrammed ahead to secure a carriage large enough to carry the pioneers and their trunks the final mile to their new home.

The little girls might discreetly whisper, stare, and point, unaccustomed to vast fields, trees, and birds. In the city, they only glimpsed patches of sky above an alley or a gray and sooty vacant lot restricted by tall buildings stacked one on top of the other.

With such a small ratio of adults to children, the youngsters could receive ample attention, sometimes for the first time in their lives. The girls might have been chosen because of their good behavior, health, and likely success: models for the victory of the venture. Some may have family they'd left behind once when taken into care, or family who now grew further distant. Others may have grown attached to a second caregiver, an elderly Sister or a nurse, only to be moved again.

For the Nuns, there was little risk. As adults, they could look forward with excitement to the undertaking ahead of them. Return visits to the city from time to time could be anticipated in order for them to remain connected to their community, friends, and family. The Sisters of Charity believed wholeheartedly that their mission would be a triumph if they created a Home where children would be given a second chance at a decent life. In clean, safe, comfortable surroundings—and if fed, clothed, nurtured, protected, and taught their Catechism—they could become devoted children of God and acceptable to society.

One by one, or ten by ten, the little girls would come. One day, they may even be able to return to their own families. Or, at fourteen or fifteen, they may be assisted in finding jobs in good homes as domes-—respectable work deemed suitable for orphans in those days. They would leave, prepared to begin their own healthy families. The cycle of poverty and destitution would be broken.

The country road was sufficiently well-traveled to prove passable, even if an early November snow had fallen. The children may have gawked at the great expanse of untouched snow mounded over dormant fields. There would certainly be no black dusting from coal and traffic to hammer it into gray slush. The travelers would see the same pastoral setting that welcomed the Reid's, nearly a decade earlier.

Accompanying Sister Mary Ulrica O'Reilly, were Sister Mary Justine Donahue from St. Joseph's Home, who would care for the house; Sister Mary Albertine McNally; and Sister Joseph Maria Leavy. In July, Sister Mary Aide Harbison would join them. Together, they would forge a new beginning, like their foundress Mother Seton had, three quarters of a century before.

At the Reid house, supplies and furnishings sent on ahead now awaited them. The party could have stepped from the wagon, mounted the few steps, and clumped across the wooden porch for the first time. Sister Ulrica would lead them in a prayer, asking God for a blessing on their new Home. Inside, all would be snug in the cottage built for the ailing Mrs. Reid's comfort and recovery. Perhaps a fire blazed.

And so their new lives began at the Little Flower House, as it came to be called. Judiciously, Sister Ulrica divided up the rooms by function for prayer, sleeping, dining, lavatory, and school activities—always with expansion in mind. The group blended their meager belongings with the furnishings left by the Reids. Mother Jerome supplemented their surroundings with crucifixes, religious paintings, and a font for holy water.

House rules and a daily routine included lesson plans. In such close, multi-purpose quarters, neatness and organization were as imperative as consideration and co-operation. With duties fulfilled, the children could play on the porch or in the yard, except in the worst weather. It proved crucial to guard against colds that could turn into pneumonia and spread among their small congregation.

Besides making up their beds, personal care, and school lessons, the girls would be expected to dust, sweep, peel vegetables, haul water and firewood, set the table, clear and wash dishes—all tasks normal to a household. They spent most of their time together.

On February 5, 1884, a welcome visitor arrived. Reverend Thomas Reid celebrated Mass in the same room where his mother had died ten years earlier. Invited to choose the name for the new asylum, in his mother's memory the Reverend chose "Saint Agatha Home for Children." The day of his visit was the feast of the martyr Saint Agatha, patron Saint of Mrs. Reid, and the name happily embraced. Reverend Reid visited his beneficiaries as often as he could over the years, until his own death on January 21, 1919 at St. Andrews-on-Hudson Monastery in Poughkeepsie, New York where he is buried. The Jesuits remained faithful supporters to St. Agatha Home in the century that followed.

By then, they had settled the practical details of life. Food provisions came by train from St. Joseph's in Brooklyn. A plentiful supply of firewood waited to supply warmth through the winter. A water pump provided sweet well water, just outside the door. They had all the basics.

The pressing need of spiritual care had to be addressed. With no regular Catholic Masses available in the vicinity, The Dominican Sisters of Blauvelt offered to share their weekly Mass. St. Dominic's Home opened about seven and a half miles away in November of 1878. The all-girl's Home, founded by Sister Mary Ann Sammon, had similar goals of providing orphaned children with a fresh start.

The rutted roads between the two Homes often iced up in winter. The Sisters huddled together—enveloped in black cocoons from head to foot—on their journey in a roughly hewn open farm wagon. Often, the Chaplain at St. Dominic's had to delay Mass for more than an hour until the frozen Sisters arrived. A Sister who endured the journey each Sunday wrote of their ordeal:

One bitter morning, one of the Sisters became so overcome by the cold that she fell faint in the wagon, and no farmhouse appearing for miles.

The Sisters could only throw their wraps over her and pray that it would not result in what really seemed to them a case of freezing before they reached the convent, so intense was the cold.

The communicants survived the trip. The Dominican Sisters were so moved by their Sisters' devotion that they forfeited their own services mid-week so that St. Agatha Home could receive Mass from their Priest. He made the journey to Nanuet. Those months of exposure to hostile climate gave way not only to spring, but also to another visitor.

Meanwhile at Catholic Charities headquarters, the Academy at Mount St. Vincent in Riverdale, Mother Jerome focused her attention on the financial matters of the fledgling Home. In a century when women had little power or respect as businesswomen, the Sisters achieved impressive successes. Besides Mother Seton and Sister Irene, the sisters who ran hospitals, schools, and orphanages were incredibly competent. They received no personal financial rewards like their contemporary entrepreneurs: Carnegie, Morgan, and Mellon. The rewards the Sisters anticipated were in the work and in Heaven.

On February 14th, 1884, Mother Superior received a somewhat terse letter from Devlin and Miller, New York City Attorneys and Counsellors at Law. She had requested that children be referred to the newly opened St. Agatha Home for Children through the New York City courts, and that funding be provided for their care. A skeptical Attorney Devlin doubted that the courts would consider referring children to a private facility outside of New York County. Further, he believed that even if children had been referred, it would be unlikely for payments to be made, particularly given current sentiment towards *Catholic* charities.

The Board of Charities formed to oversee the myriad of unregulated organizations collecting money to distribute to the disadvantaged; some legitimately, some not. In difficult economic years like 1881, careful evaluation caused the Board to deem many of the charities wasteful and encouragers of pauperism—despite all the progress made by the Association for Improving the Condition of the Poor (AICP) from 1843 until it merged with the newly formed Charity Organization Society (COS), founded in 1882. AICP had committed to improving the lives of New Yorkers in need of help by establishing the first public baths in New York State (1852), erecting the first model tenement in New York City (1855), launching the drive for pure milk laws (1862), and starting the first shelter for homeless men (1893).

The protestant-run Children's Aid Society explicitly refused to place children with the "unfit" Catholic or Jewish families. Not only did Irish politicians support the nuns, but the protestant Gerry Society, which merged with the ASPCC, found them to be efficient and inexpensive. The public coffers benefited from the nuns' vow of poverty. This may explain why the first children to go to St. Agatha Home came from the Gerry Society, which had full discretion about placement of them.

So, it is not so surprising that Attorney Devlin scoffed at the notion of St. Agatha Home receiving compensation from the City. He did suggest that St. Agatha could become a corporation under the general Act for the Incorporation of Charitable Societies. But that would not provide St. Agatha with the authority to receive children through the New York City's family courts. In fact, Attorney Devlin warned, the notion of an Institution as a sort of Protectory for girls "would bring it into opposition, or at least competition, with the New York Catholic Protectory—an outcome to be staunchly avoided."

The Archdiocese of New York had founded The New York Catholic Protectory as a counter-measure to earlier protestant attempts to teach destitute children a trade. They put them to work in local industries, such as shoemaking. The Catholic-run Protectory initially followed that practice and placed the children as apprentices in factories or private homes. They quickly found the children to be terribly exploited, underfed, overworked, and badly treated. So, they ceased it and set about raising and training the children in their own schools. According to Devlin, St. Agatha could not compete with the Protectory for resources.

Without public funds, money for St. Agatha Home had to be privately solicited. Application for the Incorporation of St. Agatha Home was submitted on November 29, 1884 and recorded on February 13, 1885 by the State Board of Charities.

> Under the Act of Legislature of the State of New York entitled "An Act for the Incorporation of Benevolent, Charitable, Scientific, and Missionary Societies," (passed April 12th 1848)—along with its supplemental acts—the Incorporation was approved. The agreement stipulated that seven trustees must manage St. Agatha Home for Children. The Certificate of Incorporation was signed by the following Sisters of Charity from the Academy of Mount St. Vincent: Mary T. O'Reilly, Maria Wallace, Margaret Mackey, Annie White, Mary Mettee, Ellen Donohue, and Mary F. Baker.

Before that ink dried, the Sisters and the girls overflowed the Little Flower cottage. They'd already converted the attic into sleeping quarters. In only six months, more than forty-five girls ate, slept, bathed, held religious services, and took their lessons in the house along with five nuns. Essential were order, discipline, obedience, co-operation, and regimentation. We marvel when two siblings get along well, let alone fifty girls confined beneath one roof for day after day.

The littlest orphans

Nine

Here Come the Boys

Hopes rose for the future in 1885. As the bad weather crept out, and spring tiptoed in, so did the children. All around, grass grew lush, trees and fields flowered. The air sweetened with the scent of apple blossoms and hay. Bees hummed incessantly, busy at their work. The girls spent more and more time outside. Little girls can usually find time to daydream and search for furry friends in the garden. Could these former urchins?

Imagine the change for these children: plucked from the city and transported to this country life. Some of them recent immigrants, they had first viewed America with family members. Full of fear and wonder at their new land, they longed for what they loved in the old. Most of them had known death, tragedy, and loss. These children were all alone now. Like the fearful and reluctant immigrant wife who did not come of her own accord, these little girls found themselves transplanted again from everything familiar. Here, they must start over again.

The tasks of supporting a family of fifty people were formidable: three meals prepared each day, laundry washed by hand, studies, gardening, and so on. A constant influx of new assorted-aged companions with stories to tell arrived mostly from the city. A few were local children whose families lost their breadwinner, went bankrupt, or got injured at work. Children who had known tragedy and needed comfort came every day.

Once school ended for the summer, the demand for farm chores increased. A vegetable garden appeared that first spring, requiring weeding, watering, and defense against local critters. A flower garden produced blooms to adorn the makeshift altar. The children received few visitors, and rarely left the Home grounds. Activities surrounding Mass, school, and preparation for feast days provided their diversions.

Sister Ulrica—sufficiently encouraged by the Home's progress—ordered the construction of a two-story building behind the Little Flower House. It would provide a chapel, refectory for dining, kitchen, and lavatory. Children and Sisters alike eagerly watched and, wherever possible, assisted in the progress.

Diseases and illnesses arrived at St. Agatha with the new inmates. Without antibiotics, infections posed the greatest threat to even the healthiest children. As construction began in April of 1885, Ophthalmia erupted. The eye disease, now generally called conjunctivitis or "pink eye," caused an epidemic affecting every child. It was further complicated by a diphtherial condition caused by bacterium that attacked the linings of the throat and sent toxins to the heart and nervous system. These highly contagious conditions invaded all of the childcare institutions in and around New York City. Children, divided by ages, required treatment and around-the-clock nursing for nearly a year. The summer produced a particularly virulent strain. St. Agatha became one vast infirmary partitioned according to the severity of the illnesses and type of care required.

The epidemic claimed the lives of fourteen children that summer. They built a cemetery, but it proved unsatisfactory because of the low positioning of the property. Underwater springs—so appealing for a well—proved a disaster to the burial site. They moved the graves and built a new cemetery up on the southernmost hill.

A large tent served as quarantine for the worst cases, with smaller tents for less severe variations. Because there was little relief, Sister Ulrica rejoiced in the help that came from Sister Mary Ernestine Reilly and four additional Sisters in September of 1885. Sister Mary Justine, with failing health herself, had to leave.

As summer yielded to autumn and then winter, temperatures hovered around thirty degrees and became increasingly difficult to heat the tent. A fifty-foot smokestack protruded from the roof. The great tent sagged on all sides from drifted snow. When the President of Charities happened to visit from Albany—accompanied by Mr. Fanning, the Superintendent of the Board—they were appalled at the conditions. They couldn't enter the tent so buried in snow.

The Sisters took turns plowing through the snow from the tent to the kitchen, dragging in water, food, and other supplies. They had no money for any more new construction. Indeed, by November St. Agatha's debt for mortgages and loans amounted to $29,000. St. Agatha's population had grown to one hundred eighty-five girls, most of whom fell gravely ill, and still the City sent no money for their care.

A barn on the property in reasonably good condition replaced the quarantine tent after some modification. On December 21, the forty worst cases marched to the barn while the Sisters chorused the Litany of the Mass. They named their new little infirmary St. Roch's, in honor of the Patron Saint of invalids. The timing of the move proved critical. A week later, a cyclone came through, carrying off the tent and its fittings—stovepipe and all.

A few days later, some improvement came, along with Christmas. Many patients were out of the tents and into the comparative luxury of the barn. Some even went back to the dormitory. Each child received a gift: a new frock and shoes from Mother Ambrosia, now Superior at Mount St. Vincent.

While they slept, "a Christmas tree was dressed for their delight, the following morning," wrote one Sister. Reverend Stephen Mackin—who administered the Sacraments and spiritual benefits to all of the Catholics from the surrounding area, including St. Agatha—offered a Mass of thanksgiving. Invitations spread throughout the community of this first midnight Mass to be celebrated at St. Agatha. It attracted young and old from adjacent farms and villages. One of the Sisters wrote:

Some arrived from as far away as 12 miles, dressed in rough farm clothes, and dusted with snow. At 11:30, Christmas Eve, everyone chorused the Adeste Fideles, (Oh Come All Ye Faithful), into the cold clear night, to awaken the chaplain and the workers. It was said that their voices could be heard for miles, in Nanuet, and Spring Valley. In the Chapel, the First Midnight Crib, a replica of the manger where the newborn Jesus first lay in Bethlehem, another gift from Sister Ambrosia. Touched, the visitors took turns kneeling before it, as if the newborn in the manger were not just symbolic.

Two months later, on February 5, 1886—the Feast of St. Agatha, and the second anniversary of the asylum—Archbishop Corrigan administered Confirmation to fifty girls. The newspapers called it "the bitterest, coldest day of the year, with snow drifts and hurricane force winds that swept everyone who ventured out of doors right off their feet."

Impervious to the weather, the Bishop set off in a sleigh to explore the long forsaken chapel in Spring Valley, of which the Sisters had told him, and where they hoped a community church could be established. This was the same chapel in Spring Valley that Reverend Reid had declined over a decade earlier when his mother died. The owner of the chapel had died, but her daughter repeated the offer so that together they could provide Catholic services to the Spring Valley community.

The normally pleasant jaunt proved treacherous on this day's outing. The sleigh overturned from gusting wind before it arrived at the chapel, now partially buried in snowdrifts. After rolling in the snow, the party turned back. Undaunted, sight unseen, the Archbishop authorized Mass to be said there each week by Father Mackin. The Sisters received the key, and the little church was blessed St. Joseph's of the Valley. The Sisters of St. Agatha provided everything to the chapel for ten years. In 1895, Reverend John Hughes—St. Agatha's then chaplain—moved permanently to the parish, and it separated from St. Agatha.

With the recovery of the children, and the sanctuary of the newly completed building, the atmosphere in the Little Flower House changed dramatically. Tensions eased with the return of spring. The kitchen of the Little Flower House no longer bustled with the collective activities of food preparation. These activities had moved to the new refectory, except for preparation of tea or warming a bowl of soup for a sick child.

Eagerly, the growing community surveyed the new refectory. Before long, added residents crowded the capacious room. The Sisters supervised the prayers, meals, manners, and serving techniques. Eventually, helpers oversaw the children, but they ate separately. The Rockland Light and Power Company formed in 1889. However, electricity was so expensive that it didn't come to St. Agatha until many years later.

The twice-monthly baths of dozens of children occurred in the lavatory of the new building. The girls filed over on Saturday, carrying their clean dress, stockings, and undergarments. Sometimes shivering in the cold with wet hair scrubbed clean with Pine Tar Soap, they made their way back across the yard to dry their long hair by the fire.

Treks between the buildings provided a welcome escape for the girls and the sisters. The duties of filling the Holy Water font, replacing bits of candles, dusting, and polishing were solemnly carried out in the peace of the sanctuary. Hushed voices responded to the Priest's Latin at Mass, "Deo Gratias," which means "Thanks be to God."

The congregation celebrated its 1886 Thanksgiving dinner in the new dining hall. Slowly, The Little Flower House loosened its corset that had been drawn so tight as to the point of snapping ribs. Young and old could spend a little time apart. In the chapel, each found a place to be alone.

In the spring, workmen built a handsome, two-story schoolhouse between the Little Flower House and the refectory. Banks of windows augmented lanterns to brighten the interior. Unadorned at first, they admitted sunlight, warmth, and views of beckoning fields. Occasionally, the clip-clop of a farmer atop a hay wagon or the ice truck making deliveries from Rockland Lake passed by.

Classrooms measured about thirty feet square, with wide wooden plank floors and rafters. Twenty feet overhead, religious pictures and small altars decorated the walls. Wooden benches seated two girls side by side.

Until 1900, many children still used slates for their writing assignments. Paper cost dearly, and slates ideal for practicing work did not need to be saved. Special sticks of slate pencils came in boxes like crayons.

St. Agatha's class size quickly grew to about sixty smaller girls and forty older ones, filling the vast room. Heat came from a coal-burning furnace in the basement, which forced warm air through a single, large register in the floor.

Wardrobes in the corners held coats and the white muslin ruffled pinafores that the girls wore over their ankle-length, woolen dresses as a sort of uniform. Black, high-button leather shoes covered the girls' wool-stockinged feet. Their long hair, secured with a three-inch-wide flat bow at the nape of their necks, hung down their backs.

As in the dormitory, hooks inside the cupboards displayed each girl's assigned number: a progressive measure by modern thinkers of the day. Designated clothing—and a specific place to put them—attempted to provide a sense of ownership and pride in their appearance. Formerly, they wore anything at hand, regardless of how ill-fitting.

Teachers tested children each day in religion, spelling, geography, history, and French, and required them to know their lessons, flawlessly. Offenders might receive a crack over their palms with the pointer stick, a pull on the ear, or a pinch on the cheek as inducement to make more of an effort. Non-English-speaking children had to learn their new tongue from the other children. Whether they spoke Gaelic, Yiddish, German, Russian, French, Hungarian, or Spanish before they arrived, they would speak only English here. They were in America, now. During prayers or at play, the children had to immerse themselves in English. In all schools, lapsing into a native language earned a stout slap across the face, as a helpful reminder. Those who clung to their native language could not get ahead.

The girls marched to school each morning in response to the ringing of a brass bell, then to the refectory for the dinner meal. Afterwards, those not assigned to clean-up chores went back to class. A little time for recess outside was afforded each morning and afternoon. Every evening, the group said the rosary together.

Though spacious at first, the rooms rapidly filled. In the ensuing years, St. Agatha added two more stories and various annexes. Circa 1904, workers installed a gravity-fed water tower on the roof—a distinct, rather oddly shaped aperture like a funnel. A cross was erected that could be seen from miles away. School offered a welcome diversion from the limited life in the Flower House, chapel, and dining hall. They enjoyed a bit more freedom as they moved between structures. The semi-circle of buildings began to take on the aspect of a boarding school.

They built a tri-level dormitory next, beyond the refectory. Passageways connected the three buildings, reducing the risk of chill. Respiratory diseases, still rampant, proved easier to avoid than to treat. Each story of the new building became one large dormitory, about thirty feet wide and triple the length. A wide center aisle divided rows of black iron-framed beds, three rows deep. Each bed had a foot of space on each side.

The coarse, tightly woven cotton sheets commonly used in institutions came from France—made of cotton and hemp with a bit of linen for extra strength. Stiff and scratchy like canvas, they sustained constant use. Boiling helped to soften them a bit. Linen sheets were usually available only to the middle and upper classes who had the money to buy them or who inherited them from dying relatives. Decorative white coverlets protected blankets of wool, which provided warmth and durability. They came from ladies' charities that either made them or supplied the fabric for the staff and girls to sew. No sitting on the beds once they were made up.

The beds themselves looked like they'd been assembled from a child's Erector Set. With no actual headboard, the frame extended upwards at each end, taller at one end to restrain the pillows. The frame was constructed of flattened, square pipes welded at right angles, and

Girls' dorm room

brackets bracing adjacent corners. Each bed had small wheels to facilitate cleaning underneath, rearranging, and daily making up.

The thick, lumpy, hard mattresses contained stuffing of excelsior (wood shavings) inside heavy cotton batting, and were covered by striped cotton ticking. They could be restuffed, and the excelsior would be replaced later with horsehair of good quality to extend their use. The mattresses rested on a bed of springs. With no government funding, the Home had to rely on churches, ladies groups, and private sources for much of what they received. Sometimes donations came when other asylums or hospitals closed or ordered new furnishings.

At each end of the long narrow dormitory, heavy doors used glass transoms at the top to admit light and air. Over the years, candles gave way to oil lamps, which gave way to electricity. The decor resembled the dining room and school. The plentiful windows remained curtainless, affording plenty of light, but little privacy. The modest girls dressed by slipping day clothes over nightgowns and removing them from underneath.

The new chapel provided a daily refuge for the Sisters. With the school and dormitory fully utilized, the Little Flower House became the Sister's convent. Finally, with the top off the pressure cooker, everyone relaxed a bit. By 1886, the Sisters had accomplished a great deal. Reinforcements arrived from Sister Mary Bertrand Kelly, Sister Mary Hilda Gillis, Sister Mary Protase Callaghan, and Sister Mary Stanislaus Daly.

Next, workmen built a laundry building behind the refectory. It had a boiler house and three separate steam plants. A coal fire generated steam for heating the buildings and drying clothes. In warm weather, drying racks sat out in the yard. The well, dug for Mr. Reid, proved so deep and possessed such good pressure that it provided amply for the Home's expanding needs.

The ongoing problem of draining sewage away from the buildings escalated. A remedy presented itself in the fall of 1886 when St. Agatha purchased from Mr. Ross and Mrs. Davidson the two-story home across the road, situated on forty-one acres. This commodious house had three stories, a wraparound porch, plenty of windows, and four chimneys to heat the many rooms. In the back sat a barn and numerous outbuildings. The chaplain and the growing population of workmen moved into it.

The land around the new building provided the solution to the sewerage problems. But an elaborate, expensive solution for processing sewage—developed by a former Civil War General named Barret of Staten Island—proved inadequate, and a cruel waste of the Home's precious funds. The Ross property extended to the eastern boundary of St. Agatha towards Nanuet; to the northern boundary into the woods; west towards Spring Valley; and south, down Duryea Lane towards Pearl River. A new frame had been placed around the original property, and the overall land stretched to more than fifty-seven acres.

Mrs. E. Fellow Jenkins—wife of the Superintendent of the ASPCC, and a great supporter of St. Agatha—planned a new expansion. She often brought Christmas gifts and sweets for the children, and became a real friend to the fledgling Home. She urged the Sisters to consider accepting boys so that families could stay together. Perhaps as a result of her financial aid, the acquisition of the Ross property was made possible for a place where the boys to live and attend school. They named it St. Joseph's Dormitory.

St. Joseph's Dorm, 1886

The first few boys came from Sister Mary Irene and the New York Foundling that overflowed with eight hundred boys and as many girls. Sister Irene served as a member of the Board of Managers of St. Agatha Home. The population of boys rapidly filled St. Joseph's, and interior walls came down to accommodate their increasing numbers like letting seams out on a dress. Each floor became one large dormitory, with a few private rooms on the perimeters for the chaplain, workmen, and classrooms.

After their chores each morning, the boys changed for class from their play clothes to uniforms, though they attended in the same building. The older boys wore black cotton leggings under grey tweed woolen knickers and shoes of black leather high tops. Waist-length woolen jackets covered snowy white cotton blouses with huge white bows at the necks, like choirboys.

Younger boys wore similar outfits, but with one difference: The boys' jackets were a bright plaid, probably the result of some excess donated fabric. In warmer weather, they doffed their jackets and wore plaid bows at their necks, instead of white. Everyone's hair was short, parted in the middle, and slicked back with a perfectly even part.

The littlest boys wore boots with silver buckles, and navy-blue sailor suits, complete with white stripes at collar and wrist. Naturally, all uniforms had to be turned in after an event. A separate outfit served for Sunday and special occasions. Worn-out uniforms became play clothes. Everyone wore hand-me-downs.

By the spring of 1887, they added a fourth floor sleeping space. Next, a shop for the carpenter and blacksmith for the increasing construction, maintenance, and repairs—all necessitated by over four hundred children. At the end of two years, St. Joseph's dormitory housed so many boys and their caretakers that the workmen moved into a separate residence they called the Lodge

The children began to learn rudimentary farming techniques. Vegetable gardens sprang up alongside the residences, providing carrots, turnips, potatoes, corn, tomatoes, beans, beets, rutabaga, and parsnips. Adjacent to the Lodge, a large barn stored hay and provided a place to milk cows and stable horses. A hand pump outside provided water.

Behind the barn, the farm expanded to teach the children the trade and to feed the ever-increasing population. They added horses to pull plows and wagons. Pigpens, hen brooders, and chicken and duck houses necessitated facilities for slaughtering animals for food. Stockade fencing enclosed the whole yard. A coal-belly stove, set atop wood floors, heated hot water in the chick brooders, and a metal smoke pipe protruded ugh the roof.

Ten

Home Farm

One of the mandates of St. Agatha's Articles of Incorporation provided that the children learn a means of becoming gainfully employed by fourteen: the traditional age of apprentices. Utilizing the expanding property, the farm became the ideal training ground for future farmers, the predominant occupation in America at the time.

The homegrown crops supplemented the produce needed to feed hundreds of children. When the Sisters asked for advice from their neighbors about how to start this endeavor, they learned that it would cost more to clear the land of stones than they would spend for vegetables in half a century. Not all of the stones rested on the surface, ready to be picked up. The Sisters devised a solution.

In the spring of 1887, many of the children—those still suffering from weak eyes and forbidden to attend school by the doctor who insisted that they remain in the open air while they recovered—started a great project. Each morning at nine o'clock, throughout the autumn and into the winter, fifty children led by one of the Sisters trudged up the hill behind the girl's dormitory. She instigated a competition to see which group could accumulate the biggest rock pile by lunchtime. With only two of the fifty-seven acres currently producing, the property seemed to be seeded with stones. "It became a great sport," one of the Sisters wrote. "After lunch, the boys began again in earnest. Two oxen, which delighted the children, carried off the heaps of rocks." The workmen constructed retaining walls and foundations with the quarried stones, which still exist today.

The following spring of 1888, Sister again led her winter-bound troops back outside, this time to plant corn and potatoes in the cleared fields. That autumn, the children harvested the fruits of their labor, plucking ears of corn from the tall green stalks. Once they harvested, they celebrated with excursions in twelve large horse-drawn farm sleighs provided by local business people. One Sister wrote, "With the merry jingle of the bells, and the still merrier songs of the classes, they sped their way some fourteen miles and back, with many regrets it could not be longer."

After four arduous years, Sister Ulrica's health began to fail. Sister Mary Ernestine Reilly assumed the role of Treasurer and General Manager of the Home in the first quarter of 1888—a post she held for nine years. Sister Ulrica died at St. Joseph's Home in New York City on September 12, 1888. The community deeply mourned her loss. Her enormous success of building St. Agatha Home in only four years live on, along with her many prior achievements. Many of the structures, practices, and programs that Sister Ulrica began lasted more than a century.

Sister Mary Ernestine faced equally monumental challenges and opportunities, as did her predecessor. The infamous blizzard of 1888 blasted the east coast from March 11 to March 14. In the days preceding the blizzard, unseasonably mild weather with temperatures of forty and fifty degrees gave way to torrential rains. By March 12, the rain became snow. Temperatures plunged. Winds howled and blasted through the little valley for a full day and a half without relief. The National Weather Service estimated forty inches of snow fell on New York City and described snowdrifts forty to fifty feet high.

Rockland County newspapers reported: "Winds exceeded forty-five miles per hour, visibility was curtailed to a quarter of a mile, and temperatures dropped below ten degrees Fahrenheit." The Great White Hurricane, as it was dubbed, paralyzed most of the east coast. Telephone and telegraph wires snapped, cutting off communication for days. The roads proved too treacherous for vehicle traffic, or even foot passage. Wind

The Home Farm

swept pedestrians over, forcing some to remain in shops for days. Residents trapped in their homes told reporters afterwards of having to burn their furniture to keep warm.

The boy's dormitory, like the rest of the County, was snowed in—up to the second story. For nearly a week, with no one able to enter or leave the front door, supplies passed through the second story window from a ladder. Even if the inhabitants could file out, they could not go anywhere. Imagine hundreds of housebound boys to keep under control amid the lure of snowball fights, sledding, and fort building just beyond the windows.

Schoolrooms inside the dormitory building allowed classes to continue as a diversion, minus some of the teachers. Each of the three floors had a Sister in charge and a teacher, so they improvised. The conditions were only slightly better on the girl's side.

Schoolbooks provided the primary distraction. *McGuffey's Readers,* originally published in 1836, had been reprinted in 1870. For seventy-five years most American school children learned to read from this series of books. Intricate pen-and-ink drawings accompanied each letter, vocabulary word, and lesson. After memorizing the alphabet and learning how to form simple words like ran, rat, and ram, there came basic punctuation and simple sentence formation. Paragraphs consisted of familiar stories set primarily on farms, in mills, and around the countryside.

While the blizzard howled outside, the youngest children read aloud *McGuffey's Eclectic Primer for Kindergarteners*. They learned to sound letters, print and write cursive, and gained six new vocabulary words per lesson. Stories described recreational activities like roller-skating, ice-skating, and sledding. Others included chores: fishing and hunting for food, chopping wood, and carrying water from the well. Girls wore dresses, usually with aprons or pinafores, and bonnets or straw hats atop long hair woven into ringlets. They tenderly clutched homemade dolls to their bosom, or transported them about in tiny carts drawn by a harnessed goat, or sometimes a dog.

The boys in the stories wore knickers, high button shoes, heavy cotton stockings, and straw hats. Some, in white sailor blouses tied with silky neckerchiefs, are content with waving flags or chasing mischievous dogs. Or they dig with small spades, spin wooden tops, toot homemade willow whistles, loft kites, pump swings, and sail toy boats. They play fifes and drums, reminiscent of the Revolutionary War.

Primly attired parents, always loving and caring, teach valuable lessons of morality. Mamas push babies on swings, or take children for picnics in the woods. Papas take time out of their busy workdays and hang up their silk top hats and canes to take their sons fishing. Families on outings discover birds' nests and dig in the sand at the seashore. All of this is contained in the Primer Reader that children must master before beginning first grade.

This house is on fire. Look! The roof is in a blaze. Run, boys, and ring the bell. Call some men to put out the fire. We may yet save the house if we work hard.

From book to book, stories become more complex with multiple themes and begin to include popular children's poems and tales about God.

Do you see that tall tree? Long ago it sprang up from a small nut. Do you know who made it do so? It was God, my child. God made the world and all things in it. He made the sun to light the day, and the moon to shine at night. God shows that he loves us by all that he has done for us. Should we not then love him?

The First Reader closes with the admonition:

Your parents are very kind to send you to school. If you are good, and if you try to learn, your teacher will love you, and you will please your parents. Be kind to all, and do not waste your time in school. When you go home, you may ask your parents to get you a Second Reader.

Most notably, perhaps, the stories depict the lives of families of the time. The harsher realities of life that befell the characters were of a more natural origin: an animal hunting for food kills the child's pet duck or sometimes lightning strikes their home: nature and death through natural causes. Imagine how these events must have seemed to the children of St. Agatha Home—children who typically had not been orphaned because their fathers set off on noble causes, but instead had been abandoned, neglected, and abused.

For these children whose innocence had been irretrievably lost, the McGuffey Readers must have proved a great escape for young imaginations during those wintry days—perhaps even offered them hope. Whether they ran out of coal to stoke the furnace in the basement, or wood for the fireplace, their plights would have been worthy of a *McGuffey Reader* with a third of their building buried in snow.

The Sisters led the children in frequent prayer to deliver them safely from their icy tomb. Food deliveries from St. Joseph's in New York halted with the trains because of the storm. Like much of Nanuet's homes and shops, St. Agatha simply ran out of supplies. A half-dozen male employees roped themselves together for a trek to the nearest inhabited farmhouse in the direction of Spring Valley. No horse could be persuaded through that depth of snow. The men carried back with them flour tied in bed sheets slung over their shoulders. For a week, the residents ate flapjacks in prodigious quantities. After this experience, Mother Ambrosia ordered an oven built on the grounds and a storehouse for flour, kept perpetually full. Thereafter, for years the morning air permeated with the warm smell of baking bread.

Along with her new responsibilities, Sister Mary Ernestine inherited St. Agatha's $25,000 debt to St. Joseph's Asylum for mortgage and operating expenses of the Home. But thankfully, in February of 1889, St. Agatha received its first money from the Finance Department of New York for the care of the children. With the money came additional help: Sister Ann Joseph O'Connor and Sister Rose Austin Galvin. The ratio improved; forty children to each Sister.

One day, a horse drew up, carrying a doctor unknown to St. Agatha. He sought spiritual comfort for an elderly couple in failing health. The wife, a Catholic, had no one in her neighborhood to offer comfort. Grateful for the opportunity to provide assistance, Sister Francina Flanagan responded to the doctor's entreaty and went to care for the couple who lived some distance away. In poor health herself, and against the admonition of her Superior, Sister Francina stubbornly insisted on being allowed to go to the aid of those in need. Accompanied by another Sister, they set off on an early morning in May as traces of spring poked through the melting snow.

Sister Francina found the couple and prepared them to receive the final Sacraments. The husband had not been baptized. Exhausted upon her return from the travel and the nursing, Sister Francina went straight to bed. She died a week later on May 15, 1891. Everyone associated with St. Agatha processioned behind Reverend Malloy to the new cemetery at the top of the hill, singing Psalms all the while.

"Her funeral was grand in its simplicity," wrote one of the mourning Sisters. She was "the favorite flower from our little circle." She came to St. Agatha six years earlier, shortly after Sister Ernestine, to restore her own good health, but stayed on and became one of the Home's most devout and tireless workers. "She had," her friend eulogized, "a most lovable character with an energy and willpower truly extraordinary for one in her delicate state of health. Her business capacity was great and her suggestions and advice beyond price, for improving the conditions at St. Agatha."

A procession reoccurred on each of her anniversaries, which began a practice by the older girls of visiting the cemetery every Sunday for prayers, weather permitting. Father Malloy, so fond of Sister Francina, said Mass on each anniversary of her death, and had a statue of the Lady of Pity placed by the good Sister's grave.

A month later, there came a happier occasion for solemnity. The Archbishop arrived to confer Confirmation on scores of children, which prompted a great celebration. His visit marked the beginning of a new religious celebration each first Friday afternoon: the Exposition of the most Blessed Sacrament, a practice that continued for over half a century. At four o'clock, everyone would congregate in the chapel, say prayers, and sing hymns followed by Benediction of the most Holy Sacrament.

Everything had to be done in large groups, with little opportunity for care and attention to the individual child. Though recognized, the benefits of reduced group size in childcare institutions seemed impractical. The goal of the "cottage plan," where groups of about thirty children lived as a family, would take another half-century to realize.

In 1891, they expanded capacity with a much-needed wing to St. Joseph's Dormitory, and a second wing the following year, along with dormers for added light and space. The improved building looked like a modern castle. Classrooms, clothes rooms, a lavatory on each floor, and other accommodations for the boys—all added to the sleeping quarters. A white split-rail fence appeared around the perimeter. Trees and hedges recently planted acted as buffers against the dusty dirt road.

St. Joesph's after addition

The year closed on a festive note. Father Malloy was ordained on December 21, 1891 amid much jubilation by his congregation. He had saved his money to buy an Angelus bell for the St. Agatha community to commemorate the occasion. On the day he returned from the ceremony, the bell heralded his progress throughout the ride from the train station to the illuminated Convent. Though delighted by the gift, the Sisters were not surprised since Father Malloy had spent even his spare time enriching St. Agatha Home.

Eleven

Raining Fish and Other Disasters

Many of the children came to St. Agatha as orphans or semi-orphans whose parents died while forging a new life in a new homeland. Other parents succumbed to consumption, cholera, and various diseases that plagued the overcrowded conditions in New York City. Alcoholics, addicts, gamblers, and other downtrodden gave birth to children who also ended up on the streets. Children left to fend for themselves took what they could not acquire honestly, and became as hardened as Dickens' young characters.

Two teenage girls set out to start life on their own. Katie, and Philomena Cooney—noted by the newspapers as runaways from St. Agatha Home—were arrested in New York on August 11, 1893 for robbing flats in Yorkville. They stole enough jewelry and clothing to value $3,000. The stolen goods turned up in the possession of an older woman believed to be an accomplice and the mother of eleven of her own children. Newspaper accounts report:

> Katie's mother died when she was only two. She and her baby brother Patrick were left in the care of their father who ignored them except when they brought home the booty that he'd sent them out to beg for. He worked on an ice delivery wagon. Two years earlier, caught begging they'd been sent to St. Agatha. Patrick remained, but Katie escaped on

July 18, 1892. She told a reporter, "I lowered myself down from a window using an improvised rope. Once in the yard, I scaled a brick and stone wall, then made my way to the train station, about a mile away. I hid in the bushes, and when a freight train came along, I hopped a ride to New York. For six months I escaped detection."

A different set of circumstances brought the Kelly children to St. Agatha on August 19, 1894. An agent of the Society for the Prevention of Cruelty to Children at 410 E. 72nd Street found them starving and took them to the Yorkville Police Court. Two went to the Catholic Protectory, and the other four to St. Agatha Home. According to a newspaper account:

> With their father in prison, their mother deserted them. They had been living for several days on morsels, which their neighbors who are very poor gave them. And the agent found them crying from hunger. The eldest tried to comfort the others by telling them that a fairy would come in a little while with a loaf of bread.

St. Agatha changed the lives of most of these children, many who thrived on their education and training as evidenced at the 1894 New York Catholic Educational Exhibit. Held at the Grand Central Palace of Industry, Archbishop Corrigan presided. Newspapers boasted that there were over one hundred tables of work exhibited, representing fifty-nin thousnd children from one hundred and two Catholic schools, including St. Agatha Home in Nanuet. Ages of contributors ranged from kindergarten to graduate level. The boys displayed drawing, painting, architectural renderings, and plasterwork. The girls presented handiwork in sewing, embroidery, tapestry and simpler plasterwork, musical composition, and transposition.

Publicity of a negative sort came on February 8, 1896 when the Nyack newspaper headlines screamed an all-too-familiar headline: "Fire!"

St. Agatha's Home, a large Catholic asylum for children under the charge of the Sisters of Charity at Nanuet, was damaged by fire today. The fire started in the store on the place, and spread to a barn, destroying both buildings. The flames then entered a cottage, termed St. Francis's Lodge, used as a quarantine, and soon that building was also laid in ashes. There were several hundred children in the home, but none was injured, as the fire did not reach the main building. The nuns assisted in carrying goods out of the burning buildings. The Loss was $10,000.

One step forward and two steps back, it would seem.

Many girls stayed connected to St. Agatha long after they became domestic help for "the best families" in New York City. They frequently sent the Sisters their savings to bank for them, until needed. The Sisters visited them at their new homes as often as possible. As the alumnus grew, an annual picnic at St. Agatha seemed the only practical solution to visiting each of them in their new homes. The Sisters began planning the first St. Agatha reunion in 1896. The following summer, more than seventy-five alumni, accompanied by fifty friends, visited their former home. One of the Sisters described the day this way:

> We devised a little plan in 1896, to have a reunion of them in their old home where they could meet together at least one day in the year. A little lawn party was gotten up and surely it was joy, more even than we anticipated, to see them again as we would wish them to be, good, respectable, and giving satisfaction to all concerned. Afterwards, each young adult enjoyed a personal counseling session with Sister Mary Bertrand. Nell Nelson, a reporter for The World newspaper, made a tour of all the buildings. She wrote a complimentary article about St. Agatha's in her paper. Through her effort, she secured several new friends for the Home.

While St. Agatha grew, the Sisters remained in the Little Flower House, steadily becoming cramped. Also, the chapel in the refectory building needed expansion—currently large enough for only half the congregation of four hundred.

From 1895 to 1905, payments from New York City to private institutions made the expansion at the Home possible. Expecting funding to continue, St. Agatha expanded further. In 1899, the design began of a large building to include a chapel on the second floor, spacious enough for the entire population to celebrate together. Below the chapel they'd build an expanded refectory where everyone could dine under one roof.

Sister Ernestine secured a loan and broke ground for the new structure on September 7, 1898—her thirteenth anniversary at St. Agatha.

New chapel, 1899

She took the first shovel of earth, and then the boys took turns digging the trench that became the foundation. Sister Ernestine transferred away in November before seeing her plan completed.

The following summer, on August 5, 1899, the Feast of Our Lady of Snows was celebrated with Mass in the new refectory. On November 1, 1899, they held the first celebration at the beautiful new altar, donated in memory of his parents by former chaplain Reverend David J. Leahy.

The new building of red sandstone brick still stands more than a century later, as do the Little Flower House and many of the original buildings.

Massive oak doors opened to a large reception hall with spacious parlors on either side. Staircases from the central hall funneled worshipers to the chapel above and into a long hall to the new refectory, separated for boys, girls, and Sisters.

A corridor connected the new building to the refectory, girls' dorm, and school. Between the buildings, walking paths quickly etched themselves into the lawn bordered by shade trees and flowerbeds. Between the new building and the Little Flower House, a grotto appeared with a curve of hedges to shelter an alabaster statue of the Blessed Mother atop a pedestal. Three shepherd children and two lambs knelt at her feet.

Life for the educated Catholic child revolved around the church, prayers, stories of Jesus, Mary and the saints, angels and devils, good and evil, morality and sin, prayer and penance. It infiltrated every hour of the Catholic child's life. Convinced God saw their deeds at all times—good and bad, wherever they were—they would one day be judged accordingly. Reward meant eternity in the glories of heaven; punishment, the perpetual fires of hell. It made life simple; a formula

Statues beside Little Flower House

by which to live and test their actions. A Catholic child's life—family, friends, and school—blended inextricably with the teachings of God and the church.

Religious events formed the core of their lives: feasts and holidays, Baptism, First Holy Communion, Confirmation, marriage, even death. Christmas celebrated Christ's birth, not Santa and gift-giving. Sunday was a day to worship God the Father—a family day of rest and relaxation, and not just for Catholics. A story in the newspaper of the time told of a man being fined $5 for taking a photograph on Sunday. At Easter Mass, Catholics honored Jesus' rising from the dead and His sacrifices. The Easter bunny and new outfits played minor parts.

At long last, on St. Patrick's Day in 1900, the congregation had their first dinner in the new refectory with the "steam" installed for heat. The kitchen of the old refectory proved impractically far away to shuttle everything back and forth to the new dining room. With construction budgets depleted, the laundry building behind the new refectory had to be refitted and annexed as a kitchen.

Workmen constructed a new laundry by digging a cellar under the girls' dormitory, enclosing the porch as an ironing room, and adding steam drying underneath. Once again, sewerage became an acute problem. The maintenance manager, Mr. Schiekel, received bids of up to $3,000 to rectify the problem: an impossible sum after all the construction.

Sanitation problems in the 1900's were obviously not unique to St. Agatha. Frequent health epidemics, largely attributed to inadequate sanitation, continued to claim the lives of one in four children in New York City. Around the turn of the century, daily cleaning became an obsession in homes that could afford at least one resident servant. In exchange for room and board, they usually worked twelve to fifteen hours a day, seven days a week.

Few homes boasted electricity at the time. Vacuum cleaners and other appliances unavailable to the average person required work be done manually, on hands and knees. In some homes, they dismantled the beds regularly so each part could be scrubbed for bacterium. It took two days each week to do the laundry and ironing for an average working class family. So, meeting the needs of nearly six hundred people must have been daunting. Naturally, it generated a critical demand for adequate water supply and proper drainage.

Before her departure, Sister Ernestine noticed a newspaper article about a Civil War veteran, Colonel George Edwin Waring, Jr. He became a highly respected sanitation-engineering expert who designed sewerage systems throughout America. Sister called on him and explained the needs and frustrations that St. Agatha perpetually experienced. After close consideration, the Colonel designed a filterbed system, which he directed to be constructed in the cultivated field behind the girls' dormitory.

Three feet of sand was poured over gravel in a pit. Pipes dispensed the liquid, and wastewater spilled into the sand beds for filtering, then was released. Rejected impurities remained in a process tank, while clean water was drawn through, and conveyed to the main collection system.

For a mere $235, Colonel Waring rectified the problem, and it functioned satisfactorily for decades.

The Colonel, subsequently appointed New York City's Street Cleaning Commissioner in 1903, rid the city of the waist-high refuse that bred diseases. In two years, every household knew the Colonel and his "White Wing" platoon, as he called his sanitation soldiers. They had made even the worst of the city's streets not only habitable, but also pristine.

As with most institutions, no buildings stood empty while they sought inhabitants. Building a shelter for needy children was like throwing a sponge into the ocean. So great was the need—and so rapidly did children arrive from various overcrowded facilities in the City—that an anxious request came from the Dominican Convent of Our Lady of the Rosary on September 11, 1899. They needed an accurate count of just how many boys had been sent to St. Agatha from them so that their records could follow. They had lost track! The unremitting demand necessitated additional sleeping quarters for boys.

Not long after completion of the Main building, a fraternal twin appeared as a boy's dormitory about thirty yards east of the first. The builders dug deep so that the new four-story brick building appeared level with the Main building. The façade of the newer lacked the porches and columns, but was meant to complement the first.

Sister Mary Albert Dwyer took over as Administrator from Sister Ernestine and profited from her predecessor's many ingenuities. Born in Ireland, she immigrated to America in 1879. By the time she was age forty-five, she'd spent twenty-four years of her religious career at St. Joseph's Asylum, then St. Paul's Industrial School—both in Brooklyn—before coming to Nanuet. For the next twenty-three years, from 1897 to 1920, Sister Mary Albert acted as Superior of St. Agatha and utilized all that she had learned in the period of rapid growth and social change that marked the early part of the new century.

Though she had no training in psychology or social work, she instinctively set as her primary goal the creation of a more family-like

Administration building, 1900

atmosphere at the Home. She wanted to increase the emphasis on the individual child rather than the group, as Mother Seton had. The new boys' dormitory used partitions and smaller rooms to enable the children to spread out and move towards more of the idealistic "cottage style" within a larger structure.

The US Federal Census, recorded June 15, 1900, enumerated four hundred fifty-six children, thirty-six Sisters, thirty-one resident employees, and the Chaplain Reverend Thomas Donaphy in residence at St. Agatha. The children, ages two to fifteen, came mostly from New York City with parents' origins listed as unknown. Whether or not these children were abandoned is unknown because of unidentified origins and poor recordkeeping. In subsequent censuses, their origins are noted. They did not include employees from neighboring towns who came in daily to work, already noted in the census for their own homes. Employees hailed primarily from England and Ireland, but some called Germany, Italy, Hungary, and Russia home.

Besides the physical expansion of the facility, food, clothing, shelter, education, and spiritual needs, Sister Mary Albert concerned herself with the emotional growth of her charges. She began a program to study the individual child and his or her particular family situation with the objective of reuniting a healthy family as quickly as possible, thereby shortening their institutional stay. This had the added benefit of making space for the newly destitute children, without having to build still more institutions.

It is difficult to comprehend the troubles faced by these youngsters separated from home and family. How lonely, baffled, and angry they must have been when they came to St. Agatha Home. Then, further isolated from their siblings, thrust into a group of fifty or one hundred children, herded about in large groups, given a number for identity, or referred to by only their last name. Teachers, Prefects, and Sisters struggled to meet the needs of up to one hundred children in their care with little assistance—twenty-four hours every day, seven days a week.

Sister Albert wondered how there could be any opportunity for love and affection under these circumstances. She began to arrange conferences with the parents of the children in an attempt to reunite the family: the most appropriate people to meet the needs of their own children.

The world was an unsettled place. In Europe, tens of thousands of people, oppressed by their governments, starved and lived as peasants. They fled to the United States for the freedom and opportunity they had read of in letters from those who migrated before them, sometimes for their very survival.

Immigrants continued to pour in through Ellis Island between 1900 and 1914, thirteen million of them from Ireland, Austria, Germany, Hungary, Russia, and Italy. Most worked twelve to sixteen hours a day for two dollars a week, even children as young as four. The population in America had grown to seventy-six million. The number of Irish in America doubled Dublin's population and fed the population of Homes that sprang up all across the country.

One such family in need of help was the Halls. It is unknown whether Laurence and Annie married in Ireland or the United States; they came from towns ten miles apart. They had four children: Anna, born in 1893; William, 1895; James Harry, 1896; and Clement, in 1898. The youngest died at age seven from tuberculosis (TB), which invaded both hips. During their nine years together, the family lived in Manhattan. Then, on

February 4, 1901, Annie died from pulmonary tuberculosis at the tender age of thirty-five. The family was split up; William and Harry went to live at St. Agatha, and Anna went to live with her aunt Mary Fitzpatrick, her mother's sister. A notation on the children's record stated that the father was "worthless and never visited the children." He died May 5, 1945 of chronic myocarditis, never having reunited the family.

In 1907, twelve-year-old William was sent to the Catholic Protectory in Westchester (now the Bronx), probably for training. Harry joined him several years later. William was educated by the Christian Brothers and later taught at the school. He went to work at Classen Point Military Academy, and Harry went to live with a gentleman on a Canadian farm, when he was seventeen years old, according to his records. A year later, he left, saying he was heading to the Canadian Northwest. He never had any more contact with his family. Anna married Ed Finn and had four daughters.

On September 3, 1901, St. Agatha further expanded when it bought from neighbors Edward and Ernestine Schubert, "a parcel of land, for $6,000," according to the deed. The nearly forty-one acres had a house and outbuildings, and extended south towards Pearl River, west to Duryea Lane; north along Pascack Road; and east behind the Ross acquisition, further towards Nanuet.

The two-story home on Convent Road had community rooms on the main floor and bedrooms above, which was immediately employed for lay teachers and office staff. A porch stretched across the front of the house and a white wooden arbor arched over the gated picket fence. Its jewel was in the back, though. A portion of the Pascack brook, fed by the Hackensack River, ran across the property, and then wandered off into the woods. A low fieldstone wall, nearly twelve inches thick, was built on both sides of Convent Road to link and define the new frontage of St. Agatha Home for Children.

For the next few decades, the land along Duryea Lane yielded several bushels of corn each year, from the top of the hill to midway down. Seasonal crops like tomatoes, carrots, and cabbage grew in the lower half. The huge field behind the girls' dorm yielded tall, waving rye grass to feed the livestock. The northern addition provided pastures for cows and horses, which meandered among apple, plum, and pear orchards.

That year, President McKinley was assassinated, and Theodore Roosevelt became President. Times became more prosperous. The Pan American Expo opened in New York City, and people truly appreciated that they lived in a new, progressive century—one of technology providing leisure time, and activities to fill it. Much of this technology resulted from the Civil War, when veterans turned engineers.

Henry Ford's creation of the assembly line made automobiles more and more popular. First the wealthy, then businessmen and farmers replaced horse-drawn carriages, carts, and wagons with autos. Eventually, emergency services and even average professional people replaced *their* horses, as time wasted traveling became increasingly more treasured. Newly developed bicycles allowed mobility to those who could not afford a car or keep a horse. The automobile demanded increased assembly line production of steel and textile production. Railroads, electric lights, telephones, even airplanes grew in popularity, as did the need for education.

Penny books and novels entertained. Children started reading *The Great Train Robbery,* fictionalized in 1903, and the historic building of the Panama Canal began in 1904. Newsreels appeared in theatres depicting life around the world and America as a great power. Circumstances did not vastly improved for everyone, though. In 1902, the average life expectancy was only forty-seven; the average wage, twenty-two cents an hour; and the average US worker earned between $200 and $400 per year. Professional salaries included a competent accountant at $2000 and a dentist $2,500 a year. Eggs cost fourteen cents a dozen. Nearly all births took place at home at a time when the five leading causes of death included influenza, tuberculosis, diarrhea, heart disease, and stroke.

The Croddick family did not share in the new prosperity. James migrated to the US about 1890, settled in the upper east side of Manhattan, and labored in the coal yards. Anna immigrated in 1888. They married and had six children. They lived in conditions so poor that only two of their five sons, Eugene and James, survived past infancy. One baby died from TB. The family moved frequently. Both parents drank heavily, according to neighbors, and bickered constantly. The American Society for the Prevention of Cruelty to Children (ASPCC) responded to complaints. James's Sister—discharged on May 15th from Presbyterian Hospital on Blackwell's Island after four months—believed him to be cured, though still weak from whatever ailed him. He attributed his bronchial illness to his coal mining work.

After he returned home, the ASPCC checked on the family for three or four days, and reported they "found the entire family to be at home. Anna seemed sober, and the children properly clothed." The house appeared in much better shape. James stayed home to watch the children, while Anna worked three days a week for $1.25 per day, though she was seven months pregnant. She "drank a little beer for her strength." On June 21, 1902, a couple of weeks before the baby came, James and Eugene—ages six and four—were sent to St. Agatha. Shortly before their fifth child in arrived in July 1902, James's sister died of consumption, age thirty-five.

Apparently the boys returned to her after her husband died. Subsequently, neighbors reported to the ASPCC that the family was in dire condition. They complained, "They're desperate; the mother drinks. While she works, she leaves the children home alone, even the newborn, in squalid conditions." The family became homeless. Baby Alice went to the New York Foundling Hospital and the boys returned to St. Agatha. Five years later, Saturday, January 26, 1907, as the boys prepared their clothes for Sunday, the first alarm sounded in the new dormitory next to the Administration building. Many of the children evacuated, still clutching their Sunday clothes. The building was entirely destroyed. Many of the boys had to be hastily transferred to other Homes, including St. Agnes in Sparkill and St. Dominic in Blauvelt.

The Croddick boys moved to St. Agnes Home, but returned to their mother in 1911. Eugene and James spent most of their childhood in and out of institutions, together and apart. As adults, they went their separate ways. What became of baby Alice is unknown, though likely adopted from the Foundling or sent out on one of the orphan trains.

Some of those years were plagued by natural disasters. Drought, blizzards, and tornadoes could not be planned for, especially their magnitudes. In October of 1903, storms and floods hit the eastern seaboard with such ferocity, it was deemed the worst disaster in Rockland County's history. Trains from Rockland County to New York City halted, and a milk famine resulted in the city. St. Agatha had not yet become totally self-sufficient, but fulfilled most of its needs from neighboring farms within easy reach. With the land at such a low point, the area separating the new little boys' dorm from the Chapel and Refectory along Convent Road flooded.

On January 5, 1904, the temperature in Nanuet dropped to thirty degrees below zero. With the coming of summer, temperatures grew so warm and humid, tornadoes followed. One cut a hundred-and-fifty-foot swath through neighboring Nyack, and the newspapers reported thousands of dead sea creatures swept up in the spout, including fish and eels. Their carcasses rained down all over town, and had to be removed by the truckload.

Regardless of weather emergencies or social crises, the Home had to care for the children at the highest standards set by the State Board of Charities and St. Agatha's Board of Directors. Not long after the latest weather disaster, on September 30, 1904, an inspection of the facilities revealed several deficiencies. In the follow-up inspection, on February 27 and 28, 1905, the improvements were noted.

- In the new corridor connecting the girls' buildings, a recreation hall was made; 20 feet wide by 100 feet long, and provided the children an indoor area to play.

- Eighty-six new horse-hair mattresses were supplied, and plans to retire all of the straw filled ones was under way.
- The girls' buildings were enlarged to achieve better lighting and ventilation in the workroom of the seamstress, the general storage area, and the clothes rooms.
- Modern toilets were added in the girls department, which could now be accessed via the dormitory above the laundry, where the little girls slept, and in the bigger girls' building.
- With the additions made to the big girl's building, adjacent to their school, a central water tower was constructed, 90 feet high, with a storage tank at the top. The elevation provided better water pressure.
- In St. Joseph's building, where the little boys' resided, modern lavatory facilities were installed, with high quality faucets and individual nozzle sprays. (This implies the older boys were in the new building, next to the Main building).
- An invalid noted as "in need of hospitalization" at the last inspection, was removed to a hospital.
- Finally, as regards Supervision, the governing body consisting of seven trustees was described. They included Reverend Mother Mary Melita, President; Sister Mary Dolores, Secretary; Sister Mary Albert, Treasurer; and Dr. Bogart of Spring Valley, attending physician. George Hornung of Jersey City was the attending dentist. Quarterly meetings were held in May at the Asylum; in August, at the New York Foundling Asylum; and in November, at Mt. St. Vincent Hospital. An annual meeting was held in May to elect officers by ballot. Supervision and Administration were merged for practical purposes.

The population at the Home gradually decreased between 1905 and 1915, when the Widow's Pension Act provided money and more children could be cared for at home. Some of the children who came to St.

Agatha came from local families who experienced many of the same hardships as their city contemporaries.

When women lost their husbands at the early part of the century, they fared no better than widows in previous centuries. Few resources existed to assist them in caring for their children. Even if they *could* find a job, finding a family member or another provider became the only solution for them. Second husbands did not always get along with, or want to raise, other men's children, so St. Agatha provided a refuge.

Many times people needed short-term help to overcome a difficult period in their family, and therefore turned to St. Agatha. That was the objective: to provide a temporary stopgap for families rather than retain children for their entire childhood.

The fire that destroyed the new boys dorm took a huge toll on St. Agatha. Afterwards, the vacant front lawn became the site for feast-day processions, graduation exercises, visitors, and performance drills. Little paths snaked to the southeast corner of the lawn, where a statue of the Blessed Mother rested on a pedestal. About ten years later, two open-sided pagodas extended four hundred square feet of shade to the children and their guests. A statue of the Sacred Heart of Jesus watched over them from a pedestal in the center of one pagoda.

A successful working model of the German "cottage plan" had been in place in New York City since 1870 at the protestant home, Sheltering Arms. Founded in 1864 for Civil War orphans, they built four smaller, self-contained cottage units to house one hundred children instead of erecting one vast mausoleum for its expanding needs. Each building contained a dining room, dormitory, playroom, and washroom, and each was run as a separate family unit.

Other Children's Homes across America—those unburdened by the constraints of large asylums—emulated Sheltering Arms. St. Agatha had no money for new construction for nearly fifty years. So, it refashioned the existing buildings and newly acquired property into a modified cottage style.

Sister Albert, although terribly disappointed after the fire, persevered. According to the board Minutes of the Sisters of Charity dated March 15, 1907, there was some insurance money, but not enough to rebuild. Besides, the goal of moving away from congregate care to a cottage plan did not warrant building another large edifice to house hundreds of children. The congregation was profoundly grateful that no one was hurt and that the chapel in the Main building was spared. They publicly recognized everyone who came to their aid.

These acknowledgements became a permanent part of the archival records of the Sisters of Charity. A resolution promised, "Brave friends would be forever in the gratitude and daily prayers for the future welfare of these kind benefactors, temporal and eternal." Public commendations went to all of the companies and their firefighters for their heroic efforts, especially the Dexter Folding Company and each of its employees. The company had actually closed the plant and sent its workers to join other volunteers in the aid of St. Agatha and its children.

Fear of fire was a perpetual reality to everyone at a time when candles, coal stoves, lanterns, and gas lamps constantly glowed. It was particularly terrifying in large congregations of children. As a precaution, they added fire escapes to the exteriors of every building, and ornate metal panels to internal walls and ceilings to help retard fire if it did occur.

With the physical safety issues resolved, attention turned back to other improvements to quality of life, including the introduction of physical training of the children—partially to relieve the boredom they endured much of the time. Mainly, they stood around when not working or studying. This was implemented to improve their self-images, as well. Prior to these years, people did not have a lot of recreational time to worry about using it constructively.

In the childcare community, military-style drills with uniforms and precise marching provided good vehicles for improving children's self-esteem. Volunteer participants entered competitions and performances in public gatherings like Independence Day parades.

The program proved successful and demonstrated another success the Home had with children: good public relations for fund raising.

On Saturday, September 25, 1909, the St. Agatha Cadets marched in uniform at the Hudson-Fulton Celebration hosted by the Hudson River Maritime Museum in Kingston NY. That weekend, the State commemorated two events: the 300th anniversary of the discovery of the Hudson River by Henry Hudson in 1609 and the 100th anniversary of the first successful application of steam, for navigation on the River, by Robert Fulton in 1807.

In full parade uniforms, the children marched while playing their trumpets and drums, and carrying the US Flag. For other festivities, St. Agatha's drum and bugle corps wore kilts, hats, knee socks, and chest sashes—all commonly associated with the Irish bands in St. Patrick's Day Parades or when esteemed visitors came to call.

The year 1909 marked the beginning of the end for large, institutional care in America. President Theodore Roosevelt called the First White House Conference on the "Care of Dependent Children," with over two hundred leaders in philanthropy, social welfare, and childcare. He included Andrew Carnegie, Jane Addams, Jacob Riis, Charles Loring Brace, and Booker T. Washington.

As Police Commissioner of New York City, Roosevelt saw the horror of thousands of children eking out an existence however they could, regardless of how perverse, and living under anything that allowed them to crawl beneath. He worked closely with Jacob Riis who uncovered and publicized all the sordid details in photographs and newspaper exposés, thus affecting real change in the removal of tenement hovels.

Roosevelt joined the Progressive Movement. It gave women alternatives when they had nowhere to turn, because their husbands died, abandoned them, or received injuries on the job. When he got to the White House, Roosevelt kept his vow to continue making drastic changes to help dependent women and children.

"Home life is the highest and finest product of civilization. Children should not be deprived of it except for urgent and compelling reasons," he thundered. He supported foster homes and the cottage plan, but, like Reverend Brace, was thoroughly against institutions, where he believed children could be dropped off, and forgotten. He devised a 14-point plan with the aim of keeping children in their own homes as a first priority, foster homes as a second, and cottage homes, as a last resort.

Existing facilities that wanted to continue to receive funding had to begin a process of converting, in competition with new Homes being built in this style. Like many plans, it took years to implement, years in which the lives of the residents, slowly improved, as St. Agatha continued to grow in that direction.

By 1910, the Federal Census for St. Agatha listed Sister Josephine M. O'Dwyer as Superintendent with sixty-three adults caring for six hundred sixteen children. The many farmhands undoubtedly reflect the efforts of getting the farm up and running. The adults' ages ranged from seventeen to seventy-nine.

Finally, approval for funding came, long sought from New York City to care for its wards. An agreement—dated January 23, 1912, signed by Michael J. Drummond, Commissioner of Public Charities of New York City, and Sister Mary Albert, Treasurer of St. Agatha—set down the following:

1. That St. Agatha agrees to receive all children or patients committed to it by the Department of Public Charities of the City of NY.

2. To furnish all inmates committed and received, care, support, maintenance, education or treatment to the standard approved by the Board of Charities. By way of proof, a monthly certificate of compliance from the Board will be presented with the monthly bill.

3. To keep a register and record of all such inmates, details of commitments and discharges, and by whom; these records are to be available for inspection at all times by the Department of Public Charities and

accountants if the Department of Finance, so there is no question about the bills presented.

4. To receive from the City payment according to the schedule of rates attached for all children cared for.

This agreement is provisional and terminable at will by either party, when submitted in writing. The existing five hundred twenty-six children are certified as meeting these contract requirements, effective January 1, 1912.

Twelve

The Preventorium

Nearly one hundred children arrived between January and the day of census taken in April. By April of 1913, another major innovation began at St. Agatha. Whether in an attempt to distinguish itself, or the motherhouse funded it, or because of the outstanding need for such a facility, St. Agatha built the Bethlehem Preventorium behind St. Joseph dormitory. The objective: to *prevent* contagion of tuberculosis by children from their afflicted parents. Rather than attempting to treat the disease in a sanatorium *after* contagion, children of afflicted parents could be separated from them as soon as a parent's symptoms appeared.

The structure, built in the shape of an "X," had at each point upstairs and down an entrance from the outside leading into dormitories. These converged on a central room on each floor, each with kitchen, dining, and communal rooms. This ingenious design maximized the number of windows, admitting light and air—over one hundred in all. The building, over three thousand square feet on two floors, had twelve entrances in all. Each point of the "X" had a wide metal staircase on the outside leading to the second floor. The building, constructed of white stucco over wood with a fieldstone base, had no chimney. The basement contained a boiler to heat the facility, a coalbunker, and the usual storage. The attic remained empty. A tall cross graced the corrugated tin roof.

The Preventorium sat well back from Convent Road

The Preventorium sat well back from Convent Road. About thirty yards from the front entrance stood a structure the size of a gazebo, with four gothic arches bound at their corners, sheltering a statue of the Sacred Heart on a pedestal. Surrounding the Preventorium, the Home's farm began taking shape: apple orchards on the west side; the woods behind; and cow pastures, corrals, and barns to the east.

TB is transmitted from an infected person to a susceptible person, via coughing or sneezing. Living in the same household with a person increases the chances of contracting it, so exposure in congregate living environments—such as orphanages, prisons, even hospitals—actually enhances the risk. Environmental factors—such as poor ventilation, unpasteurized milk, overall poor nutrition and health—greatly increase the chance of contagion.

Researchers discovered that fresh air, good nutrition, and isolation from those infected vastly improved survival rates. For those who could somehow get out of unhealthful circumstances, and into a sanatorium with improved conditions, there existed some hope of recovery. In November of 1944, antibiotics first administered to soldiers critically ill with TB showed positive results. Rapid advances followed, and the disease arrested, in those cases.

When they no longer posed a risk of infection or further detriment to the children, the family reunited. If a parent died, and no family member could take them in, the children went to a Home like St. Agatha.

This progressive facility was the first of its kind within the Catholic services in the State of New York. It proved so popular that it expanded to accommodate one hundred sixty children, some weak, delicate, or anemic. The children typically remained at the Preventorium for three to six months and were "given abundant space, fresh clean air, sunshine, good nourishing food, and kind, motherly care away from the pollution of the city," according to one report.

The inmates, considered delicate, did not commingle with the other residents of St. Agatha who may already carry the seeds of disease. They had separate programs for schooling and recreation to meet their different needs and capabilities. Mainly, they rested. Contributions for the Preventorium went to the Bethlehem Preventorium in Nanuet, or to St. Joseph's Home at 209 W. 15th Street, New York City. The children of each facility knew little about those in the other.

Meanwhile, between 1915 and 1935, World War I and the Depression dramatically increased the population of St. Agatha. On December 30, 1915, Mother Josepha, Treasurer of St. Vincent's Hospital of New York City, "transferred ownership to St. Agatha Home, of a parcel of 66 1/2 acres, for the sum of $9,000," according to the deed. The land, acquired from the former estate of Mr. Theo Babcock, was located on top of the hill, east of the boys' dormitory.

The acquisition extended the southern side of Convent Road. It took a while to decide how to best use the new property. In 1917, as World War I gathered momentum, and after some renovations, the Preventorium moved up to the Babcock property. The land held a three-story family home, a barn, a pair of two-story residences for the estate manger and staff, and assorted outbuildings. Widow Katherine Babcock (then age seventy-three)—along with her two daughters, Margaret and Anna—remained employees of St. Agatha. They lived on the grounds for several years; the elder as a seamstress, and her daughters as teachers. Later, she went to live with a married daughter in Nanuet.

The three-story building reserved the first floor for a dining room, with a boys' dormitory above, and a girls' dormitory above that. As many as one hundred sixty children lived here at the peak of the program. As the demand for the Preventorium increased with the epidemics, they incorporated other nearby buildings.

A new single-story annex provided classrooms and a separate dorm for boys. Most of the wall space consisted of windows that louvered out and afforded improved light and fresh air. Along the south-facing wall, windowboxes of flowers brightened the view in spring. The girls occupied both upper floors, with the attic for clothes storage.

A covered glass-enclosed walkway, nearly four feet wide with exits to the yards midway along either side, formed an umbilicus connecting the two buildings. This way, the children did not have to be exposed to the elements when passing between them. In fine weather, children played games on the cool floor of the breezeway, sheltered from too much sun.

The barn became bath and toilet facilities, with separate entrances for boys and girls. Hot water came from a coal-fueled boiler. The other two-story, situated closer to Convent Road, served as dormitories for Sisters and overflow of children. It even hosted some classes such as "the art of letter writing" over the years.

To raise funds for expanding the new Preventorium, a solicitation addressed to "Women of Charity" in New York City went out from the Alumni of the Academy of Mount St. Vincent where the Sisters of Charity had their motherhouse. Many of the social functions of the city revolved around these philanthropic fundraising gatherings, and the Preventorium greatly benefited from these appeals:

Consider the joy of saving one such little life. The children need warm cloaks and hoods, coats and caps, wraps of every kind, for they must spend much time in the open air. Underwear, stockings, shoes, over-shoes, outdoors playthings, small rockers, small steamer chairs. Send returns to Mrs. Henry Cassidy, President of the Alumnae, 503 west 160th Street, or Miss May Ferrall, Treasurer, 109 east 37th Street, New York City.

Children went outside as often as possible, even for classes. (Some sanatoriums placed beds on porches, and residents slept outdoors in winter.) A large canopy shaded the children in sunny weather. When they could not go out because of rain, snow, or excessive temperatures, they benefited from intermittent sunlight by being placed near the many windows.

A few deaths occurred over the years. As with the children in the rest of the Home, they buried the children in St. Agatha's Cemetery alongside

the Sisters, a Priest, and former employees. The year 1937 claimed a small group of children; TB was particularly rampant.

In May of 1917, while preparations for changes in school and dorm facilities went on, something else new came to St. Agatha to occupy the children. Clubs sprang up for different grade levels. Their

St Agatha Cemetery

goal was to teach self-control, better behavior, and skills. Children learned to make sewing repairs, clean up the grounds, and get along better with each other. This scheme may have at least part of its origin in the loss of manpower and materials, as America became actively involved in World War I. The clubs, grouped by gender and age, met one hour each week. The theory persisted that all men should understand something about farming. And since the extensive property connected with St. Agatha afforded an excellent opportunity, this encouraged the boys' knowledge of agriculture. Groups of twelve each had a garden twelve by thirty feet to tend, full of ordinary useful vegetables.

As soon as the children vacated the old Preventorium in 1917, it became the boys' school, enabling expansion in St. Joseph's dorm to the evacuated classrooms. Then, a serious threat to the future of St. Agatha arose in November of 1918. With World War I ending, the US Government wanted to lease the Roman Catholic Orphan Asylum on Kingsbridge Road in the Bronx for a military hospital, run by the Sisters of Charity. To do so, they proposed to relocate its children and staff to St. Agatha, potentially displacing the current residents, as well as some children from other institutions. A total of one hundred fifty nuns and one thousand five hundred children would need to be relocated, with the exception of the children in the Preventorium.

Mother Josepha from the Mount and Sister Teresa Alacoque of St. Agatha met with board members of the Orphan Asylum and a representative of the Commissioner of Public Charities. They successfully argued the impossibility of this task. The US Government subsequently withdrew the request and—after four weeks on heightened alert—life settled back down to as normal as possible during war time.

By contrast, after the "war to end all wars," the euphoric decade of the 20's became the "dream period," so dubbed by historians. Everyone rushed to have as much fun as possible, pursuing riches, fame, and decadence. Scantily clad flappers scandalized Victorians as much as the suffragettes had while fighting for women's rights. People picked back up where they'd left off at the turn of the century when things had looked rosy, before the war. Americans believed that the world would now be peaceful and there would never be another World War.

It proved a schizophrenic decade in the history of the United States. For many, "Happy Days Were Here Again" and ticker tape parades welcomed home the conquering heroes. More people began to acquire cars. Cheers for Babe Ruth hung on everyone's lips. Charles Lindbergh unified America's pride with his transatlantic crossing. High fashion swept away the dowdy Victorian styles.

Novelty became the fashion. People began barnstorming dancehalls across America, dancing the Charleston, playing golf, and enjoying all sorts of frivolity. Necklines dropped as hemlines rose. Speakeasies and motion pictures became all the rage. Everyone sat glued to their radios at night—even the most modest households had them—and listened to *The Shadow* and *Amos 'n' Andy.*

Once electricity became commonplace, it rapidly changed everyone's lives. Appliances like washing machines, toasters, irons, and vacuum cleaners, promised an end to drudgery. Overnight, America became a consumer society, and that defined its leisure time. In fact, most households did not have these timesavers, but everyone yearned for them and felt deprived without them. Before, people just lived simply without feeling too poor to afford luxuries like a phone. With a newfound hope, Americans wanted extravagance and the leisure time to enjoy it. Low down payments and installment plans assisted most people in getting into debt.

At the same time, the Temperance Movement resulted in Prohibition. Gangsters became celebrities. Prejudice rose against blacks, immigrants, labor unions, and women, even before the Great Depression hit. Harlem saw a great renaissance with music and nightclubs, but only whites could enjoy them. Blacks could not even be seated; they could only wait on tables and entertain. Whites owned the shops along Amsterdam Avenue in Harlem and would employ no blacks, though their clientele was almost entirely black. People toiled away in factories, working ten-hour days, six days a week.

Most of the changes took place in the big cities like NY, Boston, and Chicago. Around the rest of the country, people still played dominoes by oil lanterns, warmed themselves by pot-bellied stoves, and danced to "Skip To my Lou" at Saturday night socials. On the radio, Will Rogers made famous his lovable character, Old Shoe. People sat riveted to the national past time: baseball.

At St. Agatha, 1920 marked the opening of a first-year high-school class so that children completing eighth grade did not have to leave St. Agatha during the post war years. The coed classes taught Algebra, French, English, stenography, and typing. It is surprising that anything innovative got accomplished, given the relentless demands of running the ever expanding Home.

According to the 1920 census compiled on January 2, thirty-five Sisters were in residence—besides Chaplain Reverend Mathias Cuevas and Sister Mary Albert Dwyer serving her final year as Superintendent at age sixty-eight. Their average age, forty-eight; the oldest, Sister Edith, seventy-five; and the youngest, Sister Regina, twenty-five. All but two came from Ireland or New York City. The Sisters had the help of thirty-eight resident lay employees to care for six hundred eighty-four children.

Other employees, not on the census, lived in the surrounding area and worked in similar positions. With the shortage of help during the war, older children became monitors and acted as deputies for the adults in charge. Later, after some kids graduated from elementary school, they stayed on as Prefects to work on the farm, or in domestic work.

In those days, child psychology played a little part in childcare. Particularly when children overseeing children used fear like a Swiss Army knife. But in place of tools and blades, they used yelling, belittling, physical force, threats, intimidation, a rap on the skull, a cane to the back of the legs, and humiliation. These methods kept large numbers of children under control in schools and in many households at the time. In conjunction with what the children suffered before they arrived, the results of this treatment made for some indelible emotional scars for many of the children.

Amid fluctuating staff shortages and emergencies, the goal of the cottage plan proved elusive for decades, but it never went off the radar screen completely. When Sister Mary Albert Dwyer left, Sister Xavier Maria Hurley became Superior, Superintendent, and Sister Servant responsible for the Home and the convent of Sisters, from 1920 to 1926.

She first tackled the reversal of the disapproval reported in an earlier inspection by the State Inspectress from the Office of Charities, Miss Kautz:

Openings in the roof and ceiling of the upper dormitory; unclean conditions and a room adjoining the dormitory being used as a classroom. In a summary of the follow-up visit by Mary E. Nagle, Manager, on September 29, 1920, snippets of her findings reflect some improvements.

*... first-floor dormitory for young boys sleeping 70. ... The walls and woodwork were freshly painted last spring. Beds are comfortable and have fairly clean coverings ... a new metal ceiling, for safety sake. ... two new coats of white paint.

... clothes-room for the boys is inadequate, could be doubled for the number of boys ... all of the clothing for daily use and daily mending for the department is done here ... older girls help sort clothes ... a large table and a number of sewing machines show constant use.

... another dormitory and classroom exists over the boys' clothing room for little girls' classes ... unsatisfactory, lack of a private staircase. The upper dormitory greatly attended to ... ceiling and woodwork repaired and repainted ... iron beds recently painted and enameled, springs need to be replaced. ...The whole area, including the lavatory, was clean.

... The children's store moved to the first floor of the Administration building. ...The food found to be plentiful, considerable variety, from the working farm on the grounds. Fruits and vegetables were in ample supply. Improvement in the variety of meat and fish was observed. ... Bread was excellent and the physician, Dr. Schwartz, regularly dines here. ... Seven new cows recently added and milk is rich and abundant.

... new first-year high school class formed includes Algebra, English, French, stenography, and typewriting. Sister Vincent Dolores, Sister Marie Consilio and Miss Margaret Babcock are instructing.

...A retreat for three days before school resumed, by Father Green, S.J. assisted by Father Raines, S.J. clearly improved the morale of the children.

... As every effort is being made to remedy the objections made on the last State Report, we will add no further recommendations for the present.

---

* This refers to the original girls' dormitory built in 1884, next to the girls' school. Boys may have been moved in after the 1907 fire that destroyed the newer boys' dormitory.

Among the progressive thinkers in childcare, emphasis shifted from farming to vocational training. Between 1900 and 1909, eight hundred family farms existed in Rockland County, about eighty percent of the early households. Their number dwindled after the 1920's, then half again by 1940.

With the Industrial Revolution and the steady decrease in the number of family farms, more guild- or craft-based careers blossomed. Availability of personnel and funds increased after World War I, so in 1920, the St. Thomas Vocational School opened on Babcock Hill next to the Preventorium. Girls learned sewing, dressmaking, and cooking; boys learned carpentry, chair caning, and printing.

St. Thomas Vocational School

The Vocational School thrived according to the brief excerpts from a report made on December 10, 1921 by Sister Teresa Alacoque, a member of the Executive Board.

Over the years, St. Agatha relied heavily on the charity of others. Whenever a new undertaking began—such as relocating the Preventorium, or fundraising for buildings and fixtures—collateral needs for clothing and equipment accompanied it. The following summary of donations reveals those needs and the continual generosity that kept St. Agatha afloat through the many difficult growth years.

On July 9, 1923, Louise Joslin of Westchester sold to St. Agatha Home for $100 a parcel of land about five acres at the east most portion of Convent Road, beyond Babcock Hill. The two-story house on the property, blessed Mt. Carmel Villa, became home to the youngest inmates, with ample space for playground equipment and grass.

Both entrances facing west and south had screened-in porches where the children could play in poorer weather. A beautiful stone well stood by a stone staircase that led to Convent Road. The first floor had a reception for guests, dining room, kitchen, sewing room, and dormitories. The second floor, and eventually the attic, became more dormitories.

St. Agatha's growing reputation as a beautiful retreat and progressive institution, enticed Sisters and Priests from the city to spend a day or a weekend out in the coun-

Mt. Carmel Villa

try whenever they could. The nearby town of Nanuet had no allure for St. Agatha's guests; the allure for them came from the grounds. One of the Trustees of the Board of Managers from St. Lawrence Academy on 84th Street in New York City describes her visit in a report excerpted below, entitled, "A Day in Rockland County."

An hour before noon on Saturday, October 20, 1923, she arrived at St. Agatha Home. In the company of the Superintendent, Sister Xavier Maria, they strolled around the grounds near the Administration building.

It was a perfect day, after a heavy rain. Maples, oaks, evergreens, hedge and vines, flowers and lawns were in their final regalia of brown, russet, red, yellow and orange.

Landscape Garden—A new landscape garden at the west of the girls' school had been recently laid out. New walks had been made, choice shrubs and evergreens had been planted and a shrine was in the process of erection, to contain a statue of St. Agatha.

Cottage & Poultry Farm—Past the brick barn we visited the poultry farm and saw hundreds of leghorn chickens, placed in different houses according to age and sex. There were snow-white ducks and geese sailing around the duck pond. A new colony of pigs numbering seventeen, promised pork later, and in a few pens some were fattening up for fall killing, in late November and early December. Cows and young calves were grazing in the fields and pigeons were flying about for their snug homes.

Filtering Beds—On a walk in back of the main building, we passed the filtering beds. The system of drainage is modern and quite perfect and the land was in a healthy condition with no unpleasant odor of gas escaping.

Large fields nearby were planted with rye, cabbage, kale and other vegetables making a pretty picture with bright green rye, the vigorous drab color of the leaves of the cabbage and the deep rich green of the kale. It presented a picture of thrift and industry most creditable to Mr. Flynn, the overseer of the farm. On the slopes of the hills beyond as far as the eye could see, are the fruit orchards recently robbed of Greenings and Baldwins.

Reunion—About four o'clock we returned to the Administration building and from the office windows we beheld a touching sight. We saw groups of children reunited with brothers and sisters, as they do not receive visits from their parents, guardians or friends on this Sunday. They assembled in the shrines outside, in little private groups, running to their siblings with their hands outstretched, showing wonderful affection for one another. They moved off, arms around each other to a quiet spot where they could be alone together.

I would have liked to hear their conversations, but probably would have embarrassed them and interrupted their heart-to-heart talks. Some of the Sisters passed around candy, which made the children very happy, indeed. Then, the supper bell rang and they said goodbye and returned to their cottages.

Bakery—numerous shelves were laden with loaves of bread and the Superintendent seated herself and demonstrated the electric cutting machine that provided in a half-hour enough bread for the entire population of Nanuet, for the following morning.

Chaplain's new residence—On Sunday morning a visit was made to the Chaplain's residence, which is two-and-a-half stories of pressed red brick of colonial architecture and complete in its furnishings. It is fitted up appropriately, if sparsely, with antique furniture and carpets of subdued colors that match the decor.

His Grace, Archbishop Hayes of NY, had blessed the new house on October 18th, after he conferred Confirmation in the Chapel on seventy-four boys and seventy-one girls, the same morning. The Reverend Chaplain moved in the very evening the cottage was blessed.

The lawn in front of the cottage had gravel walks with Concolar Pines and Arbor Vitae planted in front of the veranda and about the pathways.

Grotto and Sun Dial—Next to this sunny cottage, is the Grotto of Lourdes. Newly planted Scotch Pines would soon provide shade in their place.

In front of the Shrine a circular bed of green turf with a Grecian pedestal in the middle holds a sundial, the gift of a Board Member. The time is exactly correct. The clock is reminiscent of the one at

Font Hill where veteran actor Edwin Forrest, the great actor of the last century from whom the estate was purchased, built the castle on the Hudson, and where the Academy of Mount St. Vincent resides.

On October 29, 1925, Joseph and Adele Coates sold to St. Agatha Home for the sum of $1 a small tract of land .82 acres, including a nine hundred square foot, two-story house with basement and attic. Originally used for small girls, they named it Sacred Heart Cottage. Before long, they expanded the attic and added dormers to provide additional sleeping space for the growing population.

The Grotto

Part of the original division of the Kakiat Patent, the land had been granted by the King of England to speculators in 1696 after he drove out the Dutch settlers. It divided the land into the north and south in half—or moiety, as one of the Irish partners had called it—in 1713. As the King had hoped, they subdivided further and sold off into smaller plots before it came into St. Agatha's hands.

In subsequent years, it became an employee's residence, then a visitor's cottage for Bishops, Priests, and seminarians. The porch with its white Grecian columns facing Convent Road enclosed a play area for poor weather. A white picket fence with an arbor above, and flanked by Grecian urns, added to the charming appearance of the cottage. Externally, iron staircases with railings provided escape in the event of fire.

The Pascack Brook cut right across the back of the property, proving to be its most prized feature. The land formed a sort of peninsula where Convent Road bent to become Pascack at the intersection of Duryea Lane, thus marking the new western boundary of the Home.

Little girls of Sacred Heart Cottage

Thirteen

The Schizophrenic Twenties

In 1925, Jean Brajevich—and her siblings, Anthony, Olga, Jenny, and Joseph—arrived at St. Agatha. Jean turned four years old in August. Her mother and father, both immigrants from the former Yugoslavia, arrived in America in 1922 with baby Anthony. They settled on the west side of Manhattan, and the family grew to five children. Soon after the last child arrived, her father took off with an Americanized woman and moved to Maryland.

With the Depression in full swing, Jean's mother tried hard to provide her five children with food, clothing, and shelter, with no relatives to call on for help. Pretty soon her health gave way, and an ambulance rushed her to the nearest hospital. The children went to St. Agatha, and a year passed before their mother found them, because the records housed in an office of Catholic Charities went up in flames. She located them and, little by little, they reunited after graduating from school. Except for little Jenny who ran away from St. Agatha to rejoin her mom.

Many immigrant families capsized when the father ran off, left to find work, got too sick to work, drank, or died. Few public resources existed to help mothers left with children to care for. They usually worked sporadically while the kids remained unattended except by each other. Sometimes, she became ill, pregnant, drunk, or involved with another

Girls in Pinafores

man—one who frequently wanted no responsibility for another man's children. In many cases, they ended up at St. Agatha.

The Home grew piecemeal in a reactionary fashion over the forty years after it opened. The master plan for future growth needed refinement. In May 1927, Sister Thomasina hired a New York firm, Ditmars and Reilly, who subcontracted the local services of well known surveyor, W. O. Polhemus, to survey and map all of the holdings that comprised St. Agatha Home. A plot of the buildings guided future planning.

The end of 1927 brought some happy events that touched everyone at St. Agatha. On October 10th Reverend John J. Dunn, Bishop Auxiliary of NY, administered Confirmation to one hundred eighty-nine pupils. A month later, prominent philanthropist Edwin Gould—son of the tycoon Jay Gould whose charities focused on underprivileged children—provided a bountiful dinner to St. Agatha on Thanksgiving Day.

Two weeks later, on December 11, the Board of Health of Clarkstown made their annual inspection and recorded the following observations in the visitor's book:

We have completed our annual inspection of the institution. We find that it is marching forward. Making use and taking possession of all the modern ideas, looking toward the advancement of Child Welfare.

We the Board extend our congratulations to Sister Mary Thomasina and her associates upon the matchless progress the institution has made during the past year.

So, with the seal of approval from the local health department, the congregation embraced Midnight Mass, Christmas Eve. Always a special event for the older children permitted to attend. That Christmas Day, each child received a gift, candy, and a traditional Christmas dinner, provided by St. Agatha's benefactors. And so rounded out a tumultuous year as the country battled with the Depression gripping the country.

The eighteen-car garage, 1935

St. Thomas Vocational School was needed for the expanding Preventorium. The two summerhouses down by the elementary school combined to form a vocational building for older boys to learn printing and carpentry. Another building at the foot the boys' yard, formerly used for recreation and similarly converted, became a training shop for little boys. The girls continued their lessons in preparation and food service at the lodge where some of the staff resided. In the sewing room of the girls' dorm, they developed skills in sewing and mending for themselves and the other children of St. Agatha.

The boys used the sewing room constructed over the garage, and the maintenance and carpentry shop below, for repairing the Home's furniture. The Home had several cars by now, and an eighteen-car garage went up for the various vehicles.

As the Depression progressed, more and more people began placing their children into institutions when they lost their jobs or could not afford to care for them. They became a sort of boarding school, not unusual to European immigrants.

Simultaneously, with the freewheeling lifestyle of the roaring twenties, divorce increased. As women got the vote, could own property in their own names, and file for divorce, many took advantage of the opportunity

to escape unhappy or abusive relationships. The consequences often included an inability to financially support their children. Over the course of the Depression, the population at St. Agatha doubled.

The forward-looking Sister Miriam Regina was the first chairman of the Sister's Conference of the National Conference of Catholic Charities. This organization studied and fostered women's roles in the male-dominated Catholic Church. From its inception in 1920, until her death in 1935, Sister Regina is credited with great leadership to childcare institutions throughout the country. Her philosophy was founded on two fundamental

Tom Maloney, Tony Lombardi, 1929

principles: "reverence for the children created by God, and a sense of the individuality of each child," which she had practiced with great success for thirteen years at St. Joseph's. Now, age fifty-one and full of energy, she would work her magic at St. Agatha Home.

Boys in uniform

Sister felt financially confident to implement those principles that had proved so successful to her before. Beginning with an unprecedented act, Sister Regina sent for a tailor to come in and measure each of the four hundred boys in residence for a custom-made suit of clothes so that all would look perfect for Easter Sunday. The girls chose the color of their individually made dresses and a straw hat to top it off. Sister wholeheartedly agreed with the progressive childcare policy makers that image was extremely important to a child's success.

Increased attention to the critical contribution of children's healthy-growth directed games and activities, including roller-skating and basketball. Military drills, long considered a healthy way for boys to exercise and improve their self-esteem, had languished during World War I. Sister Regina hired a Drillmaster from West Point to train the boys and acquired uniforms and band instruments for them. Music teacher Mrs. Hamilton added an orchestra. During rifle drills, the boys wore white midi blouses above their knickers, perhaps fashioned by the girls in home economics. Others wore full Cadet Blue uniforms and learned to present their swords professionally, and lead their teams. The band, in dress blues, played drums and horns as they marched. They participated in local parades with the fire departments in neighboring Counties, and even in New York City.

The Bandroom had a wide sweeping staircase across its east side, which opened onto a large play yard, later paved. From the yard, a door at the end of the Bandroom, and double doors at the center, permitted access during inclement weather and also lavatory usage. Privacy fencing surrounded the yard, and a shade was installed above benches along the south gate. Circa 1935, barbed wire enclosed it, but was removed about 1947. They added swings, seesaws, and parallel bars.

The whole proved so popular in reducing the episodes of standing around, boredom, and running away that the building was expanded. A new entrance, constructed close to the Administration building, provided visitors with their own entrance. This area doubled as a projection room when movies came along as weekly entertainment. Outside, a covered brick passageway connected the Bandroom to the refectory and kitchen at the rear of the Administration building, and a rear staircase to the chapel.

The brook after Sister Regina's efforts

In the summer of 1929, Sister Regina had workmen divert the Hackensack River to expand the portion of the Pascack Brook that cut across St. Agatha's northwest corner. It provided a place for the children to swim, and included the boys in the construction. They dug out a huge area and encircled it with fieldstones, then lined it with concrete about three or four feet deep. A rudimentary mechanical filter kept out water moccasins, grass, and leaves. Water rushed in over stones through six screened holes at the top and poured down a slope to fill the pool. The overflow ran out over a spillway, keeping the pool relatively fresh.

The spillways themselves provided great opportunities for adventure before the water rejoined the river. At the end of the summer, the diversion closed for winter. Then in spring, before the next swimming season, the pool and filter got a cleaning to weed out varmints, leaves, and fallen branches before refilling. Outhouses sprang up for boys and girls, and a cabana bathhouse to change into bathing suits for a swim. No mixed swimming occurred; genders swam separately, in groups of one or two grades.

Other of Sister Miriam's innovations included monthly birthday parties in each dormitory to celebrate all the children born in that month. A sheetcake arrived from the kitchen, and siblings were invited to share lunch and cake.

In bygone Christmases, children usually received no gifts, but sometimes a simple piece of hardtack candy. A lucky few went home to families and gifts. Others had visitors to the Home. That Christmas of 1929, Sister Miriam saw to it that each child received an individually wrapped gift with his or her own name on it from volunteers. These included college girls at the Academy of Mount St. Vincent and Cathedral High School in the Bronx, all delivered by Santa, of course. Future "Secret Santas" included the New York Telephone Company, the New York Police Benevolent Association, and local Lederle Laboratories, later renamed Wyeth Labs.

On the first Sunday afternoon of the month, the children remained in their church attire, and those with family gathered for an outdoor recreation program on the lawn by the Administration building. Siblings gathered to visit, to sustain their family relationship. Some later said that they felt like strangers to each other without a parent or other adult to facilitate their get-togethers. Many were happy just to have a break from the usual routine.

ॐ

When he was an adult, Emil Willimetz spoke of his and his sister Hanna's first days and nights at St. Agatha Preventorium from 1929 to 1931.

St. Agatha Orphanage was a large outfit, draped on the top and sides of a hill. Our unit was separate from the main complex but connected with it—we were fed from the same kitchen. The 'temporary' orphanage consisted of a dorm, a dining room, a one-room school and a large play yard. Hanna, her first night in strange surroundings, afraid to leave her bed, wet it. The Matron rubbed the wet sheet under her nose. It was not a good beginning. Along the bathroom wall was a row of sinks where the Matron would station herself with a giant bottle of cod-liver oil and an out-sized (seemed like) tablespoon with the plating worn off. She would fill the spoon, then you would step up and have it jammed into your mouth. The spoon would be perfunctorily rinsed under the hot water faucet and the next protesting kid would be hauled up under the baleful eye of the Prefect, our male guardian. Some kids would hold the oil in their mouths, slip into a toilet stall, and spit it into the bowl. What's the sense of that? I guess I was old enough to know that this indignity was in the name of our good health.

The Matron had large square black buttons on a white uniform that stared at some kids at eye level. Hanna says she still feels nauseous whenever she sees large, square buttons on a white dress. The large bathroom was split by a makeshift plywood partition that separated the sexes. As we prepared for bed I strained to hear sounds of Hanna, but never did. One night the bathroom was rent by terrible piercing screams and much frantic activity coming from the girls' side. Terrified, I rushed to the partition door but the Prefect had gotten there first.

"Stay here and keep the other boys out!" He ordered and slid past me into the other room. His appearance gradually calmed the troubled waters and after a time he returned to us. "Nothing to worry about, fellows," he said with a sheepish grin, "it was all my fault. I reached through the partition to open the window and some girl saw my hairy hand and screamed. You know how girls are." I longed to comfort my sister, but on the other side of the partition she was hopelessly out of my jurisdiction.

At 3 P.M., after school, we lined up again for another health break. This time it was a battered metal cup dipped directly into a large milk can. The milk had eggs, sugar and vanilla beaten into it, and I liked it. Hanna hated it. It did have its occasional glop of raw egg white. Our hot meals came to us from the main orphanage in large, round, insulated containers. Our daily breakfast was oatmeal with milk, butter, and sugar to liven it up—plus toast and cocoa. On Sunday it was corn flakes and milk. For lunch we had peanut butter and other types of sandwiches and for dinner we had boiled potatoes, turnips and cabbage—with butter, salt, and pepper, the cabbage and potatoes were acceptable—turnips left the dining room in kids' shirt pockets. There must have been other things, but that's all I can remember.

At the foot of our hill were great manure piles used for insulation cover for cabbages. Every day we could see the farmers digging in the huge piles for dinner. Most Sundays we had a weak beef or lamb stew with potatoes and carrots, but when we had official visitors (and for Thanksgiving and Christmas) we had chicken or turkey with sweet potatoes. We spent our evenings in a huge fenced-in playground with swings, teeter-totters and slides. These were the most difficult hours for both of us. Hanna's severe depression expressed itself in frequent tears, which of course depressed me too, and I spent most of this time trying to keep her amused. Since being pushed on the swings seemed to give her pleasure, she was swung incessantly. As we reached the apogee of the push, Hanna would shout in exaltation. The higher the arc, the more full-throated the glee. It was for me one of the few moments of solace I was able to give my young sister and I flew her in sync with her upbeat mood.

This, at times, involved the playground Prefect who was intent on flagging down the high flyers. The Prefect was a hard-nosed character and it took a certain amount of finesse to avoid his wrath. To ask for leave to go to the bathroom earned a whack, just to make sure you were committed. A major infraction of the rules brought threats of being shipped to the main orphanage next door, with Dickensian details of the harsh life to be found there. The main buildings were surrounded by high walls, and because we could never see the orthodox orphans, the happenings behind the wall took on a sinister aspect.

Fear was a constant companion—fear for my mother's life—a heavy weight of lead that settled on my chest. During the day when I was busy with tasks and school, it lay hardly noticed. In the evening play yard with Hanna, when the bells tolled for the Angelus, I would stop to look at the St. Agatha orphanage where the sound came from. A recurring thought would engulf me—what if our mother never came back? What would life be without her? Would we be sent to the neighboring orphanage? I didn't really think so, but then . . .

There were only three boys in the oldest age group—an Irish kid named Bill Gannon, myself, and a guy whose name I can't remember but will call Bully, since I felt he was a born one. Fighting with fists was one of the major infractions. One evening I had my little sister in a happy mood romping around the yard when along came Bully and knocked her down. I will never be sure that this was a purposeful act, but it infuriated me and I grabbed his coat and flung him to the pavement. Bill quickly got between us and led us to the back of the school building, out of sight of authority. I had my first fist fight, which ended in Bully's nosebleed. A bloody shirt would be hard to explain, so the fight was prudently called off. It was no great victory for me, but it did keep Bully off my back for the rest of our Nanuet stay. Bill and I became good friends. He came from a much poorer, depressed area of the Bronx than we did. His tales of life made me feel very fortunate.

We had visits from Mary and Pop, which upset Hanna more than ever, but netted us gifts from home, mostly clothes, cake, and books. Money sent by the families was placed on account in the commissary. Opened nightly, we could buy candy, cookies, toothpaste, etc. I also bought more than my share of batteries since my reading time was mostly by flashlight in bed under the blanket. Bill would never go to the commissary since he knew the cupboard, for him, was bare. By helping me entertain Hanna, I convinced him that he was part of the Willimetz family and he reluctantly agreed to share our loot with us.

In the winter we had three old Flexible Flyer sleds, one without a steering device. On the broken sled it took heroic measures and a lot of body English to avoid the dung piles at the foot of the hill. How I longed to have Anna and Unk share the sport with us!

The schoolhouse was a single, square building—a one-roomer for all grades. A nun, who had been retired, was our all-grades teacher. It would be hard to remember what I learned in my two-year stay. There are missing elements in my primary schooling—like grammar and spelling.

Some unthinking architect designed the building with a circling belt of windows—each window divided into countless square panes. I know they were countless because my only firm memory of school was washing these tiny panes. We were at Nanuet for about two years. When Mom came home, we came home. Mary came to get us and as happy as I was, leaving Bill was a downer. We both knew that the chance of his moving to the orphanage next door was very real.

The difference between the idealized programs the directors wanted and planned for the Home, and what trickled down to the children, is clear in the contrast between the public reports and private

Graduating class, 1923

correspondences, and the loss that the children express. Stories differ according to the age of the child and what circumstances he is coming from, such as death or mistreatment, which may have shaped his personality and ability to cope. Likewise, directors setting goals is not the same as achieving them.

The high school program, begun in 1920, continued for a few years and then floundered because it lacked teachers or students. It was reorganized in 1930, and became co-ed. Boys and girls, other than siblings, rarely had the chance to interact, which proved a disadvantage when they left St. Agatha.

The high school girls, who resided in the original girls' dorm, had an area set aside and furnished as a spacious social room, decorated, with patterned tin walls painted white. On the windows, below ornate wooden valances, floral drapes brightened the atmosphere. From the center of the tin tiled ceiling hung a simple chandelier. A sofa-sized landscape painting in a gold leaf frame hung on the wall above the fireplace. It depicted a mountain, off in the distance, shrouded in rose-colored mist—an early view of the Hudson River, as seen by the first settlers.

There were a number of famous local artists. Edward Hopper of Nyack was recognized as the most important realist painter of twentieth-century America for his landscape paintings including the breathtaking Hudson Valley.

One corner of the room was designated for reading. Another had tables set up for Bridge, which the Sisters taught along with knitting and crocheting. The popularity of card games like Bridge and Canasta had swept the country, and books about how to play expertly appeared on the *New York Times* Bestseller Lists for many weeks.

An upright piano provided music for dancing, under the tutelage of Sister Maria James, and the girls learned all the classics such as the fox trot, waltz, and polka. A Philco radio came later, followed by a Victrola. These introduced classical music and opera, as well as Jitterbug, radio shows, and news. A dancing teacher was hired for the girls and the boys, though they practiced separately. At an end-of-year dance recital, demonstrations of dances included minuets, Virginia Reels, square dances, polka, schottische (resembling a slow polka), waltz, and tango.

In 1930, Bill Lawson came to St. Agatha with his four siblings, after their parents died. They were Julia, Bill, Margie, Jim and Ernie.

We used to have nicknames for the nuns. We called Sister Regina "The Shadow," because she was so tall and thin, and had a hawkish face. Her garment hung down to the ground and when she walked, it looked like she was rolling on wheels. No knee movement; small steps, I guess. Other Sisters were Basalita (Bebe), and Thomasina (The Top Boss, who weighed about 500 lbs.), and Williamama.

I was born in 1919 and was about ten when my parents died. I was a resident at St. Agatha from 1930 to 1936. Some of the boys with me were Louie and Cosmo Andretta, Jacob Scheibinger, Tom Maloney, Walter Kelly, Louie Masucci (he was a good guy). Years ago, someone told me he was building houses in Rockland County. And my lifelong friend is Larry Viernstein. My sister Margie's best friend was Agnes Zimmerman and Julie's was Harriet Clapp.

I remember Charley Lee used to carry around a lined notebook in which he was writing a novel. I wonder if he ever followed up on that profession. Tom, Walter, and Charley all became Prefects after I left. There was also a Mr. Carolan that worked there.

I wasn't in the choir or an altar boy. The Bandroom was lined with dumbbells hanging on the walls, but no one ever made us use them. They looked like bowling pins. Once in a while kids would voluntarily take some down and do some exercises. The school hired a military officer who used to come in about once a week and march us around the yard, and teach us exercises with fake rifles.

We had printshop training and printed up tracts. The only sport I enjoyed was swimming. I had been swimming in the East River in New York City for years. So when I came to the Home, it was easy. They built a dam at the brook behind the school and built a hut for us to change in. They hired a swimming coach, who was a former Olympic swim champion. Once, when one of the kids sassed him, the coach decked him. No one moved. The coach never showed up after that episode, so presumably he was fired.

I turned out to be the best swimmer and won a medal. When McCutcheon gave it to me, he said, "Every dog will have his day." I believe the County made them close the 'ole swimming hole. I never saw any formal hobbies or any musical instruments. A lot of the boys played team sports. If you didn't, like me, you were not in lots of baseball. Spina was a great pitcher, and his catcher was Domas. They used to play against the local high school and win. There was a track and handball walls at the far end of the field, but very few people used them. Lack of proper coaching, I'd say. Roller-skating was big in the yard. In-line skates showed up, but they were not usable. The wheels were metal, and on concrete they just would not get a grip.

We usually just hung around the yard most of the time. There was one radio that we used to listen to serials a lot: *Bobby Benson and the*

B-Bar-B Boys and *The Shadow.* The radio was in a window of the Bandroom at the north end of the building, in an anteroom. There was a freestanding water fountain in the yard. It had four drinking spigots. Before bending over for a drink, you looked around to see who was standing near. Some of the meaner kids loved to push your head down and give you a bloody lip. Cohen's orchard up the road used to send a bag of apples down, once in a while. Then the prefect would stand at the top of the steps and fling handfuls of apples for us to scramble after. We would drop apples down our knickers legs. In the back of the school building was a "rusty" apple tree. They were my favorites.

I used to pick the locks and switch them for the cemetery and the boys' yard. The boys called me "The Magician" because I did all sorts of neat tricks. Like, I put milk in a glass jar, and shook it until it formed a clump of butter. Someone gave me two WWI army watches that didn't work, and I took them apart and got one working watch from the two broken ones. Things like that.

About 1936 I went to live with an aunt who turned me loose. I checked in with the Guardian Society who got me my first job, but I quit it and the Society, and I've never looked back. WWII, US Navy, college, then I worked for AT&T, retired in 1974, and have had a good life. My wife died in 1998, and I chose to stay where I'm a part of her large family.

I'm eighty-three now. I have had the usual health problems, but I'm in pretty good shape. My best friend up there was Larry Viernstein. He became a Ph.D. in physics at Johns Hopkins in Baltimore. He's retired now and lives in New York City with his wife, a psychologist. His daughter is also a Ph.D. in Knoxville, and his son is a minister in Pennsylvania. Some of us did okay.

Money—from charitable contributions for improvements and necessities—dried up in the years after the stock market crash of 1929. Almost overnight, people learned that they were broke. The first item people had stopped spending for was charity.

Around the nation, coal mines closed. Steel and textile mills clamped shut. From 1931 to 1939, crops died in what was called the "Black Blizzards." Dust from the overplowed and overgrazed land began to blow. Crops dried up in the fields without being harvested. Farmers poured milk on the ground for want of the resources to distribute it. No one had the money to buy their goods anyway. People lost their jobs, their homes, and their life's savings.

When the banks closed, what money Americans had saved for an emergency was inaccessible to them. Many who lived simple lives and had not gotten swept into the post-war consumerism and euphoric lifestyle of the previous decade were able to hang on longer. Those who already lived on such a small margin and were devastated overnight had to pull up roots and head for the cities or out west, in search of employment. Boys and men riding the trains in search of work became "hoboes"—boys with hoes, eager to work. Before long, even those areas like California's agricultural fields capsized under the influx.

President Hoover won over Al Smith in the 1928 election. Because of his personal wealth, he did not take any salary during his entire term of office. He believed in the American people that they could weather the storm and correct matters without government intervention. So, he did almost nothing about the financial crisis.

Unions nearly collapsed as hundreds of thousands of men waited on bread lines. They crisscrossed the country in search of work. The orphan trains ground to a halt in 1929. Families could not afford to care for themselves, much less take on other mouths to feed. Some even sent the children they'd taken in, back to New York City, or just turned them out.

When Theodore Roosevelt's presidential campaign promised rescue by the Federal government through the creation of jobs, people voted overwhelmingly for him. Some things did improve immediately under the Work Incentive Program and Civilian Conservation Corps. Thousands of people went to work right away, but it was just not enough. Businesses did not improve quickly enough. Whole families disintegrated.

More and more abandoned children went into public care as their grieving parents went in search of relief. Some left the children for a period of time while they searched for work, but did not come back. The caretakers turned the kids away, or sometimes over to the authorities. Hard times swept across America and in Europe. Times that only began to ease with American involvement in World War II. Then, slowly, rusty factory wheels began to turn once more. Finally, there were jobs.

Some people began to have a little money to buy food, then clothes, and then housing. A severe shortage of goods persisted, diverted to the war effort. Basics like sugar, milk, meat, eggs, and butter were rationed. Metal went for bombs, not cars. Gas went to fuel the war and the industry that fed it, not for Sunday pleasure drives. But at least the majority of people were no longer destitute.

Anyone who got a dollar had plenty of folks in line to share it with them. Fundraising efforts had to intensify, and only those like the Rockefellers, Fords, and Morgans had the money to help; there was no shortage of outstretched hands.

☿

Rocco Carollo witnessed the changes at St. Agatha with the onset of the recession.

I was born in 1923 and I lived at St. Agatha from 1924 to 1937. We had a very rough time of it. I was a little Italian boy, born in Brooklyn. When I was two, my mother went to Sicily seeking medical help, and she died there. Me, my brother Phillip, and my sister Carmella went to St. Agatha. My father died when I was three and we were orphans.

Originally, I was in Mt. Carmel Villa up, on the hill past the Preventorium. Then I moved to the little boys' dormitory. Sister Patricia ran the candy store outside the chapel, and she used to rush us kids in and out on our weekly visits, those of us who had a penny or a nickel to spend.

In the basement of the Bandroom, there was a big shower room where we took our weekly showers and got fresh clothes, so we were clean for church on Sunday. We each got a towel and a piece of brown lye soap called Octagon. Mr. McCutcheon or Mr. Ford would regulate the water for a set amount of time, then out, and the next group would come in. I had chapped hands all winter from that soap.

At the foot of the yard was our recreation room, next to where the third and fourth grades had their carpentry and print shop. Next to that was a huge tree that sprinkled down seedpods that we called Polly noses. We split them open and placed them on the end of our noses, like Pinocchio.

When our shoes needed repair or wore out, we surrendered them to Mr. McCutcheon. They were replaced by a repaired set that were always too big or too small, along with a lecture about being too hard on the shoes.

All of the nuns and Prefects were very tough, and it was crucial to follow the rules or there would be swift punishment. The Prefects would whack you on the back of the legs with the radiator brush. The nuns would knuckle you on the head or push you if you got out of line. If you spoke at mealtime, you were sent to the corner without your food. Then, after everyone finished and left, Sister Angelica would give you extra chores to do. If someone spoke in class and no one owned up to it, everyone had to extend their hands and get a whack with the pointer stick on the knuckles.

I only got to see my sister once each month when she came over from the girls' dorm to the boys' yard to visit for an hour. There were no other visitors. I never went over to the girls' yard in all my thirteen years there. All of the play yards were fenced with barbed wire. I remember when the new boys' refectory was built in 1931. Before that, we ate with the nuns in the Administration building.

Many nights during the Depression, all we had for dinner were two slices of bread and cocoa. We had oatmeal for breakfast every day, and once a week on Sunday we got cornflakes and an orange. It was such a prize that we gambled on the sports teams and bet that orange. We ate cabbage cooked so badly I can't eat it to this day. We got a special treat from the Dutch gardener, Mr. ViVi, who gave us a red delicious apple from the orchard behind the school at the end of our day's chores. We all wanted to be assigned to him, picking apples.

At Christmas time, the huge evergreen that stands in front of the Administration building was decorated with lights and a star on top, which we surrounded while we sang Christmas carols. We went to midnight mass, and could not have even a drink of water beforehand. Christmas morning, we got no toys, just a box of hard tack candy, and we were happy to have it. We would assemble in the Bandroom and Mr. McCutcheon would be dressed as Santa and stand up on the stage, which was decorated with a Nativity scene. We single-filed up, class by class, and accepted a box of hardtack candy from him.

When it was so cold outside, and snow piled up on the Bandroom steps, we used to go into the shower room to warm up until Mac chased us out. He poured water on the steps, and when it iced over, we sledded down them to the bottom of the boys' yard. We took turns with the sleds, and often skated with just one of the precious few skates. Of course, we never had any gloves, and our fingers froze.

Once each year, the kids that were good and didn't run away would get to go on a trip to Bear Mountain. We never went on any other outings, never went into the city. Most of the kids were pretty tough, and you had to know how to take care of yourself to fight, but I never heard any rumors about any sexual abuse.

There were about a thousand chickens whose coops we had to clean out, but we kids never got any eggs. We had chicken only at Christmas, Easter, and Thanksgiving. The nuns got the eggs and chicken once a week. We used to hold the doors for them after mass, for which they rewarded us with a brownie. We'd ask them what they had to eat, and that's how we knew they had chicken and eggs.

Besides chores, like daily sweeping of the Bandroom and yard, we had farm chores. We had to feed the pigs, cows, and horses, and help herd them from the fields by the school across Convent Road to the fields behind the girls' dorms, then back into the barns where we stacked the hay. The field along Convent Road, where they later built boy's cottages, was planted in potatoes, under the watchful eye of the farmer, Mr. Flynn. He was very harsh. At the end of our workday, he'd line us boys up and have his dog sniff us for stolen potatoes or carrots. We ate the carrots raw, but took the potatoes to a campfire in the baseball field and cooked them.

If a boy ran away, the nuns shaved his head, and for a month made him wear a dress of striped mattress ticking as an example to the other boys of what would happen if they tried the same thing. It was so humiliating.

We had an Italian barber who cut all the boys' hair once a month in one of the schoolrooms. One by one, we got out of class and went in. There were forty kids in a class. Between haircuts, the barber spit on the comb and scissor before starting on the next head.

When kids first came to the Home they stayed in Quarantine up on the hill at the Preventorium for two weeks, before mixing with the other kids. St. Roche was also Quarantine, but was for St. Agatha kids who got measles and things like that. There was a life-sized statue of St. Roche out front, with a staff or walking stick. He also had a dog which structurally resembled a Greyhound or an Afghan. The explanation for the presence of the dog, according to the nuns, was that St. Roche was the patron Saint of persons afflicted with sores, which the dogs would lick, and (enzymes from) the canine's tongue would provide an antiseptic affect to the sores. At least, that was the traditional anecdote.

I remember when Al Smith was running against Roosevelt for President in 1928. All the nuns left to go vote, and the kids were happy they were gone. Once a year, the nuns, whom they called "black crows" because of the habits, would go on a two-week retreat and the replacement nuns treated us so kindly. It was such a surprise.

In winter, the nuns wore black habits; in summer, they wore white. What I missed most was the love of a mother. The nuns were not loving.

ॐ

The same year Rocco left St. Agatha, Sister Raymond arrived. I interviewed her six months before she died in 2004, while she was still teaching and counseling. Here is what she told me of her fond memories of St. Agatha and the students she taught there, doubtless sweetened by time.

I was born October 1910, and took my brother's name when I became a Sister of Charity. I was called Sister Raymond until, about the mid-1960's when changes in the Catholic Church occurred, and many of us Sisters reverted back to our family names. I became Sister Marion Duggan, but many people I knew as children at St. Agatha continue to call me Sister Raymond.

I planned to attend college full-time after high school, but my father died suddenly. I had been working since I was twelve for $5 a day beginning in 1922. I sold hats at Stearns in New York City. With my commissions, I could contribute to my family as much as an additional $1—good money in those days. It was important to me to be helping my family.

I worked as a teacher in Harlem, giving my earnings of $60 a month to my mother. Well, except when I bought shoes for the children in my class who had none. During those depression days, the school gave students and teachers a free sandwich each day. I remember those destitute times when I saw some children sneaking their sandwiches home under their shirts, because their mother or younger siblings had nothing to eat.

While teaching during the day, I attended Hunter College at night and earned my teaching degree. When I was twenty-five, working and going to school, my brother's wife died. He was left with two children whom I began to look after, along with my mother. At twenty-six, a little older than the usual novice, I became a Sister of Charity. In the early days of our community, we Sisters renewed our vows on a yearly basis, every December 8. In 1927, Canon Law was changed, and we were required to make perpetual, or final, vows. All of us in the community at that time had to make final vows by 1929 if we wished to remain a Sisters of Charity. And so I did.

My first assignment was to St. Agatha Home, where I taught seventh grade and became a group mother to ninety boys. In fact, when I first arrived at the Home, the Sister Superior told me which building I would be assigned to, and to see if I could find a bed there, and some sheets. When I came into the dorm, there were ninety adolescent boys in my charge. They called me Baby Face, to my surprise. I promptly straightened them out on the proper way to address me, but they continued to refer to me that way behind my back.

I asked the boys if there was a bed for me to sleep in. They directed me to a vacant room where there was one. Frequently, I would be shifted to various other dorms when employees quit, got sick, or did not show up for work. Or when Group Mothers, like Sister Helen Marks of the high school girls' cottage, went away. Someone had to stay with the children. I always say that I moved around so often at St. Agatha that I felt I could sleep on a picket fence. Noise doesn't bother me, as long as I'm not responsible for it.

Food was always scarce, and I knew that boys were always growing, always wanting something to eat. I used to cook a little extra for them when I could. Or I'd make them sandwiches at snack time in the evenings. I added ice cream to their milk, or a little chocolate syrup when it was available. I loved the kids, poor things. They were always hungry, and the food, what there was of it, was not prepared in an appetizing way.

I was always full of energy and took long walks. I continued to swim when I could, though not in the company of the children. I taught the boys to swim down at the brook while I stood at the side of the pool. I fought hard for a proper swimming pool and gymnasium, which finally came a couple of years after I left St. Agatha. I was often scolded for my independence. Like the time I refused to halt the boys for Benediction in the middle of a baseball game.

I was always fighting with the Superior. We were not raising the kids to be nuns and Priests, as if they were novices, I had told her. It was so behind the times. Just let them be children, I urged. I knew that they were children of God, and what they needed more than anything was a sense of self. I always told them they could be anything they want to be.

A year after Sister Raymond arrived, the in-service training program began at St. Agatha, eventually resulting in a professionally equipped staff. Twenty-two Sisters went to conferences between March and June of 1938, offered by Sisters of Charity in social work. Ultimately, all childcare providers received training. Miss Katherine Blake of the Children's division of Catholic Charities was responsible for this aspect of the training program. Conferences held twice a month at St. Agatha discussed recent visits to the family homes by the children in residence. The progress of each child was reviewed with everyone who cared for him, as a team approach.

They held bi-monthly conferences about individual cases at St. Agatha, led by Reverend John Lennon of the Catholic Charities staff. The first lay social worker at St. Agatha was Mary Louise Foy who came in 1939 after graduation from Mount St. Vincent and remained for over twenty years. It was her responsibility to perform home visits several days each week and assist with casework at the Home. The commitment to reunite families as quickly and safely as possible once they received assistance was renewed.

As there was no high school available at the Home in June of 1938, most of the eighth-grade girls transferred elsewhere. They went to the Dominican Convent of the Holy Rosary on east 63rd Street and attended neighborhood schools there. A few girls went to Mercy Institute in Tarrytown. Others went to foster homes under the supervision of the Catholic Home Bureau. Elementary school enrollment was five hundred seventy-seven that year, down by two-hundred children over the previous five years, primarily due to lack of staff and improved benefits to families.

A significant turning point towards system-wide change at St. Agatha resulted from an extensive evaluation of the Home. The resultant report prepared by the Division of Children of Catholic Charities contained findings from March 1 to April 26, 1938. Committee members resided on the premises to afford continual contact with the subjects of the study. In May of 1938, the results entitled, *Report of Study Made at St. Agatha's Home, Nanuet NY*—a comprehensive and exhaustive scrutiny of St. Agatha—offered recommendations and direction for improvements.

To their credit, the Board of Directors implemented many of the changes suggested in this detailed critique. The report documents that the facility had moved away from the more reactive practice of taking children in and doing the best they could with them, towards a proactive, systematic plan for the future under continual revision. They had the skeleton of a full-fledged drive away from a congregate, large group setting to the smaller, intimate one, illusive for so long.

The lack of adequate staff is revealed as a constant thorn, requiring that the few employees and Sisters present be stretched too thin. Older children oversaw the younger, as Monitors. According to one of the Sisters, "The atmosphere has become one of herding—with little time, training, equipment, or energy to teach and nurture."

ॐ

The girls never enjoyed the freedom and adventures that the boys did in those Depression and War years, when few adults were around to keep an eye on kids. Life at St. Agatha Home was no picnic for Dorothy Leak.

I was born on May 12, 1926. I've never really remembered my father because he died when I was three of tuberculosis. My mother was working, but she didn't have enough money to feed my brother and me. So, we were brought to the New York Foundling Hospital, and then St. Agatha's Home in 1929. I was there for thirteen years. That was a long time.

When my brother was older, he went to another place on Staten Island, Father Drongul's Place. They had a high school for boys, but they didn't have anything for girls. Later on, they sent me there for about a year before I came out. Then I went into a foster home in Brooklyn and stayed there for a good long while, attending high school. I went off to work by myself with a lot of other girls. We had a group who were all in the same boat.

What I remember about the orphanage: Well, I was only three years old. They had a little house off from the main orphanage. It was called the Baby House. So, if you were under five, you went there. I remember one day a girl was taking care of us, and I couldn't get my shoelace open. She told me to go downstairs and get scissors from the desk. So I went, but I couldn't find any scissors.

I was so afraid because I couldn't find it, that I hid behind a whole bunch of clothes with a curtain over it. They couldn't find me, so they called the police. They looked all over the place, searched the woods all around, and they had all the kids get up out of bed and say prayers. Oh, it was terrible. They couldn't find me. Finally, somebody pulled the curtain and there I was sound asleep. I must have been about three or four.

I thought I'd be reprimanded, so I was afraid. The nuns remembered that for a long time. I think when I was around twelve they still told that story. I went over to the regular orphanage, then. It had been pretty wrenching to be taken away from my mom. She came to visit one night when she wasn't supposed to, and brought a doll carriage for me. I was screaming because she had to leave. They took the carriage away from me, and I never saw it again. In those days they didn't use psychology, you know. I couldn't have a carriage while everybody else didn't have one.

I didn't see my brother at all while I was in the Baby House. I never saw him. Later on, when we were in grade school, I used to see him like once a month, or something like that. They would send us over to the boys' side to visit. I really didn't know him. We just stood there looking at each other. It was kind of awkward. They sent me over because he was family. All brothers and sisters got together. Parents came for holidays like Christmas, but not on our birthdays. Every Sunday somebody would get some sort of visitor. That was the big thing. I didn't get too many. My mother came once in a while, but not that often. She worked at St. Luke's Hospital in New York in the laundry room. My father was a house painter before he died. They lived in New York somewhere. I really didn't know where. I think at one point they lived in the Bronx. I heard her say that one time, but I didn't know anything about him.

I had a rough time there because I had a lot of problems. I was always getting hit by some of the nuns and some of the older kids. The older kids used to be in charge of the younger kids. We used to get hit on our hands at night for whatever reason with a stick. We got hit real hard. One time I had a robe and I put my sleeve over my hand and Sister said, "For that you are going to get more." It was pretty rotten.

The musical Annie rang a note with me. I never saw the play. I wasn't a good person to be in such a place. I rebelled against them. I was kind of quiet and I thought I was such a good girl. I couldn't understand why I was getting beaten all of the time. I remember one nun, Sister B. She told us we were supposed to keep quiet in the dining room. I just happened to say something to someone. I just forgot. She got so angry. She came to hit me so I jumped out of the chair and I started running around the tables with her running after me.

She got me later and ripped off my beautiful dress that I got from my aunt in New Jersey. It was the first time I had gotten anything. She just ripped it off. Oh, she had such a temper; she just ripped into me. She beat me up all over, pulled my hair. I had another nun that did that to me when I was even younger. I didn't even know what it was all about. She just beat me. Then she went to the closet and got one of those brushes that you pick up dirt with. She kept hitting me and pulling my hair. I ran away from her, but she caught me. And oh, it was terrible. Just like a nightmare. I came back to bed and everybody was asleep. My hair was all tangled up. It was really awful.

Most of the nuns were kind. I had very good teachers along the way, especially one in the eighth grade. I remember she was very nice. There were a lot of good nuns. It was just the two of them, actually, and the older children that were in charge. I was always getting hit somehow.

There was no one to tell, but one time we put blankets over the fence and we climbed over and went into town, which was Spring Valley. We told people there that they were treating us badly. I never knew what happened about that. That was when I think they decided to send us all away, the group that was rebelling.

Dolls were a big thing. We used to make our own, these little rag dolls. I know I had a whole bunch of them. And, when I was very young, I used to say "You stay there" or "You go to sleep." I think playing with all the dolls is why I had so many children myself.

When I was sixteen they said I could go live with my mother. I was not with my mom very long, but it was an awful place. It was down on 24th Street. I remember alcoholics lying out there in front of our window. You know, it was one of those places. It was bad. She used to like to drink beer. I was doing my homework one time and she grabbed the pencil, being playful, or something. I got mad and I took it back. All of a sudden she took a big pipe. It had a big ring around it, very thin there. She hit me with it and blood kept pouring out. They had to call the ambulance; I remember that. I got stitches without any ether or anything. So I had to come out of there and go back to the foster home. There were other foster kids there. It was alright. She was a nice lady, had two daughters, and her husband was there. There were other kids, too. They got $24 a month to take care of us. It wasn't too bad.

The foster home—that was alright. I kind of rebelled at the end there. I left and went on my own at age sixteen. It was better than living with my mom. I didn't realize this when I wanted to live with her. I was always riding subways, you know, to New York and Brooklyn. It was a wonder I knew my way around.

Before I settled with friends in an apartment, there were four of us. I lived all around the place. I worked down on Wall Street for an insurance company. We had a lot of fun. The Company used to go on outings. We used to go out and eat all the time. Dancing was a big part of my life, but that was with my other friend from the orphanage, Mary Maniscalco. We used to go to the Palladium and dance and dance and dance. And we used to go down to Coney Island to go on the Cyclone over and over and over again. We had fun. We did the Lindy and all the dances of that time—the rumba, the cha-cha.

There were big bands around, like Tommy Dorsey. I never paid attention to who they were. I met Frank Sinatra once when I was living in Brooklyn. I was with one of the daughters from the foster home who was so crazy about him. She used to go into Manhattan to where he was staying and she got to know him. They got to be very friendly. She used to wait outside for when he would come out. One day, we both went in to see Frank Sinatra sing. And when he came out, the crowd was in the front, but he came out the side. We knew he was going to. She introduced me to him, "This is my friend." I'll never forget that. And, as he was standing there, he said, "I have to run. I have a benefit to get to." And all of the kids saw him from the front and they grabbed at him. He had the bodyguards take him away. That was really funny. That was something.

I don't think my mom drank too much, but she was kind of a problem. When she was older, and I was married, she went a little crazy on me. She wanted to pour boiling water on me. She said I took her home away. I invited her to come over and stay with us because she kept getting sick. And then she picked up a knife. We called somebody and they came. At first, they weren't going to take her out, but they asked her, "Why did you do that?" She said, "I was only fooling." So they knew that she had done it, and they took her away because I had two young ones, little toddlers running around. It was an awful time. They hospitalized her, then put her in a nursing home. She was a little psychotic. She was in one nursing home, then another. Her heart was failing. She died there at eighty-eight.

My brother went off to war. I think he was eighteen. He was in the Marines at Camp Pendleton. He was killed at age twenty-one in 1945 at Iwo Jima. He died when a mine exploded on him. My mother and I got a telegram, and we corresponded a little. He went over to my sister Anne's house and seemed to like all the attention, so he saw her more than he saw me. They made a big fuss over him—thought he looked great in his blue uniform when he was home on leave. He must have been maybe twenty. He wrote me a letter and said he was sorry he didn't get to see me more. That was the last letter I got from him. It was sad, but we didn't really grow up together. We didn't know each other that well.

Another girl had a brother named Tony Delaney, and when Catherine left St. Agatha, she married him. They had four children before he died of cancer, at about age fifty. Decades later, Catherine met Joe O'Connor, another former Home Kid, at an alumni reunion in the Bandroom. Joe knew both Catherine's and Dorothy's brothers, and her former husband, Delaney. They became friends and later married.

Joe told Chickie:

I always resented Dorothy's brother Arthur because when I was little, my family sent me a nice sailor suit for Christmas, and the nuns gave it to Arthur instead because he was so "cute." I cried, and never forgot it.

I have lots of memories of trips to a lake and a farm. Sometimes a dip in the lake substituted for our bath. One time a cow ate the soap and we had bubbles in our milk.

We got newly cleaned pajamas only once a month, which we wore inside out after two weeks. I remember sleeping in big dormitories filled with beds. There was no storage, so we placed our clothes neatly under the bed.

෯

The experiences and memories of the kids can be very different, even if they were at St. Agatha at the same time. It depends on whether they were a boy or a girl, what age they were, what background they came from. A child who loses a parent to disease is tragic. But one who then is moved

Paul Fabrizzi

from place to place, with no view of the future beyond the situation he currently finds himself in, can become cynical, skeptical, and defensive about the world and its inhabitants. A lucky few are so resilient that their bad experiences always have a humorous or positive side. That is their way of coping, instead of feeling victimized. One of those kids who got through the depression and war with his sense of humor intact was Paul Fabrizzi.

In 1927, Paul's parents became seriously ill with TB. He and his brother went to live at the Preventorium when Anthony was four, and Paul three. Both of their parents died, and the boys went to St. Agatha Home the following year. They remained until eighth-grade graduation in 1936 and 1937.

The little boys' dorm was heated by coal, as were all the buildings there, with a boiler and a coal bin in the basement. The coal truck dumped the coal down the chutes. I remember when I was in the first grade, we slept in a large dorm near the main building. I think it was over the laundry. It was overseen by Mrs. Graham who was the mother of a couple of boys and a girl who lived at the orphanage. She was even-handed with us boys, but she showed a preference for her own kids.

In the attached buildings behind the kitchen, there was a furnace room with a huge coal bin. I remember Mr. Williams, the night watchman, had to fill up the coalscuttles for the kitchen stove. Every night he'd bring about six of them to be filled, then carry them back to the kitchen. I can still hear the sound of the shoveling of the coal, and the noise of dumping it into those scuttles.

Our bathroom was right over this little coal shed, and there was a window through which I could see and talk to him. I remember asking him questions about what he was doing, and him answering me very kindly. Imagine a little kid, not really knowing where he was or what had happened to his life, talking through a window screen with a grown man, and he conversing very kindly.

The boiler in the dorm sent the steam up through the radiators. During the early part of the evening, when the steam came up full blast, you could hear the air pockets banging and hissing and cracking away. What a racket. I remember an incident involving the coal bin in the dorm cellar. Joe Palumbo, one of the workmen in the kitchen, had as one of his duties the task of checking out the boiler every evening.

Well, one time the authorities closed down the whole dorm because of an infestation of all kinds of bugs in the place; they closed it for disinfection. We had to sleep somewhere else, probably in the school, for a couple of days. All the windows and doors of the dorm were taped up and sealed, and disinfectant aerosol bombs were opened inside. The building was off-limits for two or three days, but nobody told Joe Palumbo. He went down through the cellar door and flew out instantly, coughing and sneezing, and wondering what the heck happened.

I also remember Doctor Schwartz, whose practice was in Spring Valley. He must have been contracted to attend to the nuns' medical

Home Kids

needs. I don't recall that he ever attended to us kids, except to pre-
scribe a general laxative, or something. He would drive up almost
every morning to the front hall in his new car, nattily dressed, cigar in
his mouth, and get out of the car. He'd go over to the rosebushes,
which lined the outside of the building—Joe Vi Vi's domain—and
clip one off with his pocket knife, put it in his lapel, and with cigar in
mouth, advance onto the nun's medical problems. A cameo.

My brother Anthony who's a year older than me—we laugh now
when we talk about our years at St. Agatha. I came from an Italian
neighborhood in Harlem, where there were gangs with strict codes
and no jobs. A lot of the boys went to St. Agatha through the Society
for Prevention of Cruelty to Children (ASPCC). Out in the country,
we thought there was nothing beyond the fences of the Home. We'd
hear the sound of the train whistle off in the distance, and it sounded
so comforting.

One kid named Devoe said he was going to hop the fence and go to
Pearl River, and take the subway to New York City. He didn't know
that no subways extended beyond the city. Some nights in the 1920's,
when there was very little traffic along Convent Road, we'd hear local
people pass by in horse-drawn sleighs, their bells jangling merrily as
they passed. It was such a romantic sound, I never forgot it.

Patriotism, next to religion, was an important part of our lives. At
the start of each schoolday we said the Pledge of Allegiance and
saluted the flag. It was not an assembly kind of thing, but was up to
the individual class teacher. The local American Legion post used to
sponsor an essay contest on what it meant to be an American. It was
open to all the boys and girls in the school. I remember a boy named
Fred Zimmerman who won it one year got to go down to the city for
a day.

For the first five years, my brother and I had no visitors—no
"friends" as they were called. But then my grandfather—who spoke
only Italian so we had a hard time communicating, and some aunts
and uncles, all on my mother's side—started coming to see us.

Except for the first Sunday of the month, which was visiting day for siblings at the Home; no outsiders could come.

Our Prefects were Mr. Callahan who was pretty tough, Mr. Fee, and Mr. McCutcheon—Cutchy, we called him behind his back. We had nicknames for all the nuns, too. Cutchy was okay; he was a strict, older man, but not mean. Once in a while, Cutchy would come to the boys' yard with a bag of apples and toss them out to us. On the other hand, unless it was zero degrees outside, he'd chase us out of the Bandroom to "blow the stink off you."

During the winter of 1934, for days we had three feet of snow with a crust on top. School was canceled all over the northeast. Since there was no traffic, Mr. McCutcheon let us take the sleds up to the cemetery and ride them all the way down Duryea Lane. One of those sleds was big enough to hold ten boys, and we rode up and down that hill all day.

The Prefects gave us a beating when we deserved it, like the time I answered back one of the nuns. I think I even cursed at her a few times. Then Charlie Lee, a former Home Kid, knocked me around pretty good, but I deserved it; I was incorrigible.

Each month, the barber—a character straight out of a Rossini opera—came to cut hair. With five hundred boys on the premises, one of their many needs was to have their hair cut. The Home engaged the services of Mr. Marcicha. One never addressed him as Mr. Barber or anything like that. He preferred to have himself addressed as "Gentleman." He lived down the road on the way to Pearl River.

He arrived with his old leather valise filled with clippers, scissors, combs, and other accoutrement. He would take one class each week. The boys would go one at a time into the little anteroom off the classroom to get their hair cut. He would sit you down on an over-turned wastepaper basket and cover you completely with a bed sheet, with your head sticking out.

I forget what it was we ever conversed about, but it was probably about events of the day. He carried on as though this sort of occupation was rather degrading for him, that he was meant for better things, but the Depression compelled him to take up this line of work. By the way, those were hand clippers he used. Metal clippers with handles like a scissor, but with a head like today's electric clippers, which had not been invented yet. He gave you a fairly good haircut. But one thing sticks out in my memory: Mr. Marcicha was given to mild doses of flatulence. Occasionally, he would let one go and he'd say to the haircutee, "Did you move the chair?"

The Sisters comprised most of the faculty at St. Agatha, but there were also a couple of lay teachers who were very good. I remember Mrs. Williams who lived in Nanuet, and whose husband was a sort of night watchman at the Home. Goes to show the depth of the Depression; jobs were hard to get, and I'm sure he was meant for better things. Mrs. Williams was not only an excellent teacher, but she was simpatico to the orphans under her tutelage.

I remember whenever there was a holiday, like Halloween, she would give each one of the boys in her class a Polar Bar, which was the forerunner of the Good Humor bar. She must have paid for them from her own meager salary. There was also a Miss Rafferty who taught the seventh grade, I think. I believe in later years she actually joined the Community and became a nun.

Boys choir

We also had a music teacher, Mrs. Schenck, who came once a week to teach us music theory. I am so sorry that I did not pay attention, as music has been a joy to me during most of my life. In fact, I have been a member of The Friendly Sons of St. Patrick Glee Club for thirty-six years. Although I can follow the line of music, I wish I were more adept at it.

I guess over the years quite a few of us played the harmonica. I don't know how we could afford one; nobody had money in those days. But somehow, the instrument would surface once in a while, probably a gift from relatives. It was quite easy to play, if you had some music in your soul. The plain ones were easy. But the "chromatic" was the toughie. I never could master that because it had sharps and flats, which one invoked by pushing in a button on the side. Sometimes the boys would gather around the harmonica player and we'd sing the old numbers like *Swanee River* and such. We also played the popular tunes of the day.

I don't recall any hobby like stamp collecting. If one were lucky to afford a stamp, he would write a letter to his relatives. Besides, where could one store such a collection? We had nowhere to put our meager belongings, except in our desk at school. A prized possession in those days was a box of envelopes and writing paper. I remember the third-or fourth-grade teacher, Mrs. Williams, presenting me with a jigsaw puzzle of the United States because I excelled in Geography. It was a prized possession.

Another good employee was Mr. Vi Vi, the Dutch gardener, who would lead us by the dozen or so around the grounds and point out "schtick, brench, pepper" and we would pick them up to keep the grounds clean. He called me "Mr. Chicken Man." I don't know why; maybe because of my freckles. Afterwards, he'd take us into the toasty basement below the Priest's guesthouse where he had his shop to warm up by the boiler he maintained, and then he'd give us an apple.

I don't remember ever smelling bread baking at St. Agatha, nor at St. Agnes. The bread was brought in by Widmer's Bakery in Pearl

River, for all the years I can remember. They stored the large loaves in a big, wooden breadbox located somewhere by the kitchen, and every so often, we boys would raid it. We all worked on the farm, picking up potatoes unearthed by the horses clumping along ahead of us. There were about a thousand chickens, a hundred pigs, and twenty-five cows to look after, too. All around us there were fields and orchards that needed to be planted, weeded, and harvested. Often, especially in winter, the supplies in the root cellar just weren't enough. Many nights we went to bed after a dinner of only two pieces of bread and cocoa. It was the height of the Depression. Everyone was poor, and St. Agatha was no different, except in the summer months when we ate the crops as fast as we could harvest them. We all worked in the laundry, too. It was huge, with its own staff, but we got fresh clothes and bedding each week, so we did our share of laundry work.

When Sister Raymond Commerford came to Nanuet, in the year before I left, she became one of the doers and shakers there. She brought a lot of innovations to St. Agatha and represented the new spirit of the age, and a new concept in institutional care. She had a breezy style, an infectious smile, and a glint in her that bespoke the future.

I remember she was very good looking, smart, and very warm. I remember her well. I was thirteen at the time and leaving to go to Sparkill, so it was 1936 when she got there. She was probably twenty-six and had an exuberant smile—and new ideas for bringing up orphans. I understand that in later years she made quite a few changes and removed a lot of the old hat restrictions. For me, it was the twilight of my tenure, but I felt the change coming, and it was in Sister Raymond's smile.

In the yard, starting at the foot of those same steps, we did some fancy footwork with roller-skates. Whenever someone received a pair of skates from relatives or somewhere else, he never intended to use *both* skates for himself. He would be entitled, under the unwritten law, to only one skate. He usually gave the second one to another boy. That single skate would be put to many uses.

The play yard was a concrete area with a slight grade downhill from the Bandroom steps to the fence by the Manual Training Building: a distance of about two hundred yards. We would put a skate on our right foot and, with the left leg, sort of pump to start going down the hill. We would ride down, either upright on one leg, or sitting down on our haunches. This was accomplished by bending the right leg at the knee and sort of sitting on our right foot, wrapping both arms around the right knee and extending the left leg straight out in front. Heavenly!

Sometimes, the enterprising one amongst us would get a flat board about six inches wide, a half-inch thick, and about four feet long. He would separate the skate halves—one would always carry a skate key in his pocket—and attach both halves to the underside of the board. We would then rig a stave more sturdy, upright at the front of the rig with a supporting truss and a crossbar for handles, and voila—we had a skateboard, fifty years prior to the skateboards of today. We sometimes attached an orange crate, or some such, to the front pole and we had a scooter. Down the yard we pumped on our scooter with the wind breezing past our faces.

Each year, we made "the outing." Everything was measured by this event. "You're not going on 'the outing' if you don't behave" or "Ten more weeks till 'the outing.'" Then, the glorious day would arrive. We would peer through the fence from the boys' yard at fifteen rented buses, all lined up and ready to take us to Bear Mountain. We had saved our few pennies for this annual trip, and oh, what a great time we had.

At Bear Mountain, we started the day under the big pavilion, with prayers and a lunch of sandwiches and fruit. The rest of the day we were free to wander all over the park. There were real bears in the zoo area, besides other New York State animals. There were motorboats on the lake for ten cents a ride, bumper cars, and scooters. Of course, there was the fabulous view of the Hudson River where we watched various crafts glide by, including the Hudson Dayliner. Bear Mountain was a terminus before West Point was. It was the ultimate fun day, and worth waiting for each year.

The only other trip I remember going on was in 1934 when a couple of nuns who always traveled in pairs took me and Walter Lipsky, a few years my senior, to St. Vincent Hospital in New York City to have cysts removed from the area above our eyes. What a thrill! I cried when, after two weeks, we had to leave. Everyone treated me with such love and care. The nurses, the nuns—they felt sorry for this poor little boy from the orphanage, and I was thinking, "There are five hundred more just like me, back at the Home."

Once, I was quarantined at St. Agatha's infirmary for measles. Periodically we went there to have Ms. Gordon and Miss Flynn give us licorice powder or castor oil as a tonic under the guidance of Dr. Schwartz's weekly visit, but there was no love and tenderness served up to us boys. And the dentist who came weekly, Dr. Gilchrist, pulled some of my teeth without Novocain!

Two months later in August, I went to live at St. Agnes in Sparkill, and attended Tappan Zee High. My brother, Anthony was a year older than me and went to St. Agnes when he graduated a year earlier.

What a change when we went to St. Agnes. Not just because it was an all boys Home, but because we were now in high school. The boys who were not academically inspired went to the vocational school at St. Agnes, but boys who had done well in school, like me (I even skipped a grade), joined the outside world. St. Agnes had a farm too, but it was not as elaborate as St. Agatha's, just some cornfields and tomato fields. There was no plan there for anyone to learn to become a farmer.

We had a very good football team at St. Agnes under the guidance of the athletic director, Coach Forks (Faulk). One of the schools we played against was St. Cecilia's, whose coach was Vince Lombardi. St. Agatha had a football team, too, but St. Agnes usually won.

One very exciting change was that there were girls in my class! At St. Agatha, since I had no sisters, the only time I ever spoke to girls was occasionally through the fence when I worked at the laundry, and they milled around in the next yard. The first time I sat behind a girl in class, I was mesmerized—couldn't even respond when I was called on to recite by the teacher.

Another major change was the freedom we had to go off campus to school and to work on weekends. Lots of us picked crops on neighboring farms or were caddies on a nearby golf course to earn money.

I joined the band and became its leader. We marched in the St. Patrick's Day parades and once, for the Holy Name Society celebration, we went to Fordham University and competed against some good schools, like La Salle. Archbishop Francis Cardinal Spellman, who was acquainted with St. Agatha, singled us out to lead the Star Spangled Banner in front of 100,000 people. What a day! It was the proudest moment of my fifteen-year-old life.

Another first came when we learned how outsiders viewed us. The townspeople referred to us as "Convent Kids," which was a derisive term and not uttered by our friends. The term "Home Kid" seemed to apply only at St. Agatha, but at St. Agnes, one never used that term. I guess it came off as sissy-ish. We referred to the entire St. Agnes entity as "The House." You were a House's Kid or a Housekid.

In the neighboring community of Grandview lived the elite. In Piermont, the Italians were considered low class, and we were below them. There were virtually no blacks in our group until a Home for black kids closed around 1937, then we got some. But the discrimination was about us as "Convent Kids"; not by race. In fact, one of my good friends was Manuel Parilla, a black kid of Spanish background. In those days, everyone was poor, or their parents had TB; there were lots of orphans. Kids that came later were more often from broken homes.

I wonder about societies that send their children away to boarding school, sometimes as young as four, to come home educated at age fourteen. Do those kids have similar stories to tell? Do their parents really believe that as long as the children are in a structured, regulated environment receiving a good education, that the rest will simply make them strong without damaging their psyche? Maybe it does, in the absence of other tragedies such as grave illness, death, and the need to survive.

ॐ

As an adult, Ed Faraday reflects on his experiences at St. Agatha with humor and good nature. Other kids may not have the ability to find the silver lining in the clouds that hovered over them.

When my four sisters and I arrived at St. Agatha in 1936, my father had died. I was three. My oldest brother stayed behind to help our mother. We remained at St. Agatha for eleven years. When I graduated in 1947, I went back home.

I first lived in Mt. Carmel Villa. These ladies helped care for us. Alice gave us our weekly bath on Saturday at noon, when the sun was warmest. We all lined up and Sister oversaw the process. If one of us had wet our bed during the week, she directed Alice to douse him with cold water from the rubber hose, which fed the bath basin. When I was old enough to go to school, I moved to the little boys' dorm.

I remember two brothers, Hector and Rubin Nieves. Their father Rubin came to visit often on the bus, and brought rice and beans in bowls. He worked as a greeter in a midtown restaurant, maybe Jack Dempsey's. He wore a uniform like they used on Phillip Morris cigarettes ads, like a bellhop. He was a tiny man, maybe four feet tall, but very tough. We called each of his kids "Papa's baby" because if any of the Prefects roughed up his boys and he heard about it, Mr. Nieves decked him.

Everyone got nicknames like that. Like one kid, Cisco, we called "Six Toes." Another was "Beanhead," I forget why, and another was "Racy," because he ran around all the time. Some of the names weren't too nice. Even the nuns and Prefects called them by the nicknames, rather than by their last name, which was the usual. You rarely knew anyone's first name, unless they were in your class at school.

In the summer, we picked our way through the cow plops down to the swimming hole at the brook. They diverted a stream from the Pascack Brook and made a nice swimming pool. At the deepest part, there were six holes, which the water poured through. There were cabanas for changing and a couple of outhouses. We had cookouts once a month, which lasted until five or six in the evening. The weather was beautiful. That was the only time we had a hamburger.

In 1947, Father Terrence Cooke came to St. Agatha right out of the seminary, and I assisted him. He was wonderful and dramatically changed things for us kids. He arranged for other seminarians to volunteer at St. Agatha. They talked to us like big brothers and they took us on hikes, which we sometimes tried to steer towards Nanuet where we'd get them to buy us a hamburger. Father Cooke hired a bus to take us on outings, like to Tallman State Park and similar places.

He developed an athletic program. I remember we did three-legged races. He acquired a bunch of lawn mowers and we learned to cut the grass, which had been the responsibility of Joe Flynn, the farmer's son and Home's chauffeur at the time. The most important impact that Father Cooke had on our behalf was that he intervened when he heard that the Prefects treated us harshly. A few were not too bad. One spoke in a loud, gruff voice, put his fingers in your ears, or scared the hell out of you when he said things like, "Hey, Hawkeye, get over here."

At school, the nuns were pretty tough. They screamed at us a lot, were very strict, but there was one nun that we boys called a "walking saint." Her name was Sister Leo. She was the kindest human being I ever met—never raised her voice, which meant a lot to those who came from harsh backgrounds.

Fourteen

"I Remember When . . ."

Federal Home Relief of 1934 helped to improve families' financial situations, and St. Agatha's census shrank back to six hundred children by September 1935. This was largely due to the intimacy and efforts between Mayor LaGuardia of New York and President Roosevelt, the City's former Police Commissioner, which created jobs. The Civilian Conservation Corps (CCC) brought a large portion of the public works projects to New York City.

A ten-year period of renovations, expansions, and change slowly began again at St. Agatha. This was much to the benefit of the children, and in spite of the negative effects of the Depression and War. There never seemed to be enough staff, money, food, clothes, supplies, or anything else to go all the way around; sort of like a baby blanket that doesn't quite cover a full-size bed. But it was worse across America, where crops dried in the fields and there was no one to buy them at market. Milk was poured out of dairy cans, onto the ground, for the lack of money to transport it.

Men walked away from their families and boarded trains, criss-crossing the country. Hoboes—in the company of other "Gentlemen of the Road," as they called themselves—emulated predecessors who had dashed west for the Gold Rush. They left everything, often forever.

Women still had too many mouths to feed, only now there was no possibility of a job.

Even seven years of the New Deal did not go far enough to improve the lives of most Americans. Shops, factories, and mills closed all over the country. More families needed assistance. Many of them gave up their children to others who could care for them and give them a better life.

It wasn't just the harsh treatment that children encountered before they came to St. Agatha, nor just the brutal losses of parents, but grueling poverty that they were facing to survive. Joe Pacheco shares his family's desperation so well.

Joe's memories of those years at St. Agatha Home are sketchy snippets of his childhood there from approximately 1931 to 1940—when he, his sister, and three brothers were inmates.

We were a destitute family. At home my three brothers my younger sister and I all shared the same bed in a basement apartment on the lower east side. After moving uptown to the east side, I remember going through the food market on Lexington Avenue with my Pop. When the markets closed or were near closing, we'd look in any discarded boxes for food thrown away. If it looked edible, we ate it. I found a jar of strawberry jam in a trash bin. We took it home, picked through it for slivers of glass, and gratefully spread it on the meager slices of bread. We had a filling meal. I remember standing in the "bread line" with a lot of other people for a dole of food from the City or Government agency.

Since we were destitute, the City of New York Social Workers sent us to the Foundling Hospital. I do remember being boarded for a period of time because that was when my brother Artie threw a rock in the air, and when it came down it hit him on the head.

Sister Thomasina was the Superior at St. Agatha's when we came in 1932. My brothers, Arthur (Artie), Raymond (Larry), William (Billy), and my younger sister Alice were up in the Home with me. Alice left after about a year. Artie and Larry left after they graduated

Boys at school, ca. 1936

from the eighth grade. When I graduated my brother Billy came out with me.

After Sister Thomasina's death, all the boys walked to the cemetery escorting the body past the girls' dorm up to the cemetery. The bell tolled all the way. They say it rang once for each year of her life. I don't believe that because it was a slow procession. I don't know if the girls ever were involved. I saw Sister Luca buried there. I didn't get to interact with many of the nuns, and those I did meet fleetingly, I never remembered. I think it was Sister Marks or Sister Carmela who broke a leg and had a profound limp as long as I was at the home.

While up at the Home we always wore khaki colored knickers, long black stockings, a blue long-sleeve work shirt, and high black brogans with four eyelets to cross over and lace up the shoes. We had Sunday clothes for church services: a white long-sleeve shirt with a red-and-blue knit tie, and another pair of knickers. These clothes were stored in a box with our names on it. We wore the same shoes and socks. All our clothing had our names printed on them with indelible ink.

In class, Catechism was the first subject taught, followed by Arithmetic, History, Spelling, Geography, Reading Current Events, Penmanship, and Grammar.

I remember between the boys' school and the infirmary there was a building called the "Baby boys." The older girls took care of us. There was a summerhouse pavilion between the cottage and the boys' school.

We were assigned cribs for afternoon naps. The girls were there for our protection. I remember one time when I wasn't sleepy and I started humming a little too loud during our afternoon nap, one of the girl monitors rapped me on the head with a broomstick to make me stop.

During the time I was there, no new buildings were erected, but before the new refectory was built and opened in 1932, I remember we all ate by grade. When they called "First Table!" we all lined up by class—two or three classes at a time—and then they let us go eat. We

went in by the main door to the Bandroom, straight past the candy shop on the left, past the stairs that led to the church, turned right, and went straight ahead to where we sat at long tables in a long, narrow hall where the food was laid out for us to eat. We all knew which table we belonged to. If

Little boys' dining room

you missed the call, you were out of luck. Once, someone complained about the food. I don't know who, but Sister Reverence lined up the classes and gave each of us just one spoonful of food.

In the wintertime, Kotchy and some of the older guys threw water down from the bottom of the steps in front of the Bandroom and let it freeze. That only took a minute or so. Then all us kids would line up, run, and slide on the ice. The leather soles of our shoes made a faster skid. It was good. Around Halloween time, the guys used to make "bouches" (stones, wet paper, and dirt rolled up into a corner of a hanky) to hit guys on the head with.

From the top of the stairs of the Bandroom in the autumn Kotchy and the guys used to throw apples to all of us gathered at the foot of the stairs. Sometimes they threw the apples like they were on the mound pitching to a batter. A few guys got their fingers broken or their legs bruised, but that was the chance you took for an apple and diversion for a few minutes.

Inside, the Bandroom was lined with dumbbells and a rack of dummy rifles. We were never allowed to touch the dumbbells or the rifles. They say a captain from West Point came and instructed the kids on close-order drills. I think I saw the kids with rifles on their shoulders once around graduation time. We never were allowed in the Bandroom unless we were going to, or from, the washroom; to, or from, the refectory; or it was raining outside. Sometimes when the weather was nasty, they would let us in, and we skated in the Bandroom. Smooth as glass. What a difference! The only other time we were allowed in was when our "friends" came to visit on Sundays and there was bad weather outside.

We never had formal hobbies while I was there. I did make scrapbooks of the boxers. I don't remember where I got the newspapers from, or the gum to paste the clippings in the book, but I had a sizable collection.

We wrote with pen nibs, which had to be replaced regularly. When I first saw a fountain pen, I was truly amazed. They had little bladders in them that contained ink. I got one that someone threw away and I took it apart. It was so simple. I started collecting fountain pens and mechanical pencils and, replacing defective parts, made new ones out of them. I kept them in a box about the size of a checkbook box. To me, that was good. I could interchange parts with different components and pen makers, and repair mechanical pencils. It was interesting to me, and I could take my time and figure things out at my leisure. No supervision was needed because the interest was there.

Most of us fixed old, worn-out, thrown-away skates. We'd bargain, trade, or steal skates or skate parts because it was one of the fun things we could do in the yard. We used to gamble for the skate washers. (If you didn't have skate washers, you couldn't skate because the skate wheel would rub against the body, so you put the washer on the skate after you put the wheel on the axel). Skate keys were a premium piece of property to be guarded most jealously. Most times, we had one skate. We'd make a run from the front gate, sit down on the leg with the skate, go past the fountain near the hud (latrine), down past the gate to the refectory, and around the basketball pole. That was a neat ride. It took only about thirty seconds to complete it, and it was a lot of fun.

We all had to learn a trade. I remember typesetting, printing press, and carpentry. I was good at typesetting and the printing press. I can't remember who the instructor for printing was. One of our projects was to set type with famous sayings, print them, and bind them in a book like a graduation autograph book. I remember the saying I had to set type to: "Strike while the iron's hot, don't make it hot by striking," by Beethoven.

In the carpentry shop I think the instructor was a man named Joe. I remember he was short in stature and very mild mannered. He made a bookshelf, which I helped with, and I took it to the sixth grade. I couldn't saw a straight line then and I can't now. Nothing's changed.

In the winter I made candy water. Every Christmas we all lined up to get a box of hard tack candy the size of an animal cracker box from Santa Claus. I'd put the hard tack into a jar, fill it with water, and keep shaking it until it was all melted. Sometimes I'd find a safe place in the snow and save it for a day when I wanted something sweet. We'd also get a new pair of long, black stockings. I think that was the only new piece of clothing we ever got while I was up there. Times were hard then. We never got or expected presents, and we were never disappointed when we didn't receive any. Anything we did get was a plus. I remember one time someone sent us a big apricot pie. I think someone said it was given by a quiz show.

Every year the eight grade—and I think the seventh, too— went on an outing. One year I went to Nyack to see Shirley Temple in The Blue Bird. I'm not sure what we did to rate a movie. I went to Bear Mountain twice. The first time I had no money at all and I visited the museum. There was nothing new or fancy about the place. It had a lot of rustic qualities about it, which is what probably kept me there in the first place. I thought that it was the greatest. Indian arrow-heads, old musket rifles, old clothes and bones. The second time I had seventy-eight cents, which took me all of about five minutes to spend. However, I remembered the trails to the museum and I enjoyed myself as if I had all the money in the world.

No one squealed on the mean people for fear of retribution. Once, they had a lot of us guys lined up with a pillow over one guy's head. When they hit him with an apple, the next guy took his place.

I never tried to join the Boy Scouts because I was told that they already selected guys to join. All the guys who joined were of light skin. I remember my buddy Mario Carione trying to sing the Boy Scout Hymn, but all he could manage was, "Be Prepared." Still we had it better than most kids in the city. As they say in the army, "We had three hots and a cot," and that's more than most city kids could claim.

The guys I hung around with called me "Black" or "Papoose" because of my color and stature. I'm of Puerto Rican descent and was a little darker than most Irish, German, Italians, and other kids of European descent. I can count on three fingers the kids that were as dark or darker than I. It was not until I was in the seventh or eight grade that we got two African Americans up there. They were very docile and never reacted to being bullied. They fought with each other a lot of the times.

I never took any guff from anyone. It didn't matter to me how big or rough they pretended to be. I guess I didn't realize how dumb and stupid I was then. However, the kids respected me. I was always in trouble or in a fight. I believe I had a fight with Paul Fabrizzi and a guy we called "Trench Ear" because he had a big hole in his ear and during swimming season he'd have to stick a piece of sponge from a sponge ball in it. John Romanchick was the only one who truly beat me in two fair fights. He was greased lightening. I really don't remember who won the fights, except for him, because after the fight we usually just went our merry way forgetting all about it.

There was one big Puerto Rican that just came from the city and thought he could boss me around. He must have been about five-feet-six. I beat him so bad he shook my hand after the fight and never bothered me again. I didn't give in to any Prefects or guys that tried to bully me. I'd just take their punishment and smile or grin afterwards just to make them madder. I was much smaller and guys who didn't know me thought they could pick on me. We all have to learn—some, the hard way.

Sometimes we were assigned to permanent duties. I was a jack-of-all-trades and master of none. I floated around—from delivering food off the steam tables to putting dishes in the racks for washing and stacking them after they were washed. I believe we all shared in the scrubbing of floors after meals. For a while, I made beds in the dorm; picked corn, potatoes, beans; stole gooseberrys; and worked in the refectory. A bunch of us guys also worked with Joe Vivi, the gardener. We'd go all over the property picking up whatever didn't grow. When finished, he selected a few of us to go down to his basement where he kept his tools and bags of sweet apples. He had the sweetest smelling place in the Home, plus he gave us an apple for doing good work, and sometimes a penny or nickel. Now that was a big deal.

Whenever we played football, we chose sides. Tom Maloney decided to play one day. I believe he played fullback. Of course I played on the opposite team. He got the ball a couple of times and made some good gains. I made up my mind and decided that the next time I was going after him. He got the ball and started running, and I tackled him and broke my back tooth. He gave me a pat and said, "Good boy." Tom was good and fair in all things. At least he never beat me for anything. Now Walt Kelly was a pretty fast and hard puncher, but he was a good guy, too. He never hit you unless you deserved it.

No one I knew ever had a radio, except the Prefects. I think it was because we didn't have the money. I remember listening to some of the Joe Louis fights outside the closed door of the Prefect's room. A few of us would huddle around the door and not make any sound for fear they'd catch us. Sometimes in the evening before we lined up to go to the dorm for bed, a lot of us kids would crowd around the main doorway window to the Bandroom, and they would put on Gang Busters, The FBI in Peace and War, and several other programs.

The Good Humor ice cream truck came around every summer and parked between the second gate and the refectory. If you had a nickel or a dime, you were rich. Most of us weren't. Of course, the ice cream man had the company of one or two of the Prefects.

Before I left the Home, I wanted to see the graves of Davies and Roy Bjork. They were the only ones that I know who died while I was up there. They say Roy died because he ate too many green apples. I never believed that, but you know as a kid you are impressionable and believe many things, whether true or not. I never got to see their graves before I left.

I learned to play the harmonica by myself. I'd listen to a tune and try to match notes to it. A lot of the kids had a natural talent for tunes and songs; they sounded like they were taught. I think the older guys had chromatics. They knew when to change scales for flats and sharps. I was in a musical in 1940 and played the harmonica. I was like spontaneous combustion. Big Sweeney was assigned to restrain me when I wanted to burst into flames. John Campbell had a high soprano voice. He was more or less the designated singer because of his high, clear voice. He was thin and tall. I remember a play the girls gave; it's when I first noticed a girl. Her name was Anna Sabelica and she sang the umbrella song.

There wasn't too much to do up in the Home after we ate supper. Sometimes we'd sneak off to the junkyard or go into the woods where we built small sheds and just hung around. Sometimes we went into Nanuet to the Grand Union or the A&P to buy candy, or sometimes we'd go to Nyack and sneak into the movies. One time Kotchy and the ushers came after us and searched every row for us. Some of the guys were caught there; some of us were caught when we got back to the Home. Many things we did were small inconsequential spur-of-the-moment things. We'd pick wild berries, strawberries, and cherries. In the autumn, we picked apples and knocked down nuts from our favorite trees. We raided the different farms around for various vegetables to eat raw. Another of my thrills was going into the second woods where the railroad tracks went past, and we'd walk the track and wait for the train to come by. These small, kid-like things meant freedom and relaxation while we were out. We liked not having to look at the barbed-wire restrictive fences in the yard and the field.

I remember the hurricane of 1935, though I think I slept right through it. It knocked a big oak tree down from in front of the dorm. In the winter when we had a big snowfall, I remember getting a shovel and throwing the ice and snow over the fence. The reason we shoveled was to clear space for playing games, skate hockey, or having snowball fights. It was wearisome but fun because I wanted to do it. No one forced us.

I don't think many of us were interested in scenery those days. However, I do remember the long flowerpots at the entrance to the driveway of the Administration building. I used to pick those flowers—petunias, I think—and suck the sweetness out of them. When I was last there in 2002, they were still there.

The road that passed the red barn and old farmer Flynn's house also passed the chicken coops and had high fencing. One time, a few of us went to the chicken coop, and while I climbed the fence to get a chicken, they were on the lookout. We took the chicken to the woods, killed it, and put it head first—still with feathers on it—into an old coffee pot we found. Poor chicken. After trying to taste the rubbery meat, we finally buried it in an honored ceremony. Never again did I do such a foolhardy stunt.

Once past the coops, we had to open the gate to the cow pasture. A long, looping right turn, then over a small bridge, and the brook where we went swimming every summer came into view. The brook was especially good when we got through with a sweaty job. When I got tired of swimming, I looked for water moccasins and copperhead snakes along the stream banks.

Near the fence by the outhouse there were berries that looked good to me. Being curious and young, I tried them once, but never again. They were hot as anything I ever tasted in my life and I don't think they were ripe yet. They were a bright, shiny green. No one else was as naïve.

One Prefect was McCutcheon who we called Kotchy. He had a stranglehold on shoes. I never got a new pair of shoes while I was up there, and the second-hand replacements I got were always too big for me. I had to wrap my long, black stockings under my toes to get them to halfway fit. Better still if I could get some cardboard and paper to put between my feet and the bottom of the shoe, and also inside the front end of the shoe toe—that would be all the better. Our shoes had to be worn to the nub to get a replacement: a repaired pair of shoes. When Kotchy got mad at you, he'd put his two big knuckles into your ears, lift you up, twist his knuckles, and say, "I'll dickle (tickle) yer ears."

Mr. Callahan, another Prefect, used to beat me with a broomstick. I don't know what got him so mad at me. I remember in the winter months he'd be at the gate going to the refectory, exercising his boxing abilities with us. When we'd get in a good punch, he'd hit a little harder and say "Epp, you dopey Spick, I'll knock your block off!" My

Pop used to call me "Dopey Sing," now I'm a Spick. What's a Spick, anyhow? One time I got him so mad at me that he grabbed me by the arm and took me up to the track in the field and made me run around it for a long time. Every time I got to where he was standing, he'd chase me with that long broomstick and whale away at me

I remember an old, gray-headed Prefect, but can't remember his name. Everyone said he had stocks. From the looks of him, he constantly worried about his stocks. If he lost in the market that day, it was woe to whoever got on his bad side. That was the impression we kids had of him. To me, he was one of the worst prefects. He remembered me most of all after I was in my PJ's, in bed, and the lights were out in the dorm. If he thought I screwed up during the day, he'd send for me, have me hold my hands out wide from my body, and beat them with a broomstick. And when that got too heavy for him, he'd change to a switch he'd cut from a tree branch and continue. Sometimes for a change of scenery he'd make me take down my PJ's, and make me look out over the hill. Guess it was a different view for him. I never cried or showed any emotion; I think that's what made him madder. He actually turned bright red several times, and with that salt pepper hair I laughed at him in my mind. He was a mean one.

There were many things wrong with the way things were run up in the Home. I guess they didn't have the money to put changes in place or to hire the right accredited professional people for the right job. They did the best they could the old way. No love or compassion. Only beatings to make and break your will for any discrepancy, no matter how minor.

Being up in the Home was one of the better things that happened to me, regardless of the beatings or the mental and physical cruelty. I hold no grudge towards the Home or the Prefects and bullies who administered them. I think that I am a better man for having suffered through the degrading indignities that existed at that period of time. It made me understand that power is good if used wisely, but it's not everything. It strengthened my will and resolve to look ahead for an enlightened future.

These writings are not intended to belittle, criticize, or fault anyone. These are memories that are fading fast, and cherished as a reminder to do unto others as you would have them do unto you. One thing that I lost forever was trust. I never trusted anyone completely. Also, I never could understand love between normal brothers and sisters, or parents and children. I know I loved my parents, brothers, and sister. We never told each other that, not until recently. It was understood, but I don't know how that love should feel.

Fifteen

The Depression and War Years

John Amlaw lived at St. Agatha from 1939 to 1947. His son tells what he knows of his father's memories.

Dad's memories of St. Agatha were among the few really happy ones he had from his childhood. He always spoke of the Sisters to his own children as having been very kindly, and would brook no insult to the Catholic Church, though he was himself a "lapsed" Catholic. Dad had two pictures of himself as a boy at the Home. One as a child of perhaps four, standing rather forlornly in front of a flagpole outside a gray building on a bleak winter's day, bundled up in his ill-fitting, cast-off coat. At least his years inside that gray building were relatively happy ones in his memory. In another photo of him, at roughly ten or eleven, he looks much happier, standing on a porch, looking as if he had been called away from play to pose for the photo.

Dad had a sister named Marion Amlaw. One of his earliest memories was of some boy at St. Agatha's telling him that there was a Mary Amlaw in the girl's section. He wasn't surprised at this; he was aware that there was such a girl. In later life, he could not recall why he felt that he seemed to know her. He had no visits with her, and the

Home had no record of any Marion or Mary Amlaw, which seemed odd. Dad always wanted to find her, sincerely tried, but had no luck.

He never knew what happened to her. She could have died young, met a tragic fate, or may have lived a long and full life—who knows? Women change their names, which makes it so difficult to trace them. Perhaps she was adopted shortly after they arrived, which is why they did not get together for Sunday visiting.

During Dad's time at St. Agatha, from age four in 1939 after he was transferred from the Foundling Hospital until he was twelve, times were especially tough. But he remembers that at Christmas, the Sisters brought the kids into their classrooms, and there was a gift for each child on each desk. After they were opened, it was understood that all the toys were to be community property.

Dad also recalled—and was influenced for life—by being exposed to music for the first time. The sisters brought all the children to a performance of Handel's Messiah at the old New York Metropolitan Opera one season. Dad was in awe of that for the rest of his life. He had never heard or seen such a beautiful spectacle.

He remembered two caretakers at the Home—probably Tom Maloney and Walter Kelly—who were drafted during the war and returned afterwards. The children were all brought out to sing a piece that the Sisters had taught them: "Hail the Conquering Hero Comes" by George Frederick Handel. He knew as a boy that if he had a son one day, he would name him for the man who wrote the music that so impressed him back then. This is why he named me George Frederick Amlaw.

Dad was always a kindhearted man. He believed that it was his years spent in the care of the Sisters at St. Agatha that were largely responsible for instilling in him a sense of the goodness in the world, something that an orphaned child in the Great Depression easily could have missed. They also gave him the gift of beautiful handwriting.

From St. Agatha, Dad went into the government-run foster care system, which didn't produce many happy memories. His mother was a mentally disabled woman in the care of the Catholic Church, and the nuns occasionally brought him to see her. He described a big, white room, and his mother sat in a rocking chair. She would hold him and ask him if he wanted to come home with her. He grew very sad as he told this story and said, "Of course, that was not to be." He never saw her again after he entered the government system. Apparently they felt this was best.

Dad did have some family. His mother's father, Bertram, signed the papers that put John into St. Agatha Home, and Bertram apparently kept them informed about his current address, employment, and income. Perhaps the Church considered the family to have financial responsibility.

After John died, his son located John's mother. I knew the name of my father's mother, and the name of the "alleged" father from the papers sent to my father by St. Agatha. I actually met his mother twice before she died. She didn't volunteer any information, and it seemed wrong to ask her since her health was so bad. The first thing she asked me was, "Where's Johnny?" and the second was, "Where's Marion?"

We heard no word on any father for Marion—only that she was born in 1928, according to St. Agatha's records. There was a reference to the data from an "Abstract of an Investigators Report" made by the New York City child welfare bureau. Further inquiries to them were forwarded to their legal office where they seem to have died.

§

By 1933, the devastating effects of the Depression drove the population at St. Agatha to an all time high of eight hundred eleven children. One of them was Marjorie Prescott. These memories are her impressions and scenes from the past.

I came to St. Agatha when I was three years old, and my sister was two. Our father was a singer on the radio in Chicago at the time. He made several albums for our dances, which the Sisters kept.

I had a hernia and had to wear a truss until I was eight, then I was sent to Bellevue Hospital for surgery. After that, I spent what seemed like months in the infirmary. Miss Gordon took care of me after the operation.

The bakery truck driver always gave me a coffee bun before he brought them into the infirmary. What a treat! When we were older, the infirmary was not even mentioned if we were sick because the nuns thought we just wanted to see the boys next door. If we got sick, we just lived with it.

At first, we lived in the cottage across the street, just a short distance from the main building. That's where all the little ones lived. I think Sister Sylvia ran it. A brook ran behind the cottage. There

Sacred Heart

never was anything to play with, and I can remember just roaming around the yard.

I was three, and on the first floor in a crib. I remember climbing out of it and someone asked, "Where are you going?" I probably was going to the bathroom or sleepwalking, which I did very often, even after I was married. Later on, I slept on the second floor, where I had nightmares. I went outside in the morning and just sat on the fire escape because there was nothing to do out there.

When I was four and five I played in the round gazebo near the apple orchards in the summertime. A group of disabled children would come around and sing songs for us. I sang these same songs to my children. One song was:

Jackie boy! (Master!) Sing ye well! (Very well!)
Hey down (Ho down) Derry derry down
Among the leaves so green, O.

My sister Joan worked with the little ones in the cottage when she got older. This was quite a privilege because it took you away from the Main House. Otherwise, it was off limits. There was no reason for us to go back to that cottage once we moved out. We were not allowed to roam about outside. When my sister got older and married, she was saving all her money to buy that house. It was her dream.

I was about six when we moved to the big house. I remember sawdust all over the playroom floor. We ate everything with a spoon; no forks or knives or napkins in those days. Once, I remember watching all the buses moving out on their way to the 1939 Worlds Fair. I wondered why I was not going.

Visiting day at St. Agatha

We slept in the two dorms that were above the girls' school, where the roof slanted down in the attics. I used to sleepwalk at night, and the girls thought there were ghosts until they found out it was me. Mrs. Klein had a small room in one dorm. One night I went to the window, which was right outside her room. Thank God she heard me because I was ready to lie down in the open window which I thought was my bed. No screen was on the window and she grabbed me just in time. She took me back to my bed and talked to me for a while. She was very nice. Another time, one of the nuns saw me walking down the stairs that led to the schoolrooms, and she grabbed me by the ear. I did not remember it, but she told me about it the next day and said I better not do it again.

I remember them paving the road, and when we came home from the movies in Spring Valley, we were all playing with the hot tar on the road. We had tar all over us.

The dorm for first-graders was off the main playroom, connected to the girls school. The monitor told us we were not allowed to get up in the middle of the night to go to the bathroom without permission. I stood by her bed one night with my hand raised, jiggling all over the place until I could not hold it any longer. Needless to say, the next morning, she wanted to know who wet the floor. I did not own up to it because I would have gotten a beating.

On visiting day, we had to line up and go to the dorms. My sister Joan and I did not get visitors very often, so we got certain privileges that the other girls did not. I worked in the Sisters' dining room and got to eat their leftover rolls, which was heaven to us. Joan worked in the Prefects' dining room.

The girls who did have visitors received all kinds of goodies. I remember one girl got a whole chicken. I don't ever remember having chicken for dinner at St. Agatha. One girl got a big chocolate cake from her parents on visiting day and put it in her locker for safekeeping. My sister had her eye on that cake. The girls lined up to go to the dorm, and Joan hung back at the end of the line. When she was alone, she made a mad dash for that locker, threw it open, stuck her hand in, and grabbed a great big chunk out of the cake. She was terrified that she would get caught, but she shoved the whole piece of cake in her mouth and nearly choked on it. Of course, the sight of my sister Joan stuffing her mouth and choking on that big piece of cake will always be one of my more memorable moments at St. Agatha.

The next day, the owner of the cake went to her locker and became furious. She wanted to know who took the big chunk out of the cake. They investigated, but never found out my sister was the one that raided the locker. Usually on Sundays we received a large cookie for dessert. So, if you had visitors that day and came back with special treats, everyone begged you for your cookie. Since my sister and I did not receive visitors, we were among the girls who begged the more fortunate girls for their

Joan Prescott: who took the big chunk out of the cake?

cookies. , I believe we enjoyed eating our begged-for cookies more than they enjoyed their special treats from their visitors.

I remember the water tower by the girl's dorm

I remember Sister Basil very well. We all had spreads on our beds with a big peacock which she taught us how to embroider. I learned to crochet from her, and have made many beautiful afghans for my family. Once, we put on a Christmas play, and Sister said I was terrific, that I should be an actress. There she was again, boosting me up. We even got to use forks and knives with her. She taught us how to tell time, which we did not learn until we were ten or eleven years old. She knew how to handle children, and we felt that she really cared for us. I never forgot her. I have an obituary from a New York newspaper for Sister Basil. Nobody deserves Honorable Mention more than Sister Basil. In part, from the Eulogy and Obituary for Sister Basil:

"What she would consider the perfect ending for a religious life began at St. Patrick's on Mott Street and ended 89 years later, doing what she loved best of all: teaching children."

I remember the water tower by the girls' dorm. We played baseball in front of it. The story went that a kid climbed up to the top, fell off, and got killed. But it could have been just a story to keep us from climbing, which I did once anyway.

When we were little and had head lice, they put kerosene in our hair to kill them. I think they stopped that when I got older. Then, I was in charge of picking nits out of the younger girls' hair.

As I look back, my bad memories are not from abuse by the nuns. Most of the terrible things that happened to us came from the older girls who were monitors. We got some really rough treatment from them. We would get beaten on the knuckles with a wooden brush for no reason, and we were such little kids. I'm surprised they didn't break. In all my years up there, only one abusive nun comes to mind.

When we went to high school we moved to the house closer to the main road. The dining room even had an ice cream parlor on Sundays—for the visitors. One night we were making a lot of noise in the dorm and Sister was so angry she marched us all out to the nearby barn in our pajamas and threatened to lock us up in it for the night. Instead, she slapped us all in the face and sent us back to the dorm. I have to laugh when I think of it now.

One person I remember well was Father Kelly. He came to St. Agatha in the 1940's—a young priest who would make a big change in the way we attended Mass on Sunday. Forming lines was a way of life back then to keep order and prevent chaos, as there were hundreds of kids to look after. Father Kelly thought differently when it came to the church. He considered that he was head of this church and wanted this church to operate like others on the outside.

One Sunday he stood up in front of us and said, "When you come up for Communion I do not want you to come to the altar row by row and in line. I want you to come out of the pews when you are ready to come." He showed us how he wanted it done. I looked at the nuns' faces and they were in shock. The next Sunday we were told by the nuns to proceed to the altar the same way we had always done. When we started to leave the pews row by row and in line, Father Kelly stopped the Mass and became so furious he was red in the face. This was his church, and it was going to be run the way he said. From then on, we went to the altar the way he wanted. I felt like we had gained a little bit of freedom and felt less institutionalized beginning that day.

And we did not have to go to Confession all the time. Living under such strict rules, what could we possible do wrong? Many times I would make up a sin like, "I stole a pencil," simply because I had no sins to confess. Father Kelly was a big Irishman and very good-looking. We always hoped he would be the one saying Mass that Sunday. Just by these little changes he made in the church, he brought some of the outside world into my life where people were free, and someday I would know that freedom. I still think of Father Kelly and how I felt that day, and I still get the same feeling I had then. He showed me that there was a light at the end of the tunnel.

After the eighth grade, I went to high school in Pearl River for one year. Later, some kids went to Spring Valley High, which must have started after I left. I loved it, but it was a little scary because we felt embarrassed that we were from a Home. Everyone thought we were bad kids. They did not know we were from broken families. I later heard that many things changed after I left.

While having lunch one day, I was one of the monitors taking the girls to the movie theatre in Nanuet. For some reason, Sister Josita kept giving me the evil eye and I couldn't understand why. I later found out that she wanted us to hurry along with our lunch because she had something to do. Everyone else was allowed to leave the table, except Mary Donnelly and me. When they all went to the movie, Mary and I were left behind, but given no reason.

We lived on the hill by then, so we hid in one of the buildings and peek out to see where the nuns were. Finally Mary said, "I am going down to the main building to see what is going on and why we were punished."

Mary happened to meet Sister Superior, who wanted to know why Mary was not at the movie. Mary told her she did not know why, and that we were being punished for no reason. Sister Josita was from Brooklyn, as most of the nuns were, and used to say "erle" for oil and "terlet" for toilet. The next day, Sister Josita called us into the room and tried to explain why we were being punished. She asked us, "T

Sister Josita was from Brooklyn, as most of the nuns were

you get my pernt?" Well, Mary and I cracked up and could not stop laughing. Then she said, "Alright, laugh, just as long as you get my pernt." And we laughed all the harder, practically rolling on the floor.

When I left the Home I found out my real last name was not Prescott but La Pointe. My mother and father were both born in Canada. Richard Prescott was my stepfather, and he was the one who put us in the Home. When I wrote to St. Agatha for my admittance records, Sister Veronica was kind enough to send them along with a dozen letters my father had written to the Superior, inquiring about us. It included all the records about when I had visitors, which was not that often in fourteen years.

In the 1980's, I heard that Sister Carmita was now Sister Mary Sheridan and working in the Bronx. I sent her a big box of homemade chocolates and assorted cheeses for Christmas. She was so surprised and delighted, and she even remembered me. In the late 80's I was also in touch with Sister Basil who also remembered me, even though she was getting forgetful. She lived in New York City, still teaching right up to the end.

ॐ

At the beginning of World War II, the Depression began to subside and many people went back to work, fulfilling the needs of the war machine. Finally, people began to have a little money, food, clothes, shelter—even niceties—and above all, jobs. But the atmosphere continued to be one of anxiety as the terror that had gripped the nation for ten years had been joined by its evil twin: the monster Hitler and his troops. Nearly all the men went off to war. The women left their homes and took over the men's jobs. Children stayed by themselves, then ended up in Homes like St. Agatha. Telegrams arrived daily with the news that the head of a family wasn't coming home. It took until the war ended in 1945 before some kind of normal life really began again in America.

As Americans all over the country did, everyone at St. Agatha carried on as best they could—coping with their own losses and disappointments.

From 1935 to 1939, Adminstrator Sister Mary Prudentia Flynn focused on renovating the living units. This was no small feat, given the hundreds of children that contributed to the daily wear and tear on the buildings. But the hope of the cottage plan still lingered.

In October 1936, the younger boys' dormitory, above the laundry, was converted from a dormitory into smaller bedrooms. New beds, installed for the twenty-nine children, came with restuffed mattresses and pillows. Shower rooms went in and an attractive dining room set up. A year later, the second grade dorm was remodeled into a home unit with four beds to a room, a living room, playroom, shower and washrooms, kitchenette, and a bedroom for the Group Mother. New beds and bed-side chairs were purchased for the thirty-two children, and their mattresses remade.

Sister Raymond's prayers for a likeminded companion at St. Agatha, with radical ideas and the energy to implement them, seemed to be answered when Sister Leo arrived around 1948. She recalled those days for me.

I admired this young Sister's dedication; she was conservative and very holy, but excellent with the children. She seemed perfect, and was a strong role model for me. We became great friends. But it was when Sister Marion Cecelia Schneider arrived that I found the ally who would energetically help effect progressive changes. We became dear friends for life. Sister Cecilia came to St. Agatha as Director of Social Services from the New York Foundling Hospital. There she had been in charge of the adoption department, and later, Administrative Assistant. Sister Cecilia became Superior and Superintendent of St. Agatha, a few months after her arrival in 1955, a post she held until 1964. She was so progressive and open to new ideas; together we forged many changes.

After twenty years at St. Agatha, in 1957 I was sent to Blessed Sacrament Convent in Long Island where I taught school. I was shocked to find the atmosphere for the nuns to be so restrictive. For instance, I once answered the phone and found it was my brother calling, so I chatted on happily. Later, I was admonished for receiving a call without permission.

When I hopped on a bike and rode around the grounds, the Mother Superior was horrified. When I said I was going for a walk, the Superior thought I meant to the end of the block, but my idea of a walk was five miles. Rather than them changing me, I managed to change the notions of the Mother Superior as I'd done at St. Agatha.

I was not accustomed to being treated as a novitiate who needed to be told every step to take. At St. Agatha, the nuns were expected to be resourceful from their first day. When Sister Bernadette Marie came to teach eighth grade, we became great friends. We both believed in being tough, strict teachers to get the most out of the kids. I remember once, when two boys were fighting, I asked them what it was over. They said it was about who had the toughest teacher, Sister Bernadette or Sister Raymond. To my surprise, they were boasting of it as if comparing battle wounds.

Some of those kids were pretty tough. You took your life in your hands. Once, a boy threw a book at me, but I was quick enough to duck. Another time, I yelled at one of the boys for something he'd done, and he said, "Sister, you better stop yelling at me; I have a temptation." I stopped mid-sentence and asked him what he meant by that. "I have a temptation to punch you," he replied. I thought it was so funny that I responded, "I have the same temptation," and the battle ended. I couldn't help laughing about the serious way he had said it. That was the way things went, but I was never afraid of the kids.

Changes at the Home continued, despite the shortages of manpower, money, and material. These can be found in an excerpt from an anonymous report to file, entitled simply, "Saint Agatha Home for Children." Within the text, the year 1943 is noted as current. It's always interesting to note the vastly different account of the way of life at St. Agatha, depending on whether it is being described by the people who plan and inspect, and the children who actually experience it.

The numbers of children needing care continually increased throughout the war years. The Progressive Movement, popular among the Charities, had as one of its primary goals to eliminate orphanages and Homes for Children. They sought the financial means and counseling for families to keep children at home. Foster homes could provide temporary care while families got back on their feet. This marks the birth of today's welfare system. Olga DeBlas, has very distinct memories of those years.

Mr. Sweeney with Tom Maloney and boys

I lived at St. Agatha from the time I was six or seven in 1939, until 1946. I brought with me to St. Agatha pictures of my family, but they were taken from me when I arrived, and I never saw them again.

I remember the Home as being very abusive. A couple of the Sisters would bop you on the head, rap you with the floor cleaning brush, and even lock you in a closet if you were bad. They'd leave you there for hours. Especially, if a girl ran away, then they cut her hair close to the scalp as a sign to anyone else who had that idea. Right behind our dorm was the water tower, and some of the kids would climb on it for a dare. That received strict punishment, too. But many of the Sisters were very kind, too.

Olga's girlfriend Mercedes recalls coming to St. Agatha in 1936.

I lived at the Home until about 1941 when I was in fifth grade. I came from Puerto Rico when I was five or six. My father had left my mother and stayed in Puerto Rico. He was her second husband, who fathered three children with her and was not very nice. Her first husband was killed in a car accident, and she had four boys and a girl by him, but the girl died when she was eight. Mom was pregnant and already had eight kids, and she became very sick, so we came to New York City to live with an aunt.

My mother had the baby at the New York Foundling Hospital, and she died there. The baby went to live with my aunt, but the rest of us went to live at St. Agatha. I didn't know my mother died until I was about ten. I just kept asking when she was coming for me.

When we came to St. Agatha in April, we had very bad measles. We went right into Quarantine for a few weeks, and couldn't walk afterwards. Since we couldn't speak English, I whispered the prayers we said on our knees at night so that Sister would not know that I couldn't speak English, and therefore punish me. I knew kids were slapped for speaking Spanish. I was left back because I did not understand English, but by the end of the summer, I could speak it well enough for school.

I was too young to go to Midnight Mass when we arrived, which I always wanted to do. When the New York World's Fair came around in 1939, all the other kids went, but I was too young for that, too. Whenever I went to Mass on Sunday, I felt like I was very close to heaven because the chapel was upstairs in the Main building.

Christmas 1941, Santa came with a present for each child for the first time. We wrote a letter and asked for whatever we wanted, as long as it was not a bike. In the years before, we got ribbon candy, but no presents. Santa distributed the toys personally, but I saw that it was really Mr. McCutcheon. I got skates and rode them round and round the yard, which seemed very big back then. I was always very active. When I returned to St. Agatha as an adult for a reunion, I was surprised at how small everything was. I saw Sister Joseph at one of the reunions, who I remembered as very tall, but was surprised to find that she was very small, less than five feet.

I left St. Agatha right after the bombing of Pearl Harbor, which I clearly remember. One of my brothers was already thrown out of St. Agatha for being so bad. All of us kids went to live with my aunt and grandmother. My grandmother was kindly, and tried to protect us from our aunt who was physically abusive, maybe because she never had any children of her own. She took in me and my two brothers. I had to learn to speak Spanish all over again because that's all my relatives spoke.

I was very mouthy, which contributed to my troubles, especially when my older sister was getting beaten. She was very timid and frightened, so I would attempt to draw some of the fire to myself. My aunt took me out of school so I could work and contribute some income to the family. I wish, in retrospect, I had stayed at St. Agatha. I do not remember that kind of abuse there.

Sixteen

Eugene's Story

Eugene Malito and his family first went to the Preventorium. Their Italian-born parents produced half a dozen dark-haired, olive-skinned children. The two oldest were tall, and the two youngest were short, but all were too skinny.

One spring in 1940, when I was four, my siblings and I were accompanied to the Preventorium at St. Agatha Home by a social worker named Miss Foy. My mother was gravely ill, and we stayed there for the summer. My brother Jimmy was seven, and my sisters Anna Marie and Joan were eight and three. There were four other children left at home.

The Prefect that attended to us children in the Preventorium was very severe. The cruel treatment I received there was an indication of the years to come. He warned me on the very first day, "You'd better sleep during nap time and not wet the bed, or I'll lock you in the basement with the rats." I was so frightened I couldn't sleep, and I did wet the bed, though normally I didn't. The Prefect made a spectacle of me to the other boys. He pushed me into the darkened storm cellar, which was filled with rows of shoeboxes. A crack between the two heavy doors that opened to the outside let a sliver of light shine through.

I was so terrified of the rats that when the boys finally came to get me, I could not walk out on my own, but had to be hauled out. That kind of bullying and terror seemed to lurk in the wings wherever I went. The Sister in charge was not a bully, but she was not a happy person, either. She seemed always sour, and I wondered why she became a nun if she did not like children. It seems I was always frightened.

I remember when my parents came to visit us one Sunday. We strolled a short way, along the path, past a field where we found an apple tree. She had to duck under its lower branches, but she caught her hair on one. Every time I looked at that apple tree after that, I thought of her adjusting her hair.

At the end of the summer, we went back home to the Bronx, but our mother continued to be seriously ill, so the Society for the Prevention of Cruelty to Children sent us to a shelter called St. Joseph's by the Sea, also run by the Sisters of Charity. There, I received equally cruel treatment. I received frequent whippings from the matrons, for reasons I did not understand.

For instance, one night the matron put me into a tub with a washcloth and told me to take a bath. I had never bathed myself before and didn't know what to do. When she came back, I was still sitting there. She dragged me out by the arm and whipped me with the washcloth. I was just four and scared to death.

One day, my father, Salvatore John Malito, came to see us. He was a short, stocky man with black wavy hair and brown eyes—a stern, opinionated man. He had emigrated from Italy with his family as a boy. I stood beside one of my father's knees, and Jimmy by the other. He told us, "Your mother died; she's never coming back." Jimmy cried worse than I did, worse than I ever saw anyone cry. He must have cried himself out because I never saw him cry again.

We remained at a shelter for a while. One day, I stood peering through the cage on the window, looking down at the Grand Concourse in the Bronx. I saw the green metal staircase that led to the underground train station, across the street near 167th Street. A woman was walking towards the staircase, to go down to the train. She had on a red coat with a fur collar, and a hat, like my mother wore. I began to call to her, "Mama! Mama!" until the attendant came and pried me away from the window. I got a whipping for that, too.

We always had head lice, and were forever scratching our heads. We absentmindedly fished out the lice and crushed them between our nails when we had nothing else to do. I could see the girls in the yard next door, standing at arms' length apart, while they had their hair combed out. They applied kerosene to our scalps to kill the eggs, but it stung so bad, we'd sneak off and wash it out first chance we got.

My brother Jimmy warned me early on that he could not fight my battles for me; told me I must learn to fight my own. And so I did.

I saw my brother and sisters on the first Sunday of each month, when siblings were allowed to assemble in the girls' yard for a visit. On one of these visits, my sister Joan said,

Anna Marie, Eugene, Joan, and James Malito

"Don't go too close to the fence; it isn't allowed." When I asked why not, she explained, "A man came there, exposed himself to the girls, and tried to grab them. So now, no one is allowed by the fence."

I told her, "You should have been a boy, then you could beat him up." I said that I would beat up anyone who hurt her, since I had learned to fight.

One Sunday when I was in first grade and gazing around, I noticed there were swastikas amongst the gold trim around the arches, between the tall columns in the chapel. When World War II was in full swing, we boys developed the theory that the Pope was in

I noticed there were swastikas in the gold trim around the arches

a pact with the Germans so that, if they invaded America, the Nazis would see the iron crosses in our chapel and know that we were on their side. We would be safe. In later years, when the chapel was renovated, those symbols were removed.

My father continued to visit us on Sundays, and part of our family was reunited, briefly. We would play on the slide, parallel bars, seesaw and swings in the big boys' yard. At first, there was a see-saw and sand pit, at the bottom of the boys' yard, too.

My father did not have a lot to say, but we kids eagerly chatted away and caught up with each other. Jimmy would tell stories. He told us once about a boy in his group, Eugene Rodriquez, put a cat in a milkcan—supposedly to feed it some milk—and put the lid on. It died. This made a big impression on me. He also told us about a girl named Mercedes who liked him and thought they would get married one day.

But when people left St. Agatha, even if they lived in a nearby neighborhood back in the city, the friendships changed. Everyone went separate ways. Maybe they wanted to forget the past, or maybe they became more involved with their own survival—like where their food, shelter, and clothing were going to come from.

Sister Leo, one of the nuns who was particularly kind, used to give us crackers to nibble at recess. We kids could go to Mass any day of the week if we wanted to, so when I was late showing up for breakfast one Wednesday, Sister Leo wanted to know why. When I told her I was at Mass, she was so pleased she said, "I'm so happy that I will see you in heaven."

We never received a hug, kiss, or a pat of any kind. We had to be content with the occasional praises of Sisters, like Sister Anna Rosaire. She was so loving and energetic that it came as a great surprise to all of us when, in June of 1942, she died suddenly. She was buried up in the graveyard.

Another Sister who was very kind was Sister Michael. She knew my mother, somehow, and I remember seeing them walk together, chatting up the path to the Preventorium, so I always associated her with my mother. She tried to help me through all the trauma by tutoring me with my spelling, but my mind was frozen in grief. I did not feel that I could trust anyone anymore.

I think of my years at St. Agatha as highlighted by cold, hunger, and fear. Not because it was all bad, but because there were bad times and you never knew when they would happen.

Summerhouses sprung up all over the property in a variety of styles, typically crafted of wood on a fieldstone base. Their wooden floors, raised up off the damp ground, and some were open on all sides, or had porch rails, others had glass so that they could be used in winter. Inside, there were wooden benches around three walls. There were two such buildings, identical, next to the boy's school, covered in brown shingles. Spacious and airy, typically used by the smaller children in summertime. The one closest to the road had a roll down shade, perhaps for privacy.

These structures went up quickly by the maintenance staff, who did much of the construction, repairs, maintenance, and updates. They built and rebuilt outbuildings for the farm, swings, slides and see-saws, pedestals for the statues around the grounds, porches and even some of the furniture, such as the children's table and chair sets. Eugene and the other children spent a fair amount of time in these outdoor playrooms.

In the beginning, at night, I would tremble in my bed, lest an uninvited whipping be sprung on me. One monitor often put in charge of a bunch of us was a ferocious brute, and needed no excuse to punch someone senseless. One night, a boy in the next bed named Norman called out to me, "Hey, Malito, could you hold my hand?" Somehow, knowing someone else was just as terrified as I was made me slightly less afraid. When Norman's hand became heavy, I knew he was asleep, and I got up and tucked his arm under the cover. Then, I was able to roll over and go to sleep myself.

There were several bully Prefects. One, who was there briefly, hung my friend Langlois by his feet out the window to intimidate him. He also molested some boys, and I barely escaped that fate, so I knew it was true, firsthand. He slept near the bathroom, and one night I got up to go. As I began to return to my bed, he called to me to come into his room, demanding to know what I was doing out of bed. I stood in his doorway and let him berate me, but refused to enter the room because I had heard from my buddy who did go in that he was fondled. But, I think someone told, because that Prefect was gone soon after that.

I remember two brothers who were his victims, and it really changed them forever. They became as mean as the meanest Prefect and bullied the other kids. I always thought that fate was so much worse than the beatings, and therefore stayed clear of him, no matter what the consequences were. As I grew older, I used to plan a career where I would work in a Home for kids or a nursing home—anywhere that people were being bullied. I thought how I would beat up the bullies and get that person out of there so they couldn't hurt anyone anymore.

But there were two other former Home Kids who became Prefects, Mr. Kelly and Mr. Sweeney. Both were so kind that I knew I would be safe from the others when they were around. Once, Mr. Kelly came upon one of the monitors who had lined us up and was hitting us with a rubber hose. He made the monitor stand still while each boy had a turn at hitting him with the hose.

This had the effect of taming that monitor for the future. Maybe it was just in Mr. Kelly's nature, or perhaps he remembered the abusive treatment he received as a boy. He went out of his way to be kind to us. Not that he didn't switch us when we deserved it, but he gave us fair warning, told us the rules, did not intimidate us, or hit us for no reason, nor did he do it excessively.

Once, while we were on an outing, an older girl named Ingram was in charge of us. Without her noticing, I climbed into the pigpen to pet the baby pigs. The mother pig began chasing me, and I was scared to death. The girl had to jump in and save me by threatening the pig with a shovel. She was scared, too—scared of the pig, and scared that I would get killed, and she would therefore get in trouble. She kept hugging me, crying, and telling me never to do that again. I never forgot that.

We learned how to do most things for ourselves. We made our own toys: skates, bikes, newspaper kites, even sleds, out of whatever we could find lying around, or at the dump. In the woodworking shop, we made toys and gifts to give. In the electricity class, I once made a lamp for my father, which he prized for the rest of his life.

We rarely received toys, gifts, or treats—except at Christmas. At first, we only got a box of hard tack candy, and we were thrilled to have it. Then, one year, we were allowed to write a letter to the

Christmas Daddy, sponsored by the Telephone Company, and request a small present, like a bag of marbles.

I loved to swim at the brook. There were stairs leading down, and a concrete platform below. I was always scared to go away from the steps, until the day I made my First Holy Communion. That day, I felt that I was in God's hands and nothing could happen to me, no matter how far out I ventured. Or, if it did, I was going straight to heaven. I hadn't had time to sin since I just made my first confession to the Priest. I dove off the steps, only to find that the concrete extended out, and I split my lip. But that didn't stop me. Even though I couldn't swim, I went out to the deepest part, which turned out to still be shallow enough for me to stand, and the water came to just below my lips. Then I learned to swim.

My best friend was a black boy named Jerome Langlois, whose big brother was friends with my brother Jimmy. We had no color distinction between the whites, blacks, and Puerto Ricans. It simply didn't exist. It was always hard when our friends left, like De Luca and Mendino; I still remember them. Some left to rejoin their families, others went to foster homes, while I stayed behind. Jerome stayed as long as I did, and we remained best friends for years, until we returned to New York City and the bigotry that existed there put an end to that.

During the war, it was a particularly frightening time. In third grade, I remember crossing the compound during blackouts. The sirens would blare, and we had to drop to the ground and nestle close to the buildings. I would peer up into the starlit sky and watch for the bombers we were sure were coming.

In 1945, when the war was declared over and a victory for the U.S., it felt like electricity was in the air. We heard promises of a chicken in every pot and a car in every garage. Great celebrations happened everywhere; you could taste it, feel it. On the radio, in the streets—everyone was thrilled, except for me. At nine years old, I thought it was a trick. That, WWII would start up again just as

WWI had. I could not be convinced otherwise, and I felt that Korea
vindicated my fears. In all the years following, the air-raid-drill sirens
still frightened me—this time about the nuclear bomb.

Father Cooke did not allow mistreatment of us kids. My brother
Jimmy got a harmonica from him once, and I had several opportunities to speak with him. He spoke at my graduation from eighth grade.

Father Burke was our Chaplain next, and also kind. So I was surprised when I was older—waiting to make my ritual, bi-weekly confession—when Father Burke came rushing out of the confessional
after one of the boys, scolding him all the way up to the altar, to beg
God's forgiveness. I don't know what the boy told the Priest he'd
done, but after that, none of the boys ever committed any sins.

Word of this miracle got back to Sister Roberta, the sweet head
nun. When she learned what had happened, she arranged for the
older boys to go to the local Catholic church to say their confessions,
if they wanted to. Father Burke died in 1957 and is buried in St.
Agatha's cemetery.

When we got a TV, a Dumont that someone donated, we saw
President Eisenhower dismiss General George McArthur. I always
remembered that. We sometimes watched movies in the Bandroom.
One time—I think I was about eight—Mr. McCutcheon was smoking while showing a movie. The film started burning. Someone
yelled, "Fire in the projector booth!" and everyone panicked. I
jumped up on a windowsill so I wouldn't get crushed. Other kids
knocked down the locked door to escape. After that, the end portion
of the Bandroom closest to the Administration building had to be
rebuilt. The chimney was removed at that time.

Also when I was about eight, a big kid jumped on me, and we all
collapsed. When we got up, we laughed that someone's teeth got
knocked out. They were mine, smashed into the sidewalk. My
brother Jimmy lost his front teeth, too, when we poured hot water
onto the ground outside and let it freeze to slide on. He fell and

knocked his teeth right out. He crushed his thumb, too, and later—coincidentally—I crushed mine with a rock.

In the fields below the cemetery, I made a surprising discovery one day. I had snuck up to the graveyard and over a low wall to say good-bye to Sister Luca, who died on April 6, 1950, and was buried there. Sister Luca worked in the laundry, and I had helped her out there. When she died, she was laid out in the Administration building, in what later became the conference room. Then the body was moved to behind the altar, for prayers, I guess.

As I knelt by her grave talking to her, a man and woman came along and asked if I was a friend of hers. Scared, I replied that I was—that she was my friend, and that I loved her. It turned out that these were her relatives, there to pay their respects. The man retrieved a box of hard tack candy from his car and gave it to me. I was so relieved that not only would I not get in trouble for being there, but I got some candy! And I was free to return on my own to the dorm.

Relieved, I scrambled back over the wall where I had entered, and galloped through the tall rye grass, which covered the length of the hill, down to the girls' yard. As I ran, up from the grass all around me, sprung into the air, beautiful multi-colored pheasants. I had never seen them before, and they were magnificent. This became a new getaway for me, running through the rye fields with the pheasants.

When I returned to my dorm, one of the monitors named McFarland told Tom Maloney what I had done. Instead of the whipping he hoped I'd get, Tom told him to mind his own business. I guess Tom thought it was a good thing, my going up to say goodbye to Sister Luca.

In fall and winter, St. Agatha had a football team, which I played on. We traveled to other schools for games. Among the competition was St. Dominic's at Blauvelt, and St. Agnes in Sparkill. Before the games, the boys from each Home compared notes to see who had the best and worst living conditions. While at St. Dominic's, I was amazed to learn that on the edge of the property was a Prisoner of

War camp. After years of cowering in fear that the Germans were coming to get us, like so many boogeymen, I found that they actually were here. We made our way and talked to these real live German prisoners through the fence, and found them to be nice, young guys. We saw the connection between them and ourselves: prisoners.

This was Camp Shanks, also known as "Last Stop U.S.A.," the final stop for 1.3 million American soldiers on their way to France and England during World War II. Towards the end of the war—from June of 1945 to July 22, 1946—1,200 Italian and 800 German prisoners of war were among the nearly 300,000 POW's who passed through Camp Shanks and were returned to their native countries. Life at the camp was better than it would have been for them back in their villages after the war's devastation.

Besides returning WWII vets, St. Agatha welcomed eight or ten adult men from the Displaced Persons program and employed them at St. Agatha. We referred to these men as DPA's without knowing what it meant. In their thick accents, they told great stories—very sad tales of homelessness—while we shared pieces of bread with them.

These people had no home to return to after the war, like those from Poland. They qualified for the June 1948 U. S. Displaced Persons Act. It permitted entrance to people of German ethnic origin, without regard to visa quotas. The program provided them with government-paid jobs. Priority was given to persons who bore arms against the enemies of the United States.

During the war years, and immediately after, the Home's population doubled, but there was still a real shortage of help. Many of the men went off to serve, and there were no replacements. Besides the DPA's, St. Agatha got some help from the Jesuit Seminarians that came in as volunteers. They took us on outings and, when Joseph John Basern and I had to get our tonsils out, one of them accompanied us to Bellevue Hospital. I was shocked to hear him curse along the way, and when he noticed, he laughed. He told me not to worry,

that he was just in the Seminary to avoid the draft. He would drop
out when the war was over.

Our favorite Seminarian was Mort Mulligan who thrilled us when
he invited us to St. Patrick's Cathedral to witness the pageantry of his
ordination. After the ceremony, there was a reception in a little back
room. There, the Priest tried to recruit some of us— get us to make a
pledge to be good, and to become Priests. I almost raised my hand,
but happened to glance out into the hall and see a pretty little blonde
girl, and realized all I would be giving up. I didn't pledge, but a couple of my buddies like Donellan did. After that, he was always saying
the rosary.

I graduated from eighth grade when I was fifteen, on June 24,
1951, with Father Burke handing out the diplomas and awards, and
Reverend Terence J. Cooke giving the Address to the Graduates. My
father took me back home after ten years. When I went home, I felt
completely inept. I didn't know anything about girls, didn't even
know how to make a phone call, or what the operator meant when
she kept telling me to dial the number. "What number? Where do I
get this number?" I asked her.

My father didn't like any of my friends because they were colored,
Puerto Rican, or Jewish. We never heard of this attitude at the
Home, but that's the way it was in the city. Even the kids at the boys
club asked me why I was hanging around with these kids. They made
it clear that my friends were unwelcome in the neighborhood.
Finally, I gave up my friends and just hung around the house. When
my father asked why I didn't go out, I told I was waiting for him to
pick me out a friend that he didn't dislike. That really made him
mad. He was very abusive and always accused me of all kinds of evil,
like stealing cars and gambling—things that I had nothing to do
with. All the rules of decency I was taught at the Home, my father
disavowed. He was so mistrustful. He accused me of lying, playing
hooky, and fooling around with girls. Ironically, the first time I kissed

a girl was when I was fifteen, and she won the right to go steady with me, in a card game.

The first semester with my father, I attended a Catholic high school, but my father wanted me to get vocational training. He sent me to Samuel Gompers, to become an electrician. He must have been very impressed with that lamp I made for him in shop and thought I had a natural talent.

I was so unprepared, coming from the Home where they taught us manners and to behave like gentlemen. I became an easy mark and was taken advantage of in the neighborhood. This embittered me, and one day while walking down the street, I stopped and said right out loud, "No more Mr. Nice Guy!" I made up my mind that I was going to toughen up, be aggressive, strike first. I took on the biggest and the baddest kids, so the others would leave me alone.

The friction with my father got so bad, so quickly, that I left home before I turned sixteen and was living on the streets until I found a job sweeping floors in a machine shop down by the waterfront. This gave me the money to rent a furnished room in what turned out to be a drug and prostitution flophouse. I was scared of the tough guys: the drug dealers and pimps. I saw a boy my own age die of a drug over-dose in the high school yard, and rejected all of those offers made to me. I began seeing a nice girl, but I wasn't ready to get married, so she broke up with me.

Eugene Malito, jumper

I decided to get my pilot's license. I had taken a few informal flying lessons from a friend. When I went to the school and said I wanted to learn to fly, a famous paratrooper happened to be there. After listening to him a while, I joined the Army's 82nd Airborne during the Korean Conflict. After I came home, I pursued a career as a machinist, but continued to jump on weekends at Lakewood Sports Parachuting Center in New Jersey from February of 1964 to July of 1966. I became a Jumpmaster and instructor there.

I was always an excellent diver and swimmer, but I broke my neck diving into a pool and became a quadriplegic. For years, the bitterness I felt after I left St. Agatha grew deeper. Through years of therapy, I gained enough mobility to work as a school bus driver, and later worked as a security guard.

While I recovered in the VA hospital with the support of a wonderful nurse who remained a lifelong friend, I came to see how fortunate I was for the care I received at St. Agatha, despite the few unkind people. The world I faced at home and in New York was much harsher. At St. Agatha, I learned the proper way to behave, and was given food, clothing, and shelter, which I otherwise might not have had. I went to school, had friends, and gained many adventurous memories.

I recalled once, seeing a man standing quietly outside the gate to the boys' yard while we played basketball, his jacket folded over his arm. I asked him if he needed directions. The man said no, he was just visiting. He said that he had been a resident there twenty-five years earlier, and things looked pretty much the same. He was just reminiscing. I feel like I understand him now.

But the most important gift came when I became a born-again Christian. I never married, and this new life allowed me to meet fine people, to release all the anger and resentment of those negative experiences, and focus on the good people—those who cared for, helped, and loved us—and remember the positive experiences I'd had. I have committed the rest of my life to helping others, the way I have been helped, and I'm a happy, happy man.

St. Agatha continued to respond to directives to minimize the congregate care living in favor of smaller cottage units to provide the children with more of a family setting. Meanwhile, many of the turn-of-the-century buildings were aging. Some were condemned by more stringent fire, safety, and health codes, as illustrated in the Report of Inspection of St. Agatha Home by the First Deputy Commissioner of the State of New York, Mary L. Gibbons, written January 22, 1945.

Seventeen

The Science of Childcare

Sister Miriam Roberta Kiernan would face difficult years as Administrator beginning in 1939, but endured the deprivations carried over from the Depression coupled with the hardships inflicted by World War II: higher prices, food rationing, the loss of the Prefects who had now gone off to fight.

Besides the addition of a social worker, counselors replaced the Prefects. Dr. William Doody, head of the Traveling Guidance Clinic of Catholic Charities, expanded the resources. His visits formed part of the fledgling psychiatric program at St. Agatha, set up fully in 1955. All of these resources contributed to the more individual attention the children received, and the growth of the structured recreational program.

Changes in childcare attitudes began taking hold by using trained social workers who emphasized smaller, family groupings of children. That there was any growth at St. Agatha during those war years seems incredible. Also, with the widespread use of antibiotics on war veterans, TB began to recede, and the need for the Preventorium become obsolete. The buildings were promptly commandeered as dormitories for older girls. From one report:

During this time, dormitory units continued to shrink into smaller groups, each with their own social rooms and activities. Cement paths and roadways replaced dirt and blue paving stone paths throughout the grounds, vastly improving the overall cleanliness and appearance of the landscape.

Sister Mary Madeleine Duffy left her position as Superior at St. Joseph Hall and came to St. Agatha for a year. Under the direction of Sister Maria Josephine Berrigan, Superior and remarkable teacher, Sister Madeleine organized an outstanding program for the high school girls' cottage.

The four buildings that the Preventorium had occupied were remodeled for the junior and senior high school girls. A complete soda fountain was installed for all children to use. They hoped to reduce frequent trips to town by children seeking the ice cream parlor in Nanuet. They got their own laundry equipment, too.

Seventh- through ninth-grade girls moved into the renovated buildings the following Easter, coinciding with the close of the Holy Rosary Convent in New York City. This meant that the high school girls who routinely went there after eighth grade remained at St. Agatha. Provisions were made for them to go to Pearl River High School in the fall. Contacts with "outside" teachers and students from the community had a positive effect.

Most of the children spent Christmas of 1945 in their own family's home for the day, or with a volunteer. Cathedral High School launched a program whereby St. Agatha students received Christmas gifts and subsequent visits throughout the year. The following year, the trend at St. Agatha continued towards more social affairs that brought brothers and sisters together.

Timothy Finn lived at St. Agatha from 1944 to 1953, and has patches of memory about his life there.

We moved from the Bronx to 54th Street between First and Second Avenues in Manhattan. We lived there until our mother died. My younger brother William, sister Mary, and I were separated from our older and younger siblings, and sent to live at St. Agatha Home. I thought the others lucky, until comparing notes years later to find out the two of them were bounced around various foster homes—locked in closets and otherwise badly treated.

Our mother died of TB. I learned this while I was in a hospital, lying naked, except for a straight jacket, because they thought I had started a fire and flood at school. The matron came in and told me to get dressed; I was going to my mother's funeral. That was my notification.

I was told that we were going to camp at St. Agatha's for the summer. I arrived when I was seven. We rode up on the train to the camp in the woods. I remember being so disappointed at the end of the summer when they told me we were staying, and wished I had jumped off that train when I had the chance.

Once, walking down the path towards the bigger boys' dorm, we passed the pigpens on the right. I was terrified of the squealing because I had heard that this was where they tortured little boys.

I joined the choir after much coercion from Tom Maloney, the choirmaster. I really did it for the milk and cookies they served afterwards. We went into neighboring towns and sang for the elderly. Tom demanded excellence, and we received severe beatings for anything less.

We stole everything from each other because we had nothing of our own. Everything was given to us to use; nothing belonged to us. I had a favorite pair of argyle socks and Sister refused to give them to me as my own. "They belong to everyone," she said.

Once or twice a month I was allowed to go visit my sister at the girls' yard. They put barbed wire around their yard because a man had escaped from Rockland Hospital, and was reportedly raping girls in the area. The kids said that he attempted to lure a girl to the fence to get her, which is why they added the barbed wire.

With very few Prefects, we mostly had bigger boys as monitors who terrorized the younger ones. It was like a concentration camp. One boy was so cruel, he used to put cats in the milk cans and close the lid. They

we had bigger boys as monitors who terrorized the younger one.

used to toss one boy up in the air and catch him in blankets. He ended up in Rockland State Mental Hospital.

Sister Bulldog was so cruel, she used to whack the pointer on our knuckles and hit us with the side of the ruler. Once, I had taken a baseball cap and stitched "NY"—as in the Yankees—and wore it all the time. Sister took it away and wouldn't give it back, so I began punching her. She doused me with holy water and would not let me say evening prayers because she said I was possessed.

I was among the last group to live in St. Joseph's Dorm before they built Loyola and De Paul cottages where the cornfields had been. I expected to go to St. Agnes in Sparkill for high school, but St. Agatha started its own program by the time I finished grammar school.

Then my father came with my older brother and took me home. My father was a truck driver and a chronic drinker who swore that he had fought to get us kids back the whole time we were in the Home. After I left St. Agatha, I graduated from Cardinal Hayes High School in New York City.

I went into the service from 1961 to 1963 to Korea. I got out just before Viet Nam began. I didn't like living with my Dad, so I went to California and worked in the Wonder Bread Bakery for many years. Then, I opened my own fire extinguisher business, which I've had for over thirty years.

Staff changes continued at St. Agatha. Sister Mary Madeleine was appointed Administrator of the New York Foundling Hospital that August, and Sister Maria Josephine Berrigan became Superior for the year 1946 to 1947. Then, Sister Mary Raymond Commerford, a graduate of Fordham University School of Social Work, replaced her from

1947 to 1949, and continued the work of restructuring groups into smaller, homelike settings.

The success of St. Agatha Home was considered exemplified in three areas: the devoted care of the preschool children, the Preventorium, and the elementary school. The latter, in two well-equipped buildings, were registered by the Regents of the University of New York and provided a complete education, according to modern standards.

For a while, once eighth grade was completed, the first two years of high school work continued on campus, providing a strong foundation for the kids before moving on. Besides regular academic work, the children had mandatory vocational training for an hour each day. Courses included dressmaking, millinery, typing, steno, and printing— skills that could be used for independent living.

In 1947, Reverend Cooke brought his extensive experience in recreational programs, implementing a summer curriculum for children. Everyone who met him was convinced that no one loved children more than he did, and everyone who interacted with him at the Foundling and St. Agatha Home remember his easy, affable generosity and good humor.

Sister Rosemarie Commerfeld remembered, "He had the ability to make everyone feel he or she was his best friend, and the children felt he was always big enough for all of them." She believed that he was more in tune with the children than anyone else, like the time he suggested watermelons as prizes in competitions. The kids loved it, despite dire warnings from the staff. One Sunday morning he asked Sister, "Would you like a pony for the children?" She replied enthusiastically in the affirmative. He led her to the front door and presented Rusty. When asked where he got it, he said only, "It doesn't matter."

Tom Maloney said that Cooke sweet-talked the pony out of a neighboring farmer who formerly had nothing but complaints about the boys. "He had such a pleasant personality when he talked about the need of the children," added Walter Kelly. "I don't think anyone ever said 'no' to him." The overworked counseling staff, already in short supply due to the war, was shocked to learn upon Cooke's arrival that he wanted to st

Rusty the pony

athletic program and get the kids off the grounds for recreation once a week. Despite their pessimism, Reverend Cooke assisted by importing volunteer seminarians from Dunwoodie in Westchester and, with a donated old bus, began taking the children on trips to parks and entertainment areas each week.

That summer, Sister Marie Josita Driscoll and Sister Agnes Carmita Sheridan came from other parochial schools to teach arts, crafts, music, and other skills to the girls. They provided the children with some fresh faces and a much needed rest for the overwrought year-round teachers. Together, Sister Mary Raymond and Father Cooke implemented a summer program from June through August for children aged seven and over.

These programs relieved the tedious boredom that plagued the kids for decades. They'd spent so much time standing around that they got into trouble doing things like tunneling underground between buildings, running away, or smashing neighbors' windows. Sister Marie Elizabeth Cassidy became Superior in September 1947 until 1953. Among her residents, she had a group of high school girls who seemed to enjoy life, move forward, and prepare to go into the outside world.

A few of them put together an illustrated booklet of their lives and signed it "The Teenagers of St. Agatha's." Perhaps used as a fundraising brochure, it spans the period from June 1947 through June 1951.

Sister Mary de Sales Collins must have been mighty impressed when in October of 1948, she began her seven-year service at St. Agatha. A graduate of Fordham School of Social Service, she joined Miss Foy in that department. Together, they laid the foundation of the social work department begun in 1939. That innovation truly began the changes of St. Agatha Home from predominately a refuge for destitute children to a progressive institution attempting to heal the child, the family, and society.

Besides organizing a comprehensive record system, Sister de Sales facilitated meetings with social workers of other institutions. The department added more and more professionally trained Sisters: Sister Marie Leo O'Brian, Sister Marian Veronica O'Connell, Sister Mary Joanne Ward, and Sister Jane Maria Hoehn, all alumni of Fordham's School of Social Work. The Alumni Association was a great asset at that time, as they assisted by working with the kids such as coaching teams and providing much needed equipment.

Insight from adults and children has already proven to be widely disparate. Sister Bernadette Marie Hagan, who served at St. Agatha for five years while earning her Bachelor's of Arts and Masters of Science in Social Service, took a hard, frank look at what was working and what was lacking, despite all the good intentions and plans. She submitted her Dissertation in 1949 entitled, "The History and Development of the Saint Agatha Home for Dependent Children, Nanuet, NY: 1884-1948." In it, she quotes Emerson as saying, "Every institution is but the lengthened shadow of one man." Sister returned to St. Agatha as a Social Worker, after completing her Masters degree.

Eighteen

St. Agatha in the Fifties

In October of 1950, Mother Mary Berchmans, Sister Marie Clotilde, Sister Marie Elizabeth, and Sister Marie Lucille met with the Right Reverend Monsignor James J. Lynch of Catholic Charities to discuss new dormitories for boys. St. Joseph's had been declared a fire hazard in a report of the State Welfare Inspection, dated May 1950, and would require extensive renovations to remain habitable. It was decided that fundraising would begin to build two new cottages for boys. Meanwhile, fire doors, fire escapes, and similar modifications would be made to the St. Joseph's dormitory immediately, until new homes became available.

Sister Mary Magdalena Doyle became Superintendent, her assistant Sister Marie Laboure O'Neill, from 1951 to 1953. The latter worked hard training the other Group Mothers and developing the summer program for girls with the help of Sister Marie Lucille. In a recruiting letter dated May 18, 1951 from St. Agatha Home, Sister Lucille enthusiastically discusses the upcoming organized Arts and Crafts Program, and solicits assistance. This was the program started by Father Cooke, which utilizes visiting Sisters for the classes, to give the year-round teachers a break.

State and City Welfare departments made frequent inspections to insure the safety and well-being of the children. In a State Department survey conducted over 1952 to 1953, the State required many improvements be made. Certain buildings became "outmoded, and must be

It was decided that fundraising would begin

vacated." St. Joseph's dormitory was found to be a fire hazard, and lacking in adequate lavatories and bathing. The top two floors could no longer be used by children, leaving only the first floor available for a limited time. Numerous fire hazards pervaded other buildings with problems such as open stairwells and insufficient exits. The result was that one hundred fifty boys had to be sent to other Homes. Additional recreational facilities could provide the full development of the children, safety, and better accommodations. Plans to build two cottages for boys began immediately.

The renovated girls' cottages, and the installation of a new fire alarm system throughout the Home, resulted from a loan of $600,000 from the Emigrant Industrial Savings Bank. The Mother House of the Sisters of Charity, friends and relatives of the Sisters, responded to requests for donations. It would cost hundreds of thousands of dollars more to build new residences. The heroic efforts of the following years are a testament to the extraordinary generosity of the local community that reached through Rockland County and beyond—to New York City, Westchester County, and neighboring states.

One of the fundraising letters, written in 1953, contained heart-rending stories about a few of the children who benefited from St. Agatha's care. One little boy told a social worker that he hated his father and mother because he knew only hate and cruelty from them. Another anecdote told of four small children, often locked in an apartment alone for hours by their parents, unfed, uncared for, and frightened. Neighbors, hearing them cry, called the parish priest to look into the matter. When he arrived, he asked the oldest where her parents were. She replied, "They are both down at the beer garden." The Surrogate Court conveyed the children to St. Agatha Home.

Not only neglect and abuse, but also poverty and sickness resulted in the breakdown of families. In one home, the father became paralyzed and could not work. He had been a hard worker. His wife was stricken ill with tuberculosis and taken to Welfare Island. The five children, neglected and undernourished, went to St. Agatha. Upon arrival, they received their first bath in a long while, and one child remarked to the attending Sister, "Gee, Sister, I didn't know it felt so good to be clean!" When Sister tucked a second youngster into bed, he remarked incredulously, "Sister, the bed is warm, and I like the eats swell!"

The brochure went on to say, "Poverty and suffering can be abated by human means, but there remains in the hearts of some of these children bitterness and hate. The Sisters play a special role in the tender care they provide while bringing Christ into these little lives, providing security and peace, acting as mothers. Many of these children have gone on to lead successful lives in their professions and in their families." Since St. Agatha opened, it witnessed a change in the type of child they received. Welfare programs, curriculums, and policies all must evolve to meet the needs of a changing population.

Sister Alphonse Mary was particularly aware of the isolation of the Sisters who served as teachers and Group Mothers. They missed time for prayer, meals, and recreation as a community. She decided to make

The Sisters play a special role in the tender care they provide while bringing Christ into these little lives, providing security and peace, acting as mothers.

arrangements so that time together was ensured for them by increasing the staff in each cottage to assist the Sisters, but this was not markedly improved until 1955.

Mother Mary Berchmans of the Motherhouse was asked by Monsignor Lynch to find a way to keep the older boys at St. Agatha's until they graduated high school, instead of sending them away. They arranged it in early 1953 with two conditions: that a new cottage be provided for the boys, and that they provide a chaplain and a counselor until St. Agatha could afford to carry the expense of having their own. It was agreed. To comply with the second condition, the former Quarantine house, St.

Roche's, was converted to a chaplain's residence, and Father Tobin was installed as chaplain. He served St. Agatha from 1954 to 1957.

In 1954, fundraising efforts raised $175,000 to build a new home for high school boys. Children would be able to remain at St. Agatha, completing their education at neighboring high schools, until Nanuet High School was built in 1959. This would minimize the further trauma of leaving the Home without a high school education.

That year, the summer program was highly effective, with approximately sixteen Sisters from the community providing instruction. St. Agatha was earning a reputation as one of the most progressive childcare institutions in the archdiocese.

The new ranch-style cottage facilitated smaller groups, more closely replicating family life. With a living room, hobby room, den or shop, bathrooms, kitchen, dining room, and five bedrooms for six boys each, it was a far cry from the rows and rows of metal beds of the past. The new fireproof beds and built-in chests of light colors were used to brighten the atmosphere. Murals of outdoor scenes graced the walls.

Door to door, fifteen thousand volunteers canvassed to raise funds for this project. On April 22, 1955, Seton Hall for high school boys became a gift from Cardinal Spellman to the Sisters of Charity. This honor was in recognition of their faithful service performed for so many children at the Roman Catholic Orphan Asylum from 1817 until it closed in 1921, and to the Archdiocese of New York, overall. The St. Agatha Boy Scouts led the procession from the Administration building. Following them was a large group of Religious, Knights of Columbus, local dignitaries, and visitors.

At the dedication, Cardinal Spellman reiterated, "While it is preferable to rehabilitate a child's home over placing him in an institution, the devoted care the children received from the Sisters was the best alternative."

Much progress was made when Sister Marian Cecilia Schneider came to St. Agatha as Director of Social Services. Sister Cecilia joined the Sisters of Charity in 1935, and was missioned at the New York Foundling Hospital where she was in charge of the adoption department. Sisters who had received degrees in social work from such prestigious schools as

Fordham University School of Social Work provided casework service to the children. They had responsibility for placing them in foster homes, and the successful transition and adjustment to life outside. Sister Cecilia became Superior and Superintendent of St. Agatha a few months after her arrival in 1955, a post she held until 1964. Her organizational skills and gift of understanding human nature made her an immediate success.

A Guidance Department was formally set up on October 17, 1955, under the direction of Dr. Frank J. O'Brien, formerly Associate Superintendent of Schools of New York City. He directed responsibility for staff education in mental hygiene to ensure that those in contact with the children in any capacity used consistent understanding of their problems and objectives. Each new child was evaluated at arrival to see what special assistance or care they might need. Afterwards, they received psychiatric evaluations, as needed.

The same year, Sister Mary Assisium Byrne was transferred from NYFH to become Director of Social Service Department, replacing Sister Cecilia after her promotion. A comprehensive program began in order to give more casework service to individual children. Also, to place more of them in foster homes. Sister Assisium took full charge of evaluation, placement, and supervision. Children, instead of transferring to the supervision of the Catholic Guardian Society of Catholic Charities once they left St. Agatha, remained in the Home's custody during their adjustment period in new homes. Miss Foy and Mr. John Flynn, now a Fordham graduate, helped make this transition successful. Sister Assisium successfully integrated the Psychiatric Services department with the rest of the Home.

A team approach began between Group Mothers, social workers, and teachers to help with children's problems. This strategy successfully brought progress for the children. Weekly conferences combined representatives of all departments who influenced the child, to co-ordinate responsibilities and goals. This helped to revitalize the staff, unexpectedly dashed by the sudden premature death of Dr. O'Brien on March 13, 1956, after only five months with St. Agatha.

Dr. John Quaranta, a psychologist at John Kennedy and St. Michael's Homes in Staten Island, jumped in and assisted several evenings each week to keep the programs going, and provided psychiatric evaluation to children in need of help. By May the following year, Dr. Quaranta could offer three days each week to St. Agatha, and was a great successor to Dr. O'Brien. Unbelievably, he too was struck down at the age of only thirty-five. It was a devastating blow to everyone who had been so hopeful and who came to deeply respect both of these men.

Mr. James Dowling became full-time Program Director in August, 1956. Under his guidance—and with added counselors, athletics, crafts, clubs, scouting, social affairs, outings, and group games—the children thrived. Girls' recreation improved through Mr. Dowling's support of the Group Mothers. Together,

Cottages along Duryea Lane

they made a special attempt to draw the more timid and unathletic children into organized activities to build self-confidence and successful teamwork skills.

Dr. Gaston Scott, a psychologist, began working part-time with the school staff towards a better understanding of the unique learning problems of institutionalized children. He too held interdepartmental conferences between the guidance, social workers, group mothers, and counselors, to ensure a consistent approach.

May 30, 1957 the groundbreaking for the new swimming pool was announced. The final completion of the construction of the 30' x 80' pool finally opened in July. Much of the credit for the pool fundraising went to Mrs. Iving P. Delappe of New City. She saw that it was impractical to frequently transport four hundred and fifty children to nearby facilities, and set about bringing summer fun to the Home.

The old watering hole at the brook, closed for swimming a decade earlier by the Board of Health, had provided over a half-century of fun to thousands of children. It remained the destination for daily hikes, catching crayfish, and sailing homemade rafts.

In 1958, five new brick cottages appeared along Duryea Lane. Each accommodated twelve children, a Group Mother, and a counselor. Initially, three housed boys aged six to nine, and two had girls of the same age. The objective was that it would provide a setting for siblings to grow up together for their full residence at St. Agatha, rather than switching to other cottages as they aged. Set among the former apple and pear orchards, across from the now empty cornfields, and still rimmed by blackberry bushes, the site offered a pastoral view of the entire Home and the community beyond.

Jackie Fox remembers those times. She writes:

I believe I arrived in 1954 and left in 1960. I have very mixed feelings about the Home; some very wonderful that helped me throughout my life, and some more negative. Having been taken from my brother at the age of eleven, and after having had the freedom of running the New York City streets, it was a big adjustment for me. Many of the kids there knew this as the only home they ever knew.

I was desperately hurt and kept running away to find my brother. I finally did find him on one of those annual Orphans' Day Outings. He was placed at St. John's Home for Boys in Rockaway, and we met by accident at Rockaway Playland.

At first, my brother and I went in the same foster home when we were four and five. Before that, we had been in seven different homes. I am the youngest of twelve kids. The other ten all were placed in the same home together, but we two were separated from them. The foster home where my brother and I stayed together had a very elderly, sick woman who really only wanted my brother, and not a girl. The New York Foundling insisted that since we'd been separated from the others, we must be kept together. She gave in and kept me, but was cruel, and my brother was aware of it. For instance, she raised us as twins until the age of ten, but only he had a cake. Later, we found out he was a year older.

He did everything for me that she refused to do. He would steal clothes from my girlfriends, get me food, and try to make my life easier. So by eleven, we became little Bonnie and Clyde survivors, and that's when they sent me to St. Agatha without even telling us where the other was going.

During the years at that foster home, my biological mother called and said she was coming to see us. I went around, announcing my mother was coming, and I'm not an orphan. She didn't come. That happened three times. So when I got to the Home and they wanted me to meet her and the rest of the family, I refused, but was forced to see her. Sister Peter slapped me, then warned me to accept and love her.

I never said a word about the past or why I didn't want her in my life. I was very angry. A few months later, they tried again with my mother, and I had to spend the Christmas weekend with her. As I walked into her filthy sty, her drunk husband grabbed me. I saw three other little kids in a corner, and thought how lucky I am not to have been raised with her. I was never disrespectful, but she was not going to be called "Mom" by me. To this day, I refer to her by her last name only.

She died when I was in a coma from septicemia, so I didn't have to attend the funeral. I met my grandmother in the hospital, as I was the charge nurse one day. She came up and said, "Jacqueline, I am your grandmother. I know it because you are me, sixty years ago." My half-brother was a patient on my floor and I didn't even know it.

I remember a heavyset nun in the sewing room, whom I liked. In the seventh grade I moved down to Magnificat with Sister Maureen Catherine. From there, I graduated to the hill. I remember very well where all the baby boys and girls units were; I was always with them. I had a special little girl named Linda Montgomery who had polio, and I was convinced I could make her leg all better, as she had one short leg. I would always find things to put inside her shoe to try to make it even. I probably did more damage to her than good. Linda did not stay long, as children with disabilities didn't have a fair chance. I still wish I could find her. I think I took on a maternal role with her, being five years older.

I had this wonderful teacher, Dr. Duffy, who taught sophomore biology at Nanuet High. For some reason, she took a liking to me and pushed me to do well. It was during her course that I developed a special interest in certain diseases, one of them being Cerebral Palsy. She encouraged me to expand my interest and do a project for the class. When I left St. Agatha, I lived with a family that had a C.P. child. God works in strange ways.

The day we learned we could wear lipstick, I wondered where every girl flew away to. Sister Deloritta and I sat in the dining room alone, as they had all gone up to get their stash. When permission was given for the girls to take driver's education, again the excitement could be heard all the way down in the Main Building.

If it were not for Sister Bernadette Marie and Sister Doloritta Marie, I would have been just a statistic today. Having had the abusive ten years before I arrived up there, I definitely was a challenge for them. Later, I no longer wanted to run away, show them my defiance, or display my anger for being up there. I enjoyed being with Sister because I knew she really cared for me.

St. Agatha truly turned my life around, but unknowingly to me at the time. One person so vital to me was Ms. Foy. She was a social worker who never got credit for her love and devotion to St. Agatha and the girls. I knew her as an older and more visibly handicapped person. I believe she dealt with the girls who had issues that the nuns didn't have the ability to understand at that time. So many wonderful people worked and lived up there. I have a picture of Ms. Foy at my wedding. I know she is in heaven now; she was a saint. I have the feeling that the nuns did not appreciate the lay social workers.

Sister Bernadette saved my life. I was brought back by the police who found me in Bear Mountain after I ran away once. I was walking back to Queens to find my brother, so I thought. Sister Marian Cecelia was at the front door with Sister Bernadette, and said she was sending me to juvenile hall because it was my third flight. Sister Bernadette said, "No, can't you see the wonderful part of her? That would make her worse, and her life would be ruined."

She begged Sister Marian Cecelia to allow her to deal with me on a one-to-one basis. I had to go to the Social Service Department every day. Sister Bernadette was my social worker, and I'd tell her how school was, etc. She gave me money and gifts, but only when I earned it. So I turned out okay, thanks to Sister Bernadette. When she left, she had the kids in her class at St. Peter and Paul School in the Bronx writing to me all the time. From what I heard, she lived well into her nineties and taught right up to the end, until she got senile.

Friends for life, she came to Rockaway where I've lived for thirty-five years to attend my daughter's communion. I wanted to name my daughter after her, but my husband didn't care for the name. I wish I had the conviction then that I have now, and she would be Bernadette. I did get the "Marie" in, though.

Sister Veronica, who recently passed on, was one that I liked because she always responded and was so predictable. There was an elderly Sister Theresa who was the principal of the elementary school when I was there. She was so frail and could barely hold the bell. Sister Ignatius took over when she left. I had Sister Dorothy in the eighth grade. I believe she also died at a young age. She sometimes let me dress in her habit because I told her I wanted to be a nun. I can't believe she believed me.

After I left St. Agatha, my mother really did not want me to live with her, so I was on my own after a year. I started working in the restaurant field, which I had learned from working in the nuns' dining room. I worked my way up to hostess and manager of some of the finest restaurants in New Jersey. At my first job, I was a waitress, and the owner could not believe how terrific I was.

Once I left the Home, my sister ran away, and when they caught her she was placed in a different Home. She finally got out and went to live with Ms. Foy, who had a couple of other girls living with her.

She was a nice lady. My sister never got over being placed in a Home, and once tried to kill my mother. She became an alcoholic and died at forty-four years old.

I have never come to grips about my childhood. I've been gathering information over the past year about my family, which I was never told before. I always knew that I was told many lies as a child, and that they hated when I asked questions. I had a gut-awful feeling about them all, and recently found out through research some horrible facts that I always suspected.

My husband died at the age of forty-two from alcoholism. At the age of thirty-nine, I started drinking. Before that, I never drank at all. The disease hit me furiously, and I needed help. I am three years sober and have found what I needed, spiritually. I became a Eucharistic minister and now have peace in my life. I can't hate anything I didn't have, but I don't pretend to love them because they are family.

The St. Agatha newsletter, published by the children in the print shop, and called "Sagatana" Vol. I, No. 6, was issued. It was subtitled, "Our 75th Anniversary and Dedication Issue," with illustrations by V. Coriano, the same artist who illustrated "High School Girls' Story, The Hill." It contained editorials by some children about Mother Seton, and the importance of May—the month of the Blessed Mother. Sister Maria Ignatius, Principal at the school enclosed a beautiful note to the children.

Following a tribute to Mother Seton for the Sesquicentennial, elaborating the works and examples of her in a most loving way, some children offered poems and letters like the following:
"The House With Somebody In It"

Whenever I walk to Suffern, with my knapsack on my back
I go by a large red building with trimmings brown and black.
I supposed I've passed it a hundred times, but I always stop for a
   minute

And look at the house, the happy home, the home with the children
    in it.
I have never seen such a happy home, but now I know there are such
    things;
That they hold the laughter of children, their mirth and sorrowings.
This home has done what a home should do, it's a home that has
    sheltered life.
It has put its loving arms around those children who have known
    such strife.
So whenever I walk to Suffern a-carrying my pack
I never pass St. Agatha Home without stopping and looking back.
It makes me very joyful to see such happy hearts,
And I know this home is for one and all and no one is left apart.
–James Beaner, Grade 8

Dear Blessed Mother, teach me to say "yes" every time Jesus asks me a
favor. He only asks little things of me. Yet sometimes I find them so
hard. With your help, I am sure I could learn this great lesson.
–Maria, Grade 7
This is the lovely month of May. The blossoms are out on some of
the bushes. The birds are building their nests. The grass is growing
green. It is the beautiful month of Our Lady. –Michael Dowling,
Grade 3

The boys in Sister Kevin's group have formed two baseball teams. We
call them the Braves and the Yankees. So far, the Braves are winning.
–Nelson De Jesus, Grade 2

Spring Thoughts, I hope they can finish the swimming pool before
the summer, but until then, the boys play on a lot of rafts down by
the brook. We go up and down the brook. Sometimes we fall in.
When we get on land we get dry. The boys go fishing and catch gold-
fish and other kinds of fish. The apple blossoms are beginning to

grow. After the blossoms come the apples. We eat them with fun.
–Felix Alejandro, Grade 5

When I Was Alone With Jesus. One day I went to the chapel to pray and to ask Jesus if He would help me with all my problems. As I went in, I noticed that there was no one in the chapel. But I was not afraid because I knew that Jesus was there. When I entered, I knelt down and thought of Jesus. After that, I said a few prayers. When I was coming out, I felt happy because I had talked to Jesus and I knew that He understood my problems. –Nidia Cancel, Grade 6

We made some lovely birds. They have wings. The colors are pretty. They look as if they could fly. –Edwin Perez, Grade 3

Three 8th graders—Rose Santiago, Regina Lyons, and Olga Sandoval—composed this poem:

S is for the Sisters whose love we, and others, have cherished through seventy-five years of hard work, patience and constant labor.
T is for the time spent trying to make St. Agatha's a pleasant and more cheerful place.
A is for the absorbed interest in making us good Christians and children of God, and good citizens of our wonderful America.
G is for the gratitude we show in return for the love and care, which we receive so frequently.
A is for the good advice we can always seek from our Counselors and Sister when trouble comes our way.
T is for the tenderness we have experienced, one and all. We have come to count on it, and we want to show it to others when the time comes.
H is for the happy hours we have shared together.

A is for all those who have helped make St. Agatha Home a true home. Put all the letters together. They spell St. Agatha, the place that means a home and love to me.

St. Agatha is a Home for children whom God placed here for some reason. When I came here to St. Agatha, I was sad to leave my parents where I was happy. But as time passed, I realized that I would not be sad all my life because such things do not last. I began to cheer up and played with the other boys and girls. After I was here about a week, I wanted to see all the big buildings and play yards. I began to notice the lovely trees and bushes. I admired the beautiful grottos where the children go to pray. I went from grade to grade until I finally reached the eighth grade and realized that I was a teen-ager. Time has passed quickly and I am grateful to be here. –Douglas Rodriquez, Grade 8

What I like best :
The things I see about me, the fields, the barn, the brook,
Sister Patricia's little candy store,
Sister Ramona, our famous cook.
The steeple and the chapel
Our trials that end in tears,
The love that has been growing
Through all these seventy-five years.
–Donna Krish, Grade 8

We are happy because we've got lots of toys to play with, and a big, big room where we can make lots of noise. –Armondo Mercado, Grade 1

It's nice because Sister Marian Cecilia and all the workmen made them for us. God helped them. –William Marrero, Grade 1

The teachers in school teach us about God, and all the other subjects we must know before we go into the big world around us. The Social Service Department, I am sure, will help me later on in life when I have to leave. –Neil Perry, Grade 8

The girls in our group went to Sebago Beach with some friends. We made castles in the sand. We had hot dogs, soda, and ice cream. –Dorothy Loon, Grade 3

Our baseball team is practicing for the games that are coming this summer. The field is not quite ready. We work on it on good days. When the field is ready, we are going to win every game for St. Agatha's and we will get the trophy. –Harold Vivos, Grade 7

Sister Gabriel is doing a good job with the Garden Club. Have you read the sign on the lawn? "Your feet are killing me." Watch the little blades of grass when you put your feet down! –James McGinley, Grade 7

The newsletter closes with, "St. Agatha's big day for the dedication of the new cottages comes on May 14. All are preparing for the Cardinal. The boys and girls who are participating in the program have to practice over and over, but they do not mind because they know that something worthwhile takes time, and I am sure that it will turn out beautifully and both God and the Cardinal will be pleased. Now that graduation and promotion are approaching, I am sure that everyone is studying and aiming to get a good mark. Then all will have a wonderful summer. I think that's all the news for this month. Until the next time, God bless you and keep you."

Nineteen

The Turbulent Sixties

A merica changed profoundly in the sixties. Poverty moved to the fore-front again. Renewed emphasis on government programs to help alleviate the suffering inspired President Johnson's Great Society programs. As in the Great Depression, intervention by the Federal government was necessary. The free market economy's failure to provide jobs for everyone who needed them conspired with the lack of state and local funds available to aid those most affected.

After the war years of deprivation, the prosperity of the 50's materialized at St. Agatha in the form of physical improvements. The 60's focused more on the children's academic and social education. The Social Services department continued expanding, group homes opened, and resources became available to reunite children with their families. St. Agatha began actualizing the goals they had been striving towards for decades.

Home Kids frequently appeared in local newspapers accepting awards. For instance, the pre-teen girls took first place in the fifth annual CYO Cheerleading Contest. They competed against ten nearby schools, including Albertus Magnus, St. Dominic's, and St. Margaret's. Liz, our "Goody Two Shoes" award winner, was among them.

Under the direction of Mr. Dowling, the current program offered competitive sports for fifty-three high-schoolers participating at outside schools, which include a complete cycle of major sports, football, soccer, baseball, and basketball. They competed in two leagues: the CYO, against elementary public schools; and other Catholic Homes. There was also a swim team. Everyone joined up for the Nanuet teams.

Sports were not the only venue for children's recreation. The once-strong music program, revived under the direction of Sister Seton, afforded the children individual lessons and the opportunity to play in the St. Agatha Band. An art program formed in conjunction with the Social Services Department under Mrs. Dorothy Fitzpatrick to aid in the individual child's expression.

Amidst the growth and progress, St. Agatha took a giant step backwards on February 9, 1961 when St. Joseph's dormitory caught fire. Flames began in the kitchen of the historic wooden building, causing thirty children to lose their homes once again. This disaster greatly impacted their resources.

St. Joseph's after the fire

Water from Pascack Brook was used to fight the flames. The snow all around was blackened with ash for weeks as the burned-out hulk waited for the wrecking ball. The fire was detected by the building's recently installed alarm system. Besides the boys, two Sisters and ten counselors had resided there, though no one was hurt. Six fire departments responded, including a thousand-gallon water pumper, which drew water from the Pascack Brook, laboring to squelch the fire. Nearby buildings went without heat and light for several hours.

Rockland County residents quickly rallied. They opened their hearts and pockets to help replace the children's possessions, and to put a roof over their heads. Middle-school children amassed clothing and blankets. A Spring Valley restaurant collected bedding. Collection containers appeared in area restaurants and taverns for the St. Agatha Fire Fund.

Rockland Theatres pledged assistance in the rebuilding effort. Local churches began drives within their parishes. The White House on the Lake Hotel in Spring Valley temporarily housed some of the boys, for whom there was no room on campus.

For weeks, the children had to work their way to school past the burned-out buildings. The crossing guard and a Sister watched their progress carefully. The front wall had collapsed from the heat of the fire, and tons of water was used to extinguish the rest. The demolition progressed slowly. First went the outer shell, then the walls yielded to a wrecking ball, swung from a huge crane. At one point, an exterior metal staircase stood alone like a dinosaur skeleton in a museum. Then, nothing remained but bits of ash. But, as before, the little Home persevered.

As time went on, so did St. Agatha. In December of 1963, the scope of childcare needs could be gleaned from a report published in a New York newspaper:

> In New York City, there are over 21,000 children in care. Another 2,000 are awaiting placement. Of those, 45 %, or 938, waiting for care are the most neglected and rejected in New York City. They are the *acting-outers, aggressive, truant, profane kids given to temper tantrums, children of out of control parents.* They are *educationally handicapped, functioning two to four grades below normal, despite average IQ's, essentially and sociologically damaged.* Over 13 years of age, many have lower than institutionally accepted IQ's, but higher than those accepted by the State schools. *Physically handicapped and emotionally disturbed children* are recommended for residential treatment that is unavailable.

St. Agatha began to think about how they could help these needy children in the coming years. In January of 1964, volunteers began receiving training from the Director of the Guidance and staff Psychiatrist. He counseled the adult volunteers, who took children into their homes on the third Tuesday morning of each month at the Home, to help them understand the children. He explained to them:

are bad and that's why they are here. They distrust and despair because they have been unloved. He urged this work, not for themselves, or their own benefit, but . If you come, begrudgingly, the child will sense it and resen... pulation.

That was the old atmosphere of charity. These children feel deserted, they may know that their parents are sick or imperfect in other ways. They are wounded and anger at their inability to measure up, will aggravate the problem." He assured volunteers that bad behaviors are not indelible, as Freud believed, that "loving relationships *can* be formed and a child *can* change. Volunteers must keep their promises to the children, no matter how trivial, in order to recondition their reflexes from destructive, to trusting and believing behavior.

A strong service program existed to help the children, which included two psychologists, three psychiatrists, twelve social workers, and thirty-nine nuns. The average turnover was about one hundred children per year. About twenty-five of them returned home to their families, another twenty-five went to foster homes, and the rest left to make their own futures at college or at work.

The Sisters had no training for professional jobs before the 1950's. Then, the Sister Formation Movement required education to nurse and teach others. Before that, even study of theology and the Bible was discouraged. Many religious women, though not content, served quietly in a male-dominated hierarchy, despite their own untapped capabilities.

Men had charge of home schools, the military, the government, and the workplace. Nuns disavowed their families to serve God through the men of the Church. In large part, women of the 30's and 40's had babies or became secretaries, schoolteachers, housewives, or nurses. After the war when the men came back, women gave up their much-needed jobs to the returning men and went back to homemaking.

Sisters were sent anywhere, anytime, to do anything. After Vatican II, they began to have some say in their destinies. Vatican II was the work of

Cardinal Angelo Roncalli who became Pope John XXIII in 1958. He worried that the inflexible church would break. Changes had to be made to coincide with the women's movement. Roncalli asked for input from Church members, irrespective of the papal infallibility of the nineteenth-century Vatican I. A vast overhaul was needed to make the Church, priests, and nuns relevant to the times in which they lived. Many practical changes took place, such as in Mass. The Sisters wanted education, choice in their work, and updated habits, which did not require so much attention.

As with most extensive organizational changes, casualties resulted. Sisters self-divided into traditionalists, progressives, and those in between. Some valued the traditions of the Church, such as chastity, unquestioning obedience, and modest clothes. They didn't see these as only ideas that had grown old-fashioned. Consequently, many left the order now that they had other options, or because the Church no longer represented what they had dreamed of as young girls.

Many young novitiates hailed from small rural towns. They were sheltered and unaccustomed to the poverty and rebellion they encountered from the children in their care. Familiar with people like themselves, these multiracial, poor, inner-city kids seemed mysterious. The expectation was to transcend the differences and treat them simply as the sick, the poor, and God's children.

For the first time, the Sisters began identifying problem areas—such as a lack of homeless shelters for women with children—and received support to open facilities. The homemaker-types stayed at the rectory to care for the Priests. The entrepreneurial types boarded planes to their new lives, empowered. Many Sisters left the order and fewer joined. Their ranks diminished by a third in twenty-five years. This took a harsh toll on teaching and childrearing. More and more providers had to turn to lay people.

Some Sisters began to feel that communion with God did not require a chapel and a congregation. A pause on the staircase of an orp\ served just as well. The very thing the Catholic Church ha(wanted—its members interpreting for themselves—was now

Some Sisters agreed with St. Thomas Aquinas who said that the ultimate authority in moral issues is one's own conscience. There resulted contrary thinking to the official position of Rome on matters of birth control, abortion, and the women's roles in the Church.

The pull-and-tug felt by the Sisters was felt equally by church parishioners. Some thought, "If all of these hard and fast rules that we have lived our lives by are subject to change, why bother with the others? Weren't they just interpretations of the Bible that may change?" Some of the exiting nuns felt that few female leaders existed who could take them into the new Catholicism. Fortunately, among those who remained included many innovators who helped with the adjustments.

The exodus did not happen uniformly or in one fell swoop anymore than the nuns changed their habits for one new uniform. The changes percolated—coughing up one here, another there—and some Sisters escaped in the steam. Others conformed and fell back into the pot. Among the conformists and non-conformists who remained, a differing ideology became evidenced in their dress. Some Sisters began to avoid each other. Solidarity in many cases was lost.

Over the same period of time that the nuns had been going through their changes, women were going through similar image upheavals. Before the turn of the century, a pregnancy was referred to as "confinement" and women stayed out of sight until after the child was born. In the 1960's, women nine months pregnant began to be featured in popular magazine covers. None of the women on *Donna Reed, Ozzie and Harriet,* or *I Love Lucy* ever wore slacks before, much less the hot pants and go-go boots that modern moms donned in the late 60's. Imagine in 1960 wearing shorts and a sleeveless blouse to Church!

All of this upheaval was felt at St. Agatha. Sisters leaving and church rules abolished added to the uncertainty for children who already craved stability. Over the next three decades—as the Sisters received solid educations and their reputations for excellence as school teachers, social workers, and administration expanded more professionally than spiritually—Catholics and non-Catholics began to send their children to Catholic schools for the improved education and for the Sisters' cultured refine-ment. Often, the Sisters came from well-to-do, upper-class families, then went on to college and joined the convent. These young women became the leaders in social reform and industry.

Twenty

The Worst Blow of All

This turbulent atmosphere surrounded our family when we came to St. Agatha Home, but we were oblivious to most of it. We saw only what was closest to us. Our weekend visit to St. Agatha became permanent. We had, in fact, been tricked into going quietly.

On Monday, we started school at St. Agatha. During the first week, they took us to the Home's store to get a full wardrobe of clothes. Sister Agnes helped me make my choices from the clothes she had stocked the shelves with. For Mass, I got a pair of red patent-leather slip-ons with a bow. Aside from Dorothy in *The Wizard of Oz*, no one could carry off that embarrassment. I also received a blue-and-white herringbone A-line dress, and a tan one of a similar style with a long brown bow down the front. Forty years later, I still recall every detail of these costumes.

I had three more months to finish the eighth grade. It was my third school in this grade because we had moved so often. Helen and I remained together, as did Tommy and David. Jack, a freshman, rode the bus to Nanuet High School, so we saw him only at canteen and Sundays during visiting hours. To their credit, our relatives took turns coming to see us every weekend.

Mom stayed at the hospital for six weeks. She wrote short notes to one or the other of us telling us some activity she had—like going to the movies, or taking a class—and reminding us to be good. She was like our old,

April 17/65   *Saturday*

Dear Nancy,

I was very happy to hear from you. The letter I received from you was the first one that I got.

How are Jackie, David, Helen and Tommy. Is Tommy turning on his charm for everyone. Tell them all that I miss them and I love them, you included.

We were taken to the movies by the nurse the other night so it helped to relieve the monotony. The saw a picture called "the Lion". It was good.

What do you do with yourself. All you told me about is what you ate I gather you eat very well.

Well honey I want to get this off in the mail so I'll say goodbye for now. I'll write Jackie as soon as I can get another letter off.

Lots of Love
Mom

Mom's letter, April 1965

gentle mom. She signed herself out, feeling she could handle her drinking, and moved in with Gram and Bill. She looked great, got her hair and nails done, wore new clothes. We were ecstatic when she came to see us in May for David's Confirmation. She was so proud of him.

But slowly, we began to see it flake away. The few drinks she had before she came "to steady her nerves" turned into showing up drunk. This humiliated us, especially in front of the nuns and other kids. When mom settled in with Gram, we took turns spending weekends with her. At first she wasn't as bad, but the frequency of her drinking increased over the following year. I considered bitterly that having us put away made it easier for her to drink. No one knew what to do with her, except to protect us kids from a repeat of the life we had before.

Long before I arrived at St. Agatha, the girls had established a secret smoking place—a treehouse of sorts. Down below the field behind the cottages, at the edge of the woods and amidst all the wild blackberry bushes, there were huge oak trees. One in particular had loads of thick branches, some so low that we could use them as a ladder to climb up to the higher ones. Girls draped in the branches like leopards, puffing away, while the view from the cottages was that of a massive green canopy. Even in winter, though it was cold and no greenery hid our presence, there was sufficient distance to get away with it. This is where I made some of my friends, up in the "smoking tree." It was sort of the equivalent to "down on the corner" back in the Bronx. You could find a little peace and quiet. Or before long, someone came along and you had someone to chat with.

When I graduated eighth grade from St. Agatha elementary school in June of 1965, all of my relatives came, and mom did behave. It was a glorious day. I had a new powder-blue dress and heels—provided by the Home from and outside store—the same color as our caps and gowns. I hadn't felt so special since I made my Confirmation four years earlier. Sister Lucy gave me a special present—a puppy, which I named Tippy. She also gave me the vacant counselor's room, as I was the oldest in the cottage. Every bit of it was done in pink, and it was tiny. It had a door, a cupboard for clothes, a tiny sink, and two windows all my own. One looked out towards the fields along Convent Road. The other to the back fields, where the deer indeed snuck out at dawn and dusk. I couldn't believe how happy I was.

About a month later, they told me a place had opened up and I was moving up on the hill to Duryea Lane with the girls my own age. I knew a few of them from eighth grade who already lived there. I was reluctant to leave Helen, but she had made friends and settled in as best she could. Besides, I had no choice.

Moving up to fourth cottage turned out to be good, except I couldn't take Tippy since they already had a dog there. Sister suggested that I leave him at St. Agnes. After I was gone, one of the girls, Patty, asserted herself over the group and took over the puppy. Patty had a real anger problem. In the brief period while I was in St. Agnes, I was shocked to see both she and Miriam physically assault Sister Lucy, then Sister Raymond, her successor.

Sister Henry got a few of us girls jobs as candy stripers for the summer. We earned money and went shopping with the counselor on the weekends, and had a leisurely summer before school started. I took the bus home many weekends, rotating with my brothers and sisters, usually to

Gram's, but sometimes to Aunt Mary's or Aunt Terry's. While I was home, I saw Mom, Gram, Bill, Jerry, Billy, Ginger, and my old friends. Of course, my friends went on with their own lives and, though I traipsed after them for about a year, we finally had nothing left in common. New friends had joined the group; others moved away; a few started high school—all the usual stuff that happens in a group of kids, but makes less of a ripple when you are ensconced in the group. Once I moved away, I felt like I was always on the outer rim, looking on, and we had little left in common except for history.

The day finally arrived, and off we went to high school. That morning felt like the backstage of a dress rehearsal. Sixteen girls rushed about, getting dressed, using only three sinks to primp and prepare. Corky the bus driver pulled up in front of the cottage door. With the squeal of brakes and the whoosh of the pneumatic door opener, we climbed onboard, off to our new lives. In new outfits, and with butterflies darting about tummies, we slid into the cool, green leather benches. Unflappable, Corky had a schedule to meet. The first day of the school year was always the same, except for "Outside Kids" to be met.

The two-story school was so modern compared the Victorian we left behind at St. Agatha. The granite floors gleamed beneath the onslaught of thousands of feet. We passed down halls seeking our assigned lockers amid hundreds clanging open and shut. They sported combination master locks. The cafeteria, filled from wall to wall with spacious tables surrounded by plastic molded chairs of orange and yellow, offered both hot and cold lunches daily, and the Home provided us money to purchase ours so we could blend in.

BOCES, the vocational training taken off campus, offered courses in cosmetology, auto mechanics, and food preparation for some of the eighty percent of Nanuet's kids who would not go on to college. Art and drama classes held exhibitions and put on plays. Pep rallies happened in the gym on Fridays before the games, and dances throughout the year. I knew nothing of what went on in high school and thought the whole place was Shangri-La. More and more, I saw my future with Nanuet and not the Bronx. This was my chance to start over, to leave all the squalor and drama behind.

For the first time, I played basketball, softball, jogged, did anything physical besides walk or dance, and it was fun. I discovered I was a pretty good player, if not a strong athlete, and enjoyed being chosen for teams. I felt like a dormant flower bulb, beginning to bloom.

Like most kids, I saw no relevance for Algebra, History, or Geography. I did not join any clubs, sports teams, or the school newspapers. Instead, I worked. To my surprise, St. Agatha hired me as the relief switchboard operator on Saturdays, and two nights a week working for Sister Jude—a scary older nun who dressed in black. Now it was me who sat in the creaky little chair by the purring equipment box, where I'd been a year-ling only six months ago. It was a big responsibility. At first I worked only a couple of hours on Saturday, but later this expanded into two nights a week from six to nine and all day Saturday. I could bring my books and study when I wasn't taking calls. I loved it, and I got an actual paycheck instead of cash.

The switchboard was the same, with the cords and switches and gur-gling box. The internal buildings could call each other without an opera-tor, but all outside calls had to go through the switchboard. Any calls for kids had to go to the Group Mother or social worker, and no kids could make outside calls.

I was nervous that an incoming call would be one of the head Sisters, even though I was always professional in the way I answered the phone. The operator was also the interface in the event of a fire at the Home. The alarm behind the operator's chair would ring, as well as indicate the loca-tion of the fire so that the operator could tell the fire department exactly which building to go to. When the alarm did ring once, I was relieved that Sister Jude was nearby to handle it, as I was not even authorized to call the fire department.

Occasionally, anxious parents called for kids, but I just put those through to a nun without any discussion. Sister Jude explained that sometimes parents upset and frightened the kids, and that was why the nuns screened the calls. They could be calling to say one parent died, which was best handled with intervention. I also witnessed similar pitiful vignettes as I had starred in not so long ago. New children brought to the Home were left gaping in the waiting room across the hall. I reached out to them like Mrs. Mauro had to us. She was a volunteer, I later learned, and her daughter attended Nanuet High School when I did.

I never wandered anywhere else than the little office, but I could stand by the open window and breathe in the night air, sneak a smoke, and look at the night sky. Plus, I was away from all the strife of the world. Sister Joannne and Sister Maureen sat across the hall, and Sister Jane even closer with the social workers and administrators. The Sisters passed by on their way to prayer and meals upstairs, and sometimes stopped in briefly or waved as they whisked by. It was a little cocoon.

Working kept me out of trouble, too. Since I wasn't around a lot of the time, I didn't get tested for conspiracies like sneaking out. Or embroiled in the frequent tiffs that seemed to erupt over someone taking something that didn't belong to them, or for not washing the frying pan. Plus, I had money to buy clothes when school started, and bus fare to the city. Having my own money meant freedom. But after a while, the newness of the job wore off, and I got bored.

I applied for a job at W.T. Grant in Nanuet and they hired me. I never did get Saturdays off, but I could walk to work right after school. The night watchman picked me up. More and more, my life was settling in to Nanuet and became fairly comfortable and routine.

It was difficult to fit in with the "outside" kids because they had the normal freedoms of high school kids. Many of them had cars and the freedom that went with driving. Home Kids could not get cars, though they could take driver's education their senior year. They had to ride home on the school bus, not in an overstuffed VW with a bunch of kids after an outing.

Instead of jobs, most outside kids had moms waiting at home with milk and cookies, or in their absence, an empty house to bring their friends to—friends they'd grown up with, gone to elementary school with, and played little league alongside. It's hard for any kid moving into both adolescence and a new school to break into established cliques. Add to that the stigma of the Home, whose purpose ranged—in the minds of outside kids—from an orphanage to a reformatory for minorities from New York City.

From 1965 to 1968, high school was a turbulent time, wherever you lived. This was a predominantly white, middle-class community of collegiate kids, with a few fledgling hippies in drama or art class. When the country suffered the mind-numbing loss of Martin Luther King in 1968, everyone was shattered. As kids, we felt invincible, but this somehow shook us. Then, Robert Kennedy was shot before there was a chance to process King's death, and Viet Nam began taking everyone's brothers, sons, and friends. It was a frightening time.

But in those first high school months, we concentrated on ourselves. At the end of the school day, we cast our school stuff in our lockers and changed into play clothes. Some of us went off to work while more studious kids began their homework. Mostly, we wanted to hang out, go down to the canteen, and cling to a little of the fading summer.

My brothers, sisters, and I took turns going down to the city for weekend visits with my mother or another relative. I was so disappointed to see her drinking again. On one occasion, she and I went out to eat. How I could believe over and over that she would not drink is beyond me now. Wishful thinking or lack of courage to stand up to her, I guess. I hated to take a chance on the humiliation again, not after all that had happened.

We sat down at a table in a nice Italian restaurant on Fordham Road in our old neighborhood. We scanned the menus, and when it came time to order, Mom ordered a Manhattan—no food. I felt powerless to do anything to stop her. I tried to persuade her to eat, and she said she would order in a bit. My food came along with her drinks, but she never ordered a meal. She became drunk and belligerent, slumping further into her chair, pounding the linen table cloth, making the silverware jump as she emphasized some complaint. She was so loud we were asked to leave. I hated her.

I had to try to keep her from falling down on the sidewalk by propping her against a building while I hailed a cab. I loaded her in and got her up in the elevator to Gram's apartment. They'd escaped for the weekend. I was fifteen years old and humiliated. I held my tongue until we got inside Gram's apartment. Mom was blubbering and incoherent, and I finally exploded.

"I hate you! You're disgusting! You always say you're not going to get drunk and then you do. You always break your promises. I hate you! You don't even care enough about us to quit drinking!"

I finally said what I had wanted to for years.

She stumbled from the couch to the chair I sat in, and fell on me with limp fists, trying to pummel me, but she was so hysterical, so hurt, and began sobbing again for my father. She disgusted me all the more, but I maneuvered her onto the couch—being the adult, once again. I patted her until she calmed down, and told her I didn't mean it, thinking all the while that the old Mom was completely gone, and mess had stolen her body. Maybe this is how it is for people who have to care for someone with Alzheimer's, to watch the person they once knew and loved be taken over by a stranger. I would never go out in public with her again.

Now I dreaded that we *would* get out of the Home, that I would have to go back to live with her. To myself I declared I wouldn't go, but I knew that I would. Finally, we had a decent life. The Home wasn't perfect, but they took care of us. We had clean clothes, regular meals, went to school and church, to the doctors and the dentist. We had friends and nothing to be ashamed of. Finally, a little self-respect. Since the other kids in the Home had been through similar traumas, we helped each other out and understood. The kids at Nanuet High School grew up normal. They didn't know about our past, so it was a new lease on life.

Not long after that, around January of 1965, my mother became quite ill and my grandparents had to call an ambulance to take her to the hospital. There, she had an emergency tracheotomy because she couldn't breathe. She'd had hay fever all her life, so they thought it was asthma. But between the heart murmur from rheumatic fever, drinking so heavily, and the pills she took, no one knows. For years, she had taken lit-tle orange pills called Darvon, prescribed by the doctor because she was "low on energy," she said. Today, we know this medication as Speed. All this, and having given birth to nine children, maybe her body was just wearing out.

I went to see her in the hospital, and she had to write notes to commu-nicate with us. She had a hole in her throat with some kind of tube stick-ing out, and it scared me to death. It scared her, too. After this, mom was back—the old Mom who visited us at camp and wrote us little notes. The Mom who had visited briefly last year—docile, sweet, smiling—and who had turned frightened eyes towards me from her hospital bed. This illness had scared her solemn, and she seemed determined never to drink again. Finally, at forty-two, after a ten-year slide into hell, she got a grip on herself. For the next six months, whenever she came to visit us or we went there, we saw no sign of alcohol.

In fact, Mom looked better than she had in years. She went with Gram to get her hair colored and styled regularly, wore lipstick and nail polish, dressed fashionably, and seemed happy. It was like she had hired a personal groomer. I don't know what she did otherwise—watched soaps with her Mom, went to lunch and shopped, or to a show, as she called it. And as far as I know, she never took another drink.

In June, Jackie and I visited her for a three-day holiday weekend. Gram and Bill went to visit friends for the weekend, due back Wednes-day, so we had the whole place to ourselves. She hadn't felt like doing any-thing all weekend, so we just stayed put in the apartment. On Monday, she was still resting in Gram's bed when we left. Still not feeling well, she said that her throat felt like it was closing up again. I offered to stay, or call Gram to come back early, but she dismissed it and said she would call Gram if she felt worse. She didn't want to spoil her vacation.

I told her I would call Saturday before I put David on the bus to come for a visit, as was planned. Since she wasn't drinking, we had started a new scheme for the little kids to go there for weekends. When it was their turn, I would take one of them to Nanuet and put them on the bus, and

Mom met them at the George Washington Bridge bus terminal on the other end. She would pick them up and take them to Gram's on the other side of the Bronx, by bus or cab. I called her Tuesday and she said she was still under the weather, but that Gram was due back tomorrow and, if need be, she'd go to the doctor then.

On Saturday morning, I walked David to Nanuet for the bus. On a hunch born from years of disappointment, I called Mom before putting him on the bus. I wanted to confirm that she was feeling up to Dave's visit, and that she would be there to meet him when he got off the bus. After all, he was only nine, and she had not lived up to her side before. There was no answer. I told myself that she may have already left for the terminal to pick up David, but rather than put him on the bus alone, I went with him. I figured I'd just say hi, then turn around and ride back. I called the Home and got approval from Sister Jane, who would inform the Group Mothers.

When we got to the bus terminal, Mom was not there, and there was no answer at the apartment. We took the bus to my grandmother's, hoping we wouldn't cross paths in transit. All the while, I had a sense of dread. There had been so many scenes of disappointment that it becomes automatic for anyone who has dealt with an alcoholic. When there was no answer at the doorbell, we went around the corner to the store and phoned. No answer to the endless ringing.

On the way back, we stopped by the superintendent of the building who knew all of us all our lives, and he gave me a key, which I promised to return right away. I unlocked the door and scanned the kitchen and living rooms. Everything was tidy, in order, but no one was there. No radio played. The television sat silent. No coffee permeated the air, nor toast or eggs frying. No water ran in the shower or the sink. There was no note.

We walked towards the bedroom. As soon as I stepped over the threshold, I saw her in my grandmother's bed. I knew something was wrong and I wanted to shield Dave's view, so I sent him to return the key. He wanted to push past me and come in, but I had a bad feeling and insisted we take the key right back like we promised.

"What's wrong with her?" Dave asked.

"Nothing, she's sleeping. Now be quiet before you wake her," I hissed back, corralling and herding him back into the tiny, carpeted hall.

I walked with my body just an inch from his like a battering ram or a shield. After all but shoving him out the door, I dead-bolted it behind him and walked back through the apartment calling softly, "Mom," hoping for her reply. "Mom, I'm here. Mom?" When I got to the bedroom, I saw her face again. She looked the way she did when she slept: eyes closed, head back, mouth open. But no soft snores emitted. She looked like a deflated balloon, with everything gone out of her.

I walked slowly to the bed, still calling to her. I reached out and touched her arm, which lay on top of the cover. It was cold and somewhat hard. I turned and rushed from the room, terrified.

Looking back, I knew she was dead all along. I felt something was very badly wrong all the way back in Nanuet, though I did not give it a name, but instead pushed it away. I rushed to the phone on Gram's desk in the foyer and called my sister Ginger at Aunt Mary's. My heart pounded so hard I could barely speak.

"Gin, it's Nancy. I'm at Gram's with David. I think—I think Mom's dead," I said it with a question mark, like maybe she could make it not true. I was choking back tears, knowing David would be back in a moment. "Please come right away." She kept her voice calm while I told her what happened, and she tried to reassure me that I was mistaken, that mom might be unconscious. She said she would come right over and told me to stay calm. I wanted to believe her, but I knew she was wrong. I recognized that she was trying to shield me, like I tried to shield David.

I stood there in the hall, waiting for my brother to return. It was so still, not even a clock ticked. I knew I had to keep him away from mom until Ginger came—no small feat with David who was still perpetually restless. In a couple of minutes, the phone rang so loudly, amplified for my nearly deaf grandfather, that it was like the crack of a rifle. I jumped. It was my brother Jerry. Ginger had called him. He lived with Aunt Rita Mary and was closer, so he would come. He was calm and said he'd be right there. I urged him to hurry, and told him I didn't want David to see her, mindful that it was his mother, too.

Now the bell was ringing and David was pounding on the door, calling for me. He knew something was wrong. None of this was normal behavior. I let him in.

"What took you so long?" he asked suspiciously. To keep him calm, I told him that Mom was sleeping and he had to be quiet. He asked why I didn't answer and I told him that Jerry called and he was coming over. He thought that was odd, but I forced him down on the couch to watch cartoons. He kept trying to make excuses to go in to see if Mom was awake. He said he had to go to the bathroom, and I escorted him down the hall after I shut the bedroom door. I waited for him outside the bathroom, then escorted him back, keeping myself on the side of the hall lest he bolt into the bedroom. Once he was seated on the couch in front of the TV playing Saturday morning cartoons, I opened the window that looked down on the street four stories below. I leaned out, peering through the window guard, trying to reach the approaching rescuers, sooner. I wanted to will them here.

A cab pulled up. Jerry and Aunt Rita Mary jumped out and rushed into the building. "They're here," I gasped, further raising David's suspicions. "Come on," I gripped his hand and dragged him out the apartment door, which I left open.

"What's wrong? What's wrong?" He became panicked by this unexpected turn of events, but I wanted to meet them at the elevator and turn over the responsibility to someone else. I think I was so close to relief from this hideous responsibility, that I just stopped answering David. My mind was unable to come up with replies. As they stepped off the elevator, I collapsed into Jerry's arms, sobbing, still holding David's hand. My aunt rushed past us and into the apartment. She came out shortly thereafter to the hall and nodded to Jerry, confirming my diagnosis.

David wanted to know what was going on, and I calmed myself enough to sit him down on a step to tell him, "Mommy died." He kept shaking his head, "No, no," as he fought back tears, looking at me as if to ask why I would say such a thing when it couldn't be true. He wanted to go in, see for himself, but there was nothing else to say. Jerry led us down to the cab they kept waiting, while she stayed behind to make arrangements. It was June 3, 1967.

At Aunt Rita Mary's house, my aunt and then my uncle, arrived soon after. They knew I was close to my grandmother and asked if I wanted to be the one to convey the terrible news. I did. She was devastated. She told me what had happened after Jackie and I had left.

On Tuesday night, she called Mom, apparently after I did. Mom said she still wasn't feeling well. Gram was so enthusiastic about the weather and what a great time they were having. She asked if Mom if she would mind if they stayed until Saturday. Rather than spoil their fun after she'd brought them so much grief, Mom said fine, that she had a nice visit with Jackie and me, and that David would be coming on Saturday. Sometime between that phone call and Saturday morning, her heart failed. Perhaps if one of us was there, we could have called an ambulance in time. But she was all alone, with no one to help her.

I think I was in a state of shock at Aunt Rita Mary's, keeping a stiff upper lip and quaking only as I delivered the news by phone to Gram, and then to Uncle Bill. Ginger told Aunt Mary. Uncle Eddie called and spoke with Sister Jane, who would have the Group Mothers tell Jack, Tom, and Helen. I felt guilty about having left my mom, and later learned Gram felt the same way.

Uncle Eddie asked me what I wanted to do, and I said I wanted to go back to the Home. He took David and me back to our cottages. Thankfully, my room was already dark. The kids were already in bed with lights out. I buried my face in the pillow, but the sobs would not be suppressed. My roommates spoke softly to me in the dark, but were at a loss as to how to assist in the face of so much grief.

We went back to the city for my mother's wake and funeral. Numbly, I shopped for a black dress to wear with Ginger. I don't remember where we stayed—I think with Aunt Mary. I was still in shock, realizing that the tiny flame of a dream that still flickered somewhere inside me—the one that believed we would all get back together again, and live happily ever after—was extinguished forever now. It took me a long time to go stand at the side of the coffin to say goodbye. When I did, I stood transfixed. I consoled myself that there was nothing left of my mother here. This shell was completely lifeless. I thought the energy—the last bit of life had gone out of my mother—was now mixed with all of the energy of the world, though it had been leaking out for ten years. I thought about my sober mother who never wanted to bother anyone, or to be of any trouble.

If she would have just asked me to stay there while she was sick, send Jack back alone, or let me return when I offered to, I could have taken her to the doctor. Maybe she would have lived. Or at least, I could have been there without David when she died. At least he would have been spared that eternal glimpse, now etched in his young brain. If she had only told Gram she wasn't feeling well, they would have come home and taken her to the doctor, and she might be alive today, I thought. I vowed never to do that: never be afraid to ask for help. But Mom didn't want to be any trouble to us in her death, maybe considering how much trouble she made for all of us already.

I kept thinking of the words from a poem in an English assignment the previous semester. It was called "Lucy," by William Wordsworth. Part of it reads:

She lived unknown, and few could know
When Lucy ceased to be;
But she is in her grave, and oh,
The difference to me!

I wish I could tell you how my brothers and sisters felt, but each of us was like a cocoon, wrapped tightly in our own feelings. One or the other draped an arm over a shoulder, but there was nothing to say. We never spoke about it, except in terms of arrangements: going to get funeral clothes, who would ride in which car, who would stay over which house. I suspected each of us felt pain, loss, guilt—and there was no point in picking the beginnings of a scab.

The best weapon kids have against grief is their enthusiasm and curiosity about what comes next. When my father died, lots of things changed, and the new arrangements distracted me while the pain took years to subside. With mom, the new arrangements had already taken place. In both cases, there was nothing to do but grit my teeth and bear the pain. I imagine it was the same for my brothers and sisters. We each marched forward, eyes on our individual futures, and were never reunited as a family again. But for the rest of our lives we were always available to each other.

In Memory of

Rita C. Canfield

June 3, 1967

May her soul and the souls of all the faithful departed, through the mercy of God, Rest in Peace.
Amen

Twenty-one

More Growth and Change—For Us

After my mother's death, I dreaded stepping back across the threshold of my grandparents' apartment, yet I knew how badly Gram needed me to do so. I don't know if I thought the apartment was haunted, that my mother's spirit hung there. Mostly, I just didn't want to relive that dreadful day.

I did go back though, often, and I always felt ill-at-ease at night. I was never alone there. My brothers and sisters felt the same, but we came anyway. Gram gave me a few little mementoes of my past that she had uncovered among mom's meager possessions: letters we'd written to her from the Home, a cheap watch she had, a newspaper obituary about my father, a clipping from the Daily News when our house burned down. Before this, I had nothing that tied me to my life before we went to the Home. With all the moving since the fire, I had no tangible links to the past.

I understood that mom was Gram's only child, and that while she never understood how to help her, she treasured her and felt that she had failed her. Her skills did not extend beyond love and cooperation. It was the only tool she had needed with her compliant daughter before my dad died. When as an adult my mom did not yield to the recommendations my grandparents made about her lifestyle, Gram sat back down, out of ideas.

Gram missed my mother terribly, but she was inclined to hide her feelings and not sob or cry like my mother always had for my dad. She had married young and starry-eyed, had one sweet-natured little daughter, and was shattered when her adult princess turned into something of a frog.

The school year ended right after mom's death, and we plunged back into the unstructured days of summer. I didn't feel carefree, though; I felt depressed. I tried to enjoy our newfound freedom, and take my mind off my mom and my future as much as possible.

By tenth grade, I settled in knowing we were not going back to the city. Having made my peace with that, things generally went pretty well. I got a new job at a shoe store a couple of miles from the Home. I walked to work, and the night watchman picked me up and drove me home. I loved working there. Everyone was older, but got along like one big loosely knit, happy family, and it helped me not to think about my mother.

By the end of my junior year at Nanuet High School in 1968, I had friends and had put down roots in several places. It felt good to feel a part of something and plan for the future. Since I came to the Home, I had a routine and began to know what to expect. Finally, I could relax a little, at least for a while. And then we were uprooted again.

Jack graduated from high school and planned to get an apartment in town with another boy. He had a girlfriend at Nanuet High School and was finally happy. We were promptly told that we were going to a foster home in New York City where I would spend my senior year in a high school with total strangers, and have to start all over again. I had no idea at the time what precipitated this move. Ginger explained that we were private residents and our trust fund was paying for our care. At the current rate, there would not be enough money to keep us there until we each graduated. Whereas in a foster home, Jack, Ginger, and I could afford to live for one year, Tommy for two, Helen for four, and David for the five years until he graduated high school. But if we stayed at St. Agatha and the money ran out, the younger kids would be at the mercy of the bankrupt Child Welfare System. They could be sent anywhere to live, even split up, and my relatives did not want that. Ginger and Jack did not have to go at all, but the goal was to keep as much of the family together for as long as possible. Jack may not have been ready to be out on his own, or maybe he just wanted a chance to live as a family again.

Of course, the kids I would leave behind thought we were lucky, just like the kids in the Bronx thought we were lucky to be going to boarding school. All I knew is that we had adapted to our new environment and didn't want

Mercedes and group

to make another change. Instead of the feelings of apprehension I had felt three years earlier when we arrived, I felt anger and resentment—and powerless, as usual. My mind understood the facts, but my emotions were fighting like a horse avoiding a trailer. In the end, there was nothing I could do, except go.

First, they had to find someplace to send us. There was a wealthy couple, the Bostwicks, who wanted to adopt all five of us. We went to their home in Scarsdale. They showed us our rooms, and we even went out on their cabin cruiser with them. Once again, I was stunned with the rapidity at which these plans were made, and the complete absence of any word to us—the pawns whose best interest would be served. Maybe they didn't want us to have too much time to dread the moves.

After much discussion and consideration, my uncles decided that the Bostwicks were not right for us. I wondered if partly my uncles felt that they would lose control of us completely if we were adopted. Instead, we went to live with Loretta in the Pelham section of the Bronx. She was an elderly woman, a longtime friend of Judge McGrath of the surrogate court who handled our case. Her sister was a head nun at a convent. There could be no better endorsement of Loretta's morals and character.

My uncles approved of her and her home, so we went to live with Loretta the summer before my senior year. The kids at the Home thought we were lucky because, after all, we were "going home for good"—the mantra of every kid there, and the realization of only few. I felt torn between being happy to live as a family with most of my brothers and sisters and having to start all over again. Each of us had moved into an individual survival mode at the Home, whereas before we came there, I was in a group survival mode. Maybe we had moved from a survival to a maintenance mode, no longer in immediate danger.

Helen and I shared a second-floor bedroom. It was freshly wallpapered in a huge pink-and-red rose pattern with matching bedspread and draperies. The spacious room had a queen-sized bed to share, a closet, and two dressers. The window looked out onto the street below, and quite some distance towards Pelham Bay Park. Ginger, the oldest, had her own room next door to us, and Loretta's equally small bedroom was on the other side of Gin's. She already graduated from high school the year before and remained at Aunt Mary's while she worked and attended business classes. But she, too, wanted the chance to live as a family again and to help the rest of us transition.

Jack, Tom, and Dave shared Loretta's paneled basement—a former recreation room, plenty big enough for them. We ate dinner together in the dining room every night, watched TV in small groups, and became reacquainted with each others' lives, but we always felt like guests in Loretta's house. We never fought, although Tom and Dave had never ceased their bickering. We helped each other out, but the bond that existed when we all lived under one roof three years before had been changed. Now we were individual orbs circling near each other instead of all being in the same circle. I don't know if that happens in normal families, like when one child gets a job, goes away to school, or into the service. But we had each turned towards our individual lives at the Home, instead of our common family, which no longer existed, especially after Mom died.

We saw my other brothers Jerry and Billy for dinners, birthdays, and holidays—along with aunts and uncles—but these "mobs" in her home made Loretta nervous. So, mostly we went to their houses. I should have been grateful, but it was staggering to start all over again, and I continued

The Canfield kids together

to feel very resentful. Loretta was moody, and you never knew if you would find her crabby or cheerful. We were strongly discouraged from turning on the television in the living room, or helping ourselves to more than a cup of tea or glass of milk. Even then, she'd come on the run when she heard us in the kitchen. Ginger and I took tons of Di-gel for nervous stomachs, which Loretta kept in the kitchen cupboard. She'd dash in like the sheepdog guarding the sheep when we went in for that.

"What are you doing there?" she'd squawk. Like a parrot, she either squawked or whined most of the time. When told we were getting a cup of tea, she'd sometimes join in. A glass of milk though, and she'd cluck and shake her head that we were eating her out of house and home, and she'd have to get more money to cover these expenses. The house was immaculate and nicely decorated, although there were uninviting plastic slipcovers on the furniture that made us feel like we were unfit to sit on the actual sofa and chairs.

She had a small, black poodle named Pierre that she doted on and took to have groomed every week. Loretta's little granddaughter Debbie came for babysitting every day. She was the daughter of Loretta's only child, now divorced. Even though Loretta adored the little girl, she got cranky with her as she did with us. But she truly loved her. I guess she was just old and irritable, and had pictured her final years a lot differently than a foster home for stray children.

In September when we began our new schools, Debbie went off to kindergarten, so Loretta had peaceful days—at least for a few hours. Every evening, Loretta went to Mass, but she did not force us to go, except on Sunday. This wasn't a suggestion, but a requirement. She went up to visit her sister, Sister Alphonse, every few months, and made frequent donations to the convent. We never went, but Sister Al came to meet us once. She was formidable, like a head mistress of an all-girls' school from the previous century.

We thought Loretta was such a hypocrite to be so cantankerous to us, and then run to Mass every day, or to Sister Al to do charity. Loretta was the tie that bound us now. We griped to each other about her, complaining about the latest infraction, mimicking her behind her back. It was us against her. Of course, we didn't dare say these things to the relatives, just to each other and Jerry and Billy. It gave us that sense of conspiracy and somehow unified us.

I missed Rockland County like I missed the Bronx when I'd first gone to live there. I thought of that as my home now, and felt alien in the city. I didn't know how the buses and trains worked here. My friends had long since disbanded. I guess in the same way that St. Agatha's became the villain in our having been taken away from the family, Loretta became the enemy.

I saw Mercedes occasionally, but not many of the other kids from the Home. It's like a time warp closes up when you leave a place, and you no longer belong. I tried to renew my friendships with the old crowd, but most of the kids had moved on and the others had changed, as I had. There was just no going back.

One nice thing about living back in the city was seeing my grandparents more often. The trip up to Nanuet was too hard on them. Neither of them drove. For them to go across the city, then up on the bus for over an hour, visit a bunch of whooping kids, and make the journey back, was physically too much for them, especially after they became sickly. So, they appreciated our visits to their apartment.

Grandpa would take me around the corner to Fuhrman's and buy me a little girlie thing, like a string of fake pearls or a linen handkerchief. Gram would press a folded five-dollar bill in our hands, "For carfare," she'd say, like it was a big secret just between the two of you. It was their way of thanking us for the visits that meant so much to them in their isolation. I don't think Gram ever recovered from my mother's death.

I went through that year like a square wheel. Feeling out of place, behind on the schoolwork, and just trying to get by. In earlier situations, I always started open, like this was the rest of my life. But this year, for the first time, I knew that as soon as school was over, I would never see these schoolmates again. I would leave Loretta's and move back to Rockland County.

The thing that I disliked most about living at Loretta's—besides having been yanked out of the nest I had begun to build for myself—was her disdain towards us as if we were not only intruders, but low class, beneath her. I felt that she had been talked into taking us and was receiving a good deal of money for each of us, so she tolerated our noise and easement on her household.

In March, Ginger married Jerry's best friend Mike, who had returned from Viet Nam the year before, and whom she'd been dating. I was her maid of honor. Our sister Helen and Gin's best friend Carol were the bride's maids, with our brothers as ushers. Sharing this big event was unifying. We shopped for dresses, dyed shoes, got our hair done, and attended showers and rehearsals together. Gram and Grandpa and all of our extended family were there, which was unusual. Uncle Johnny gave Ginger away in a beautiful ceremony with a High Mass in our old parish, St. Peter. They left immediately afterward on a honeymoon to the Poconos. Six months later, Jerry married Ginger's best friend Carol in a similar traditional ceremony.

As soon as I graduated High School, two things happened. Jack moved in with a buddy, and I got a call from my friend Mercedes reminding me that we had planned to get an apartment together after we graduated. I was elated to have a way out of Loretta's, but totally unprepared, not having had a job for the previous year. My bigger concern was that with Ginger and Jackie gone, the three youngest kids would be left alone with Loretta if I left. I had the same torn feeling as when we left the Home versus getting the family back together.

That became immaterial since Loretta's daughter-in-law remarried and moved away, so Loretta was no longer needed to babysit. She announced her plan to retire and move to Queens Village, and wasn't taking anyone with her. I guess she saw the same handwriting on the wall. Tommy and David moved in with Uncle Eddie and Aunt Rita Mary, while Helen went to live with Uncle Bill and Aunt Terry. This meant more moves and changes of schools for them.

In May of 1971, Uncle Johnny died of a heart attack while rocking his long-awaited son to sleep. It was a terrible shock to the family. Uncle Johnny, always good to us and loving to his children, had finally gotten the little boy he longed for five years earlier. Aunt Mary had gone back to work so that they could buy a house. Unlike so many other women who fall apart with the loss of the family wage earner capsized, Aunt Mary struggled through with her three children. She worked hard, supported them, set high standards for them to live by and to achieve in school. This family would never end up at St. Agatha's.

After I left, the Home went on without me, of course. There were still hundreds of kids being cared for, and a tidal wave waiting for entrance. But radical changes were taking place. There was an overall sense of flight at the Home. Many of the nuns had left, and the new counselors that were being hired were no longer the social worker students, but entry-level people with no particular skills looking for a job. We began to hear stories of girls marrying counselors, counselors marrying counselors, and nuns getting married and leaving the church. It was all so strange. St. Agatha was about to undergo as profound a change as any events of the past decades had done, including the Depression and both World Wars.

Twenty-two

Merger with the New York Foundling Hospital

One pivotal period for St. Agatha was already in progress while our family made its hasty departure. Perhaps the two were related. We were actors, caught up in our own roles, and didn't see the set changing around us, except as it affected us: changes in the nuns, the mass, and our situations. Money for caring for the children of St. Agatha Home had been drying up.

In 1968, the Administrators of St. Agatha Home, St. Joseph's Hall, and New York Foundling Hospital, as part of a representative group of voluntary childcare services, wrote an "Extraordinary Appeal" to the Mayor of New York, John Lindsey. It outlined their grievances, the laws being broken, and what they expected to improve. They made it clear that the next action they would take would be legal for "non-payment, and underpayment of reasonable fees, for the care of ninety percent of the city's dependent and neglected children in voluntary child care institutions."

Because the City only allows St. Agatha to value a Sister's service at $2,900 per year, contrary to the policies of the US and New York State Governments for Medicare and Medicaid, the real deficit would equal $706,000, if properly and legally charged as allowed by Federal and State agencies. Calculated by all of the voluntary child care institutions dealing with New York City, the total deficiency by the City to all, ranges between ten to twenty million dollars per year.

The Sisters did not undertake a religious vocation, a vow of poverty, and a life of community service to have the benefit of such personal sacrifice accrue principally to the tax revenues of New York City. The practice is unjust and adversely affects morale. The costs of training the Sisters for their works of charity, their physical support, education, health and hospitalization, and old age support, require greater selectivity in how and where their work will be applied.

One hundred and fifty years of charitable work freely given to New York City, will not cease. Our highest moral obligation is to see that the religious vocations directed to us by God are spent well in works of charity, and to see that they are not dissipated because of the devious working of complex reimbursement formulae.

We are heirs to a shared responsibility for rearing these children. The state financially, and the voluntary institutions, for the daily care. The institution has as its background and motive, a religious and moral quality which gives them a concern for the children that transcends the material. The law represents the cumulative experience of human reason, the religion represents the cumulative experience of the human spirit. This represents a cumulative judgment as to what is best in the upbringing of children. In the absence of the ideal normal family situation, the human race has learned through the centuries that it is best to give a child training in values more than just material in nature, if it is to survive.

New York City is forcing the voluntary child care institutions of the City out of existence. By these continued policies and practices, through omission, neglect, or default, it is effectively abandoning the shared responsibility of the care of abandoned children. New York City was the home and first love of our foundress, Elizabeth Seton. For one hundred fifty years, New York City and its people have been the beneficiaries of the continuous service and devoted love of our Sisters. There is a bond between the Sisters of Charity and New York City, which we shall always strive to persevere.

Perhaps the lack of resolution with New York contributed to the departure of other kids, like us. On September 5, 1968, Sr. Helen Murphy succeeded Sr. Joanne, after fifteen years as Administrator at St. Agatha.

In parting, Sr. Joanne characterized her years at St. Agatha as a consistent move towards more individual care for the children, and an effort to understand the total picture of their needs. Enrollment dropped from five hundred children to three hundred thirty-six, in the effort towards individualized care versus congregate care. The social services department grew from three to fifteen, and a guidance clinic which provided psychological evaluations and therapy. Individual plans were developed for each child including social work, education, child care, health and psychiatric ser-

Sister Joanne

vices. They attend the Home's school from Kindergarten through eighth grade, then went to local public schools.

St. Agatha had evolved into a Foster Home Program to serve children in their own communities who might otherwise be institutionalized when, in fact, they may only need foster care. Institutionalization was still an option, but only after a child had attempted to live in a group home.

Group homes, where seven to ten children placed as early as age five and up to age eighteen live as a family, existed to permit the child to continue the use of services, including health, education, welfare, recreational and religious facilities as in their own community. St. Agatha had success with these programs.

In August 1970, a review of the Education Department at St. Agatha indicated that at a time of greatest need, resources were dwindling rapidly. For some of St. Agatha's children, school had meant failure and further alienation. Programs needed to be individualized to include vocational counseling and opportunities for personal growth and achievement.

A community outreach opportunity came in the summer of 1972, when a group of alumni and residents assisted local volunteers in building a new barn for the horses that provided recreation and learning opportunities for children. There was a "Summer of 72" festive program with fireworks on the 4th of July and a presentation of the progress of the barn.

That same year, another event had an even more profound affect on St. Agatha. The needs of the "difficult to place" children skyrocketed, perhaps precipitated by Geraldo Rivera's radical exposure of Willowbrook, which blasted into the media. Here's what he saw when he entered the Staten Island mental ward:

> The ward was crowded with children. Mostly naked, some were smeared with their own feces. Essentially unattended, they were everywhere, under sinks, knocking their heads against walls, one even lapping water from a toilet bowl.

Day after day, the stories and photos blared from the front pages of newspapers and magazines. Edward Kennedy's exposé of the same place in the sixties, had little impact because without photos, he was made to seem like he was exaggerating, campaigning, making a sensation. This time, Rivera didn't ask for permission, he busted in with cameras rolling.

Other institutions had their doors thrown open to reveal similar circumstances. Once exposed, the places were shut down, patients removed, and intensive treatment begun to try to erase lifetimes of abuse. Homes like St. Agatha, ill-equipped for the worst cases, scrambled to assist at least some of the evacuees by placing them in surrounding communities in small group homes, some for retarded children, some for severely emotionally disturbed children, and chronic runaways with specially trained counselors—all supervised by St. Agatha's Board of Directors.

This may have precipitated the catalogue of changes that followed over the next decade. The more children with special needs, the more specialized the programs became, which then branched out to include satellite programs in Rockland, Westchester and New York City: therapeutic and specialized programs, Rockland's first Non-Secure Detention Shelter, providing an alternative to secure juvenile detention center programs, and, a Pre-Adolescent Treatment Program as an alternative to secure psychiatric hospitalization for children.

Most of these events were invisible for the residents at St. Agatha, where the staff felt it important to insulate the children from the challenging special-needs newcomers. Many of the original programs continued: a Bike-A-Thon for Muscular Dystrophy, the Ponderosa Club for horsemanship competition, and membership in the community 4-H program. Field trips were still planned: a trip to Belmont Racetrack to meet jockeys, watching the riding in the Summer Olympics, and a trip to see the famous Disney horse "Holy Smoke." And, of course, children still made their First Holy Communion.

Boys in hand-me-down suits for First Communion

The special-needs programs were proving effective, and in 1976, several more were begun, however also in 1975 and 1976, many emergency referrals to St. Agatha were placed in foster homes, directly. Small group homes did not suit some children unable to handle the freedom inherit in this type of living.

With special needs kids, came special schooling and recreation. A review of the Department of Recreation at St. Agatha in 1976, by its Director summarized its purpose in the lives of the children.

The children cared for by St. Agatha Home are dependent, neglected children who suffer a lack of self-worth, and in some cases, a lack of identity. They need constant, positive reinforcement as they seek to discover who they are, and to become healthy adults, and opportunities to excel individually and as part of a team, through recreation.

Many of St. Agatha's residents came from environments where they had to spend their time surviving, defending themselves, fighting and struggling for parental love and attention in large families of five or ten children. Now, children have a chance to feel good about themselves, as they excel in a variety of recreational activities. Trained professionals reinforce successes on an individual level, according to personal growth.

As most of the children are minorities, their chances to succeed in the majority population are improved by increasing their abilities, which may lead to careers in photography, mechanics or sports. Overall, life becomes more meaningful and enjoyable. In a recreational environment, children have the opportunity to observe adults who are firm, loving and helpful, and the children accept rules as necessary and helpful rather than with resentment.

In 1976, Denis J. Barry became the Acting Executive Director at St. Agatha Home for one year, after Sr. Helen Murphy left. He was the first lay Director of St. Agatha Home, then described as:

An agency serving single and family groups of children up to age 21, designated dependent, neglected, abused or PINS. The program includes Residential Care, Foster Care Services, Community Services and provides services for more than four hundred children. Referrals are accepted seven days a week including evenings, and come through the Social Services or Family Courts in the five boroughs of New York City, Westchester and Rockland Counties. Most are for emergency admission, and transportation is provided for them.

A contract with New York City guides the intake of children up to age sixteen who are able to benefit from an open treatment-oriented program. Older and younger siblings are also accepted as a family group. The Residential program for children has a capacity of 180 and provides therapeutic child care for groups of eight to fifteen children, residing in sixteen separate cottages on one hundred acres of land. [about seventy acres of land had been sold off] Each cottage is a complete home. There is an on-campus school with a specialized and remedial program, operated by New York City Board of Ed and community schools are available for selected elementary students, including High Schools with BOCES [vocational] programs.

All children have caseworkers and receive medical and clinical services. They enjoy year round recreational facilities, volunteer tutoring, job training and vocational counseling, religious development and denominational services. The New York Foundling Hospital Adoption Department handles adoptions for St. Agatha. There are five psychiatrists and three psychologists to provide diagnostic and prescriptive evaluation, therapy, consultation and staff development. A diagnostic Reception Unit with capacity for ten, serves newly admitted children, most of whom are received through emergency referral. A Special Cottage for ten provides a program geared to meet special needs of moderately retarded children. Two Special Needs cottages, each with a capacity of ten, serve children with exceptional development difficulties, such as mild or profound retardation.

There are 130 children in 59 Boarding Homes, 68 in 8 Group Homes, 11 in 2 Agency Operated Boarding Homes.

In 1977, children placed with St. Agatha through New York courts ranged from three to eighteen. The emphasis was on the inherent worth of the child and his family members. Sr. Mary Christine, a Group Mother and teacher at St. Agatha since September 4, 1964, described their goals:

St. Agatha works with children and their parents towards effecting changes in their environment, relationships or in behavior, to enable the individual child to:

- understand him/herself better
- realize his/her own self-worth

- conquer his/her problems
- develop his/her potentials

so that s/he may make a satisfactory adjustment to life. Inherent worth of the child is all important and applies to each member of the family.

With the decline in Religious staff, the Board of Education of the City of New York assumed total responsibility of the school. Over three years, grades six through eight were phased out. Sr. Christine joined the Religious Development Department in September, 1976 with two goals: To better co-ordinate and provide for the religious development of all children in care, (including non-Catholics) and to re-establish the importance of religion in the total development of children.

A new Center was established where the resident children could drop in for music, reading or just to visit. It provided religious instruction for Catholic children in preparation of the Sacraments. Students from the Nyack Missionary College provided special programs for non-Catholics. Some children attended the Aloha program at St. Catherine's Parish in Blauvelt, and all children were encouraged to worship in their own persuasion. Staff visited the cottages each week to exchange ideas of mutual concern for the needs of the residents.

By January 6, 1977, the Board of Trustees, committees, administration, and staff of Catholic Charities had met repeatedly to discuss the merger of St. Agatha and the NYFH (New York Foundling Hospital). Everyone agreed that the following July would mark the date of the merger, once all legal steps had been taken.

Accordingly, on July 1, 1977, St. Agatha merged with New York Foundling Hospital to provide more effective care for children and families, through a more united effort. Sr. Cecilia Schneider served as Executive Director of the merged agency, now called St. Agatha Home of the New York Foundling. All trustees of both agencies would serve on the new Board. By the following year, St. Agatha's Residential Program included 250 children living on the grounds, primarily adolescent and dependent/neglected children. After a six month evaluation of the program, several short and long term goals were established.

- Reduce overall population and per cottage capacity
- Increase the number of staff per cottage
- Develop a geographically separate unit for those developmentally disabled
- Reduce the age and pathology so that St. Agatha is primarily servicing pre-adolescent, mildly to moderately emotionally handicapped population
- Develop and enforce relevant in-service training of direct care staff
- Realign the caseloads of caseworkers
- Remove all children who present a chronic threat
- Establish a program for professionals to meet more regularly
- Intensify and restructure support services
- Establish new Children's Court and Crisis Intervention Team
- Establish program for middle and upper management to meet regularly to resolve problems and achieve goals.

Most of these goals were begun or met by 1988.

Twenty-three

The Growth of Group Homes

In August, 1979, the newspapers were full of stories of the newest destitutes: the Boat People, 400,000 Indochinese refugees adrift for days at a time, no food or water, near death before rescue. Outstretched hands of communities around the world wished to help them. In 1975, 4,000 refugees were airlifted from Kuala Lumpur in the first week after the war, for permanent resettlement in the US. Pope John Paul II urged that all of these displaced people "be assisted, comforted and helped to a future of hope and tranquility." President, Jimmy Carter lived up to his promise to use the US Navy and Air Force to rescue boat people from the icy seas, while Hanoi condemned what they called a display of military domination.

The churches of the US launched campaigns for members to sponsor families, with particular emphasis on those with children, and find them homes. Many of the children were separated from their parents, who may have died, or could only afford passage to save their children. This exile was not unlike the children of America's early immigrant families migrating from Europe, where parents often died from horrid conditions en route, leaving their children in need of foster care.

St. Agatha received twenty-four refugee children. Two Vietnamese child care workers, one a recent refugee, the other arriving in 1975, had joined St. Agatha's staff, and could interpret and put the newcomers at ease. Just two days before, they were encamped along with 50,000 others on Pulau Bidong, Island of No Hope, where the Malaysian government was housing escapees from Vietnam. They had left their family in Viet Nam and escaped to Malaysia, then Tokyo, San Francisco, New York, and finally a home at St. Agatha. Thus began an ongoing program at St. Agatha, for new refugees to the US. Community Services expanded to include several new facilities throughout Westchester and Rockland Counties, in 1981.

In August, 1983, other short-term programs opened in Westchester, and the next year, the first Rockland County Runaway Program, Project Turning Point, opened, expanding in the following year to include homeless youth. From thirty youths served in the first year to one hundred-fifty in 1986, this much-needed program proved a great success.

In September, 1984, the therapeutic riding program, commonly called Hippotherapy, was hailed as a huge success at St. Agatha's. The program offered disabled children the opportunity to bond in a loving relationship with a horse, while developing physical and motor skills that may be lacking. Residents who were able to, cared for the horses and assisted other riders in exchange for a small salary.

Longtime friend, counselor, and role model at St. Agatha, Richard Royster headed up the program, and observed, "You have to always be positive and give everyone a chance." The late Cardinal Cooke continued to suggest to those he met who were in the position to do so that they donate one of their horses to St. Agatha. Now if they could just get the funding for an indoor ring so that the riders did not have to hang up their stirrups for the winter, the program would be complete. But they never did.

Donations were the backbone of St. Agatha from its inception. In another innovative move, New York Mets player George Foster began a program whereby, for every homerun he hit, a donation was made for the children of St. Agatha Home. He converted his career total at the end of each game to dollars, which he then donated. Career Homer No. 328 netted $328 for the Home, bringing his total donation for the year to $5,000. As an added bonus, Foster's contributions were matched by his agent, attorney Lonn Herney. Together they contributed nearly $10,000 the first season! Besides the financial contribution, the role model he provided to the children was of incalculable benefit.

With all of the children helped over the years, the Sisters periodically received special thank-yous that surely reached into the depths of their hearts. In 1993 one such letter arrived from a former resident thanking St. Agatha for helping him.

Dear Sisters,

I am writing you to offer my long-overdue gratitude and thanks for what you have done for me. I was one of your children which you raised in St. Agatha's Home for Children in Nanuet, NY. I lived there with my brother Frank during the years 1954 through 1959. I was approximately three years old when I arrived, my brother was 2 years old. We were both mal-nourished and very sick when you took us in. But we flourished with your care. I remember the Home as a place of warmth, love and security. I remember Sr. Mary DePaul who loved us with a genuine mother's love. I loved her dearly and I have always thought of her and always miss her. There was Sr. Charles and Sr. Mary Kevin and Sr. Mary Joseph. There was Sr. Ignatius, the school principal.

I remember them all with thoughts of love and gratitude. They all gave me a set of morals and values which have withstood the tests of time. Today I am a resident physician at a Medical Center in Brooklyn, and am almost finished my specialty training in rehabilitation training. I am recognized among my peers as a person of unusual compassion, and dedication to my patients and my profession. Rarely a day goes by when I am not complimented by a patient or staff person to whom I offered some attention.

When I left the Home in 1959 I went to live with my father in the south Bronx. Since then I have been on an incredible odyssey which would be worthy of a book. But to make a long story short, to get to the "meat of the matter," I have long realized that behind all the obstacles I have overcome, all the hardships I have survived and endured, and all the successes I enjoy can be traced back to that intangible something that the Sisters of Charity gave me in the home. I have never forgotten any of them even though I cannot remember all their names . . . and never will. I am eternally grateful.

Please find enclosed my small contribution and rest assured that when I become a successful private practitioner my contributions will be more substantial and dependable. Today, I only wish I could thank the Sisters who were responsible for me personally. But if that never happens just tell them that they have my heart.

With sincere love
LPC, MD
P.S. Thanks for the Hymn Book!

Twenty-four

The New Millenium

It was Saturday, July 21, 2001, when my brother Tom and I arrived at St. Agatha early to help set up for the alumni reunion after our absence of over thirty years. We parked by the gym and stood on the spot where we'd stood that first Sunday decades before, mugging for the camera, taking photos of each other as keepsakes, mementos of what we believed was a weekend visit to a boarding school.

Many things had happened since that time, but with the advantage of hindsight, I came to realize that the most important thing was that we'd been rescued. Like thousands of other kids brought to that very spot for over a hundred years—some kicking, screaming, and rebelling—all were saved from a world where we were powerless to rescue ourselves.

Thirty years later, people's faces were like popcorn they way they turned around, stretched their necks up to survey faces, and greeted newcomers in a way we would have never dared when we were kids. All around me, people could not contain themselves, they were so overjoyed. It was a joy to see all these people, some of whom I had been corresponding with for months, like Rita and Myrna. I had to urge my brother to be quiet, as Sister Robert was right behind him and could roll up that song sheet and bop him just like in the old days.

During the mass, I began to truly see what a heroic story the St. Agatha story was. Now I understood what C.S. Lewis meant when he said, "We read to know that we are not alone." Certainly, as a minimum, some of the other "Home Kids" would be interested in the story of St. Agatha, and so would their families. Maybe others who had shared simi-

Sisters Christine and Robert

lar fates would be, too. I kept thinking how, like me, these kids had holes in their histories. Most did not know about the place they had called home, some for their whole childhood.

After the Mass, I stayed to take pictures of the beautiful chapel for one of the alumni who couldn't be there. He had been at St. Agatha from 1929 to 1944. Tom Maloney came over to me while I was taking pictures in the Chapel and Sister Joanne introduced us. Tom had been President of the Alumni for decades, and was still actively involved. He made so many contributions to the Home over the years, he was considered a true patron.

Before leaving the grounds for the American Legion Hall and dinner and dancing, the group assembled in the field to sing the St. Agatha Alma Mater. Amazing how the words come right back to you.

Dear Alma Mater, St. Agatha it's you
We pledge our loyalty, we will always be true
In all our hearts, Love is overflowing
In all we do, proof of it is showing
St. Agatha so grand, kindness and a helping hand
St. Agatha so grand, finest in the land
We'll always love you so, Wherever we may go
We'll always love you so, Wherever we may go.

As adults, we could rationalize and see that the Home was not to blame for us being there, but at the time, many kids did feel imprisoned by the Home, as if they were being kept away from the people who wanted and loved them. Instead, the Sisters were often protecting us when the people who should have cared for us could not.

Every person I spoke with told me that while they were not always happy during their time at the Home, and some bad things hap-

Rudy Polk and Rich Royster, longtime counselors

pened to them, they were glad that they had come there to live, and were better off because of it.

I could see that the problems do not change with the generations, only the people. The basic needs of children do not change. And thankfully, the people willing to open their hearts keep coming, too. Continuous threads weave through this story—from 1873 when John Reid first purchased sixteen acres in Nanuet for his ailing wife, then donated it a year later to children in need of a home—right up until this moment. There is still a steady stream of children in need after all these years.

I learned how successful many of the Home Kids had become, both in their careers and families. They had weathered the gut-wrenching origins that brought them to the Home, and in some cases, continued in their families. But through the change in their situation, they reached inside themselves and created something good, and became responsible adults. They had their share of divorces, drinking, and drug problems reflective of society—and a few got in trouble with the law. But most of them seemed to have found their way.

Postscript: June 2005

The inevitable but dreaded news has just come to St. Agatha alumni: St. Agatha is closing its doors. The City of New York will no longer pay for the care of the disabled and troubled children living there, and the New York Foundling Hospital cannot afford $300,000 to $400,000 annually to keep the facility open.

The last reunion on the grounds is scheduled for October 15, 2005. A mass will be said in the chapel by Father Oliverio, if the building is still standing by then and if he's able to. In the evening, a dinner dance is scheduled at a Nanuet hotel. For many of the alumni, the loss of this oasis they called home during the most troubled time of their lives will live on in their hearts and minds. But it doesn't have to be constrained there. It lives on in the friendships that have been forged over so many years. The other Home Kids, their families, the Sisters, and former volunteers and employees, provide a web of memories that is St. Agatha Home for Children.

I can't help thinking of all the immigrants who have bravely come to America over the course of its history. They left the homelands they loved, family, everything familiar to create a new life. They never forgot those roots that lived on in their hearts and in the stories they tell their children. St. Agatha will live on inside everyone who was touched by its uniqueness.

This book was written to help you remember, even if it does not contain your particular story. Everyone who lived here will find something of their experience in these pages. This is your memory book, your family album.

Resources

The Children's Aid Society of New York, An Index to Its Federal, State, and Local Census Records of It's Lodging Houses (1855–1925) by Carolee R. Inskeep, offers former residents and their descendants the opportunity to review census records for 5,000 children who lived in the Lodging Houses of the Children's Aid Society. ISBN:0-8063-4623-X

The New York Foundling Hospital: Federal, State, and Local Census Records 1870-1925. Carolee R. Innskeep. The Children's Aid Society of New York
Federal, State, and Local Census Records of It's Lodging Houses 1855– 1925

The Sisters of Charity of NY. Sister Marie De Lourdes Walsh. Fordham Press.

The Discovery of the Asylum. David J. Rothman. Little, Brown and Company.

Blessed Elizabeth Ann Seton. Joseph I. Dirvin.

For The Love Of God, The Faith and Future of the American Nun. Lucy Kaylin. HarperCollins, 2000.

A Short and Remarkable History of New York City. Jane Mushabac and Angela Wigan. Fordham University Press, 1999.

How the Other Half Lives. Jacob A. Riis. Dover Publications, 1971.

They Cage the Animals At Night. Jennings Michael Burch, Signet, Penguin Putnam, 1985.

The Changing Face of the Priesthood. Donald Cozzens. The Liturgical Press, 2000.

Records Information Office
http://hscareers.com/agencies/ agencyoftheweek.asp?id=37
Attention: Wendy Freund

New York Foundling Hospital
18 W 18th St.
or
590 Avenue of the Americas
NY, New York 10011.

Websites:
http://stagathaalumni.family-feliciano.com/
http://www.stagnesalumni.org/

"Goodnight, all you Princes and Princesses of St. Agatha ."

Appendix

*T*his is a sample of an agreement that the family signed before the child was handed over.

Indenture/Adoption Form
Children's Aid Society
(PLACING-OUT DEPARTMENT)
United Charities Building
105 east 22nd STREET, NY

I, the undersigned, _____ hereby agree to provide for _____ of the age of ____ years, until the said boy shall reach the age of 18 years, according to the following terms and conditions, and with the full understanding that the Society reserves the right to remove the child previous to legal adoption if at any time the circumstances of the home become such as in the judgment of the agent are injurious to the physical, mental or moral well-being of the child.

The terms and conditions for the retention of the boy in my family being as follows: to care for him in sickness and health, to send him to school during the entire free school year until he reaches the age of 14 years, and thereafter during the winter months at least, until he reaches the age of 16 years, also to have him attend Church and Sunday School when convenient, and to retain him as a member of my family until he reaches the age of 17 years, and thereafter for the final year, until he is 18 years old, to pay the boy monthly wages in addition to his maintenance, the amount thereof to be previously determined after consultation with the Society's local agent and his approval.

In case he proves unsatisfactory, I agree to notify the Society and pending his removal, to keep him a reasonable length of time after such notice has been given. I agree, moreover, to use my best endeavor then and at all times, to detain him, should he try to leave me, until the Society can take steps for his removal. I agree to keep him at all times as well supplied with clothing as he was when I received him.

I agree to write to the Society at least once a year, and should I change my address, I will notify the Society.

_____

Witness, _____

Date, _____

HAVE THIS NOTICE AND RECEIPT IN YOUR HAND WHEN THE TRAIN ARRIVES

Sample notes pinned to abandoned babies.

Most Holy Redeemer Church, N.Y.
December 10th, 1869
Sister M. Irene, Superioress

Respected Sister,

You would oblige our R.F. Rector Leimgruber in taking the poor child in
the Asylum. It has been happily saved from being murdered this morning
by his unfortunate mother. She told me that she gives up all claims on it. I
gave private baptism to the child.

Respectfully yours, Francis Eberhardt, C.S.S.R.

July, 1870
To the Sisters of the House,

Necessity compels me to part with my darling boy. I leave him, hoping
and trusting that you will take good care of him. Will you let some good
nurse take charge of him and will you try to find some kindhearted lady
to adopt him and love him as her own while he is young that he may
never know but that she is not his own mother? It would break my heart
to have him grow up without a mother to love and care for him. God
only knows the bitter anguish of my heart in parting with this little dear;
still if it costs me my life I am obliged to give him up.

He is just from the breast, he has been sick with his bowels, they have
not been right for a long time. I have cried and worried over him so much
that I think my milk hurt him. I think a change of milk with good care
will make him well soon. I got these things thinking I could keep him but
as I can not they may be of use to you. I shall always take an interest in
this Institution.

He is 4 weeks old. Will you please remember this name and if he is adopted, request that they will not change his name; so that at some future day, if that name should be asked for, you will be able to tell what became of him or where he is. Perhaps you will think me very particular, but if any mother will take it home to her own heart and think how she would feel to have her dear little boy torn from her breast, I think they would excuse me.

This is the last time I can speak of him as mine, and if in years to come if I could hear that he had a home and kind friends, I could die in peace. On the other hand, if I should never hear, it would haunt me to the day of my death. Please excuse all that you think is not right but for God's sake remember the last request of a heart-broken mother.

(Day-old infant left by Dr. J.J. Brennan)
70 Rivington Street

The little baby which was left in the crib last night, if you for the love of God and his holy mother will keep it for me I will give anything you require. Her father is a wicked Orangeman. I told him it was dead because I want to have her raised a Roman Catholic and have her nursed out. I will pay all the expenses.

Will you, dear Sisters, remember a kind mother's heart? If I do not see her again I will never do any good on this earth. I work at dress-making for a living. My husband gives me but a third of his earnings because I am a Roman Catholic. Write to Father Farrell, Barclay Street Church, state circumstances to him. Pray to the Blessed Virgin for me to help me through.

Dear Sisters,

By the love of God be so kind as to take this poor orphan child in and if she should die, please bury her for me and I will be very happy. You must not think that I have neglected her; I have worked very hard to pay her board but I can't afford to bury her.

So, by the love of God, take this little child in. May God Bless you all for your kindness to all the little sufferers. This little child has suffered since she was born and I have paid debts, but I have not paid all, but I shall. My husband is dead and I have nobody to help me. Be kind to my little lamb. May the great God receive her into Heaven where she will be loved by God.

This two Dollars is to have this child christened Willie. Do not be afraid of the sores on its face; it is nothing but a ringworm. You will remember this babe.

(Included with the letter: colorful cloth badge that reads: "General Grant our Next President")

Police Department of the City of New York
Precinct No 20 NY, August 5, 1872
To the Superior of the Foundling Hospital

We have arrested a woman named Mary Gallagher for intoxication and vagrancy at 11 this P.M. She has this infant about three weeks old, she wanted to destroy it. So it is not proper to leave it in her charge and even if she were sober, she is not in a fit state to take care of it. The child will not live if it does not have nourishment. If you will take care of it, also the older one until tomorrow, I will then have them sent to Commissioners of Public Charities. We have tried to get some of her people to take care of this infant. They all refuse. I do not know what else to do with these children then to leave them in your kind protection for this night and by so doing very much oblige.

Yours Respectfully,
    CHARLES W. COFFRY, CAPT. ⁓

And this brief note of explanation:

"This offspring is the fruit of a brutality on the person of this poor but decent woman and to cover her shame and being too poor to support the children—there are two from her husband—she is obliged to resort to this extreme measure. The child is not yet baptized."

The Sisters cared for over 2,500 infants in their first two years, and were forced to move again, in November, 1873, to accommodate their ever-growing population.

St. Patrick's Cathedral New York
August 28th, 1875
Sister Irene,

    The child in question is indeed an object of charity. The mother is in danger of death, is but fifteen years of age and without means of providing for the child. The child has been baptized in this church.

Yours in Christo,
REV. WILLIAM HOGAN ⁓

December 1, 1875
Dear Sister,
Alone and deserted, I feel to put my little one with you for a time. I would willingly work and take care of her but no one will have me and her too. All say they would take me if she was 2 or 3 years old, so not knowing what to do with her and not being able to pay her board, I bring her to you knowing you will be as kind to her as to the many others who are under your care, and I will get work and try hard to be able to relieve you of the care, when she is so I can take her to work with me. She is only 3 weeks old and I have not had her christened or anything.

No one knows how awful it is to separate from their child but a mother, but I trust you will be kind and the only consolation I have is if I am spared and nothing prevents and I lead an honest life that the father of us all will permit us to be united.

A Mother

November 1876
Miss Brock,

You can keep the baby or you can put it in the street or not for I will not pay for it for it has no father nor any one to look after it. So you better put it away for I will not pay for it.
Child's name: Alpheus.
Left by Father Reilly.

St. Patrick's Church, NY
July 15, 1884
Rectory 263 Mulberry Street

Dear Sister,

I have an unfortunate girl in my parish who has given birth to an illegitimate child. She is so circumstanced that if it were known it would greatly
injure her and at the same time give rise to a great deal of scandal among
her friends. She is truly repentant and has brought the child to me to be
baptized. (It's name is Louis.)

I therefore request of you the favor to receive the child in the asylum
and free her from the burden which she has been so unfortunate to bring
upon herself. Greatly Obliged.

Yours respectfully,
REV L.A. MASSIATTA

In a letter of farwell, the full text available on the following link, Archbishop Cooke reminds the reader of the sanctity of life and thanks all
those who have provided childcare over the years <http://priestsforlife.
org/magisterium/ cardcookelter.htm>.

About the Author

After leaving St. Agatha, Home Kid Nancy Canfield married the owner of a Nanuet candy store in 1972. They moved to California in 1977, where Nancy raised her son, Danny, and her daughter, Eva. She became a business woman and then a writer. She is now a Realtor with Prudential California Realty in Rancho Bernardo, California.

She was inspired to write *Home Kids* after she found a former St. Agatha roommate on the Internet. Their correspondence kindled Nancy's interest in exploring the meaning of St. Agatha for herself and her family. Following the 2001 reunion at St. Agatha, she resolved to chronicle the legacy of St. Agatha for herself and her classmates. It took her four years to bring Home Kids through the research, writing, and editing and into the light.

She thanks her patient family, friends, St. Agatha alumni, Sisters of Charity, and everyone who contributed so much to making this book a reality.

While Nancy and her fellow Home Kids no longer need their help, hundreds and thousands of children in foster care still do.

Contact Nancy at www.NancyCanfield.com.